T0254683

Fundamentals of Secure System Modelling

Raimundas Matulevičius

Fundamentals of
Secure
System
Modelling

 Springer

Raimundas Matulevičius
Institute of Computer Science
University of Tartu
Tartu, Estonia

ISBN 978-3-319-87143-1   ISBN 978-3-319-61717-6   (eBook)
DOI 10.1007/978-3-319-61717-6

Printed on acid-free paper

This Springer imprint is published by Springer Nature
The registered company is Springer International Publishing AG
The registered company address is: Gewerbestrasse 11, 6330 Cham, Switzerland

To Sigita, Mantvydas and Vygantas.
To my parents for all their trust, love
and support.

Foreword by Andreas L. Opdahl

The security of ICT systems is becoming more important by the day. In the last decades, cyber crime has established itself as a branch of international organised crime. Computer and network security breaches—often combined with social engineering attacks—have become tools for industrial and political espionage, and electronic warfare has moved computer and information security into the realms of international politics and terrorism.

The new security threats have emerged as modern societies have become increasingly reliant on information and communication technologies. Industrial corporations depend on computing and information systems to store and process business-critical information about customers, processes, products, markets, and employees, and reliable ICT systems are needed to support essential public infrastructures such as energy, health, transportation, waste, and water. Besides being an important concern in itself, security is also a prerequisite for other aspects of dependability, such as safety and privacy. Safety-critical systems that used to run bespoke software on specialised hardware in isolation from the Internet have been re-engineered into or replaced by networked, standards-based systems, making them vulnerable to a broader range of security threats than before. And without the information confidentiality and integrity provided by secure ICT, there can be no personal information privacy.

In the old days, computer security was often treated as an implementation and infrastructural concern. Software was secure if it was securely coded, tested and maintained, and if it ran in a secure operating environment: on secure computers, basic software, and networks—preferably behind a firewall. Information was secure if it was encrypted. Modern ICT systems have long since become too complex for handling security only on the software and infrastructure levels. In a modern system, a single weakness can be used as an entry point to incrementally expand an attack to any of that system's parts: the only thing a prospective attacker needs is a single weak link in the security chain, and the chain keeps growing longer as system complexity increases. The emergence of systems-of-systems that span smart cities and multi-national corporations has only added weight to the problem.

The new situation calls for defence in depth, designing security into every component and every level of modern organisations. In addition to hardware, networks, and basic software, security must be woven into all the organisation's information systems, business processes, and its enterprise architectures—cross-cutting technological, individual, organisational, and social concerns. Such defence in depth cannot be added as an afterthought, but must be ingrained in every organisational development, redevelopment, and maintenance activity that somehow involves information management, information processing, or ICT. The new situation also calls for broader collaboration about security than before, starting from the earliest project planning stages. Whereas security of the past could be treated as a technical issue to be left to the experts, defence in depth requires collaboration between new groups of stakeholders: not only security experts, but also involving software developers and experts from many other domains, bringing new types of expertise, perspectives and vocabularies into the security work.

Future generations of security experts, risk analysts and software developers need new security skills to deal with the challenges. Dr. Raimundas Matulevičius' book provides a coherent core around which such skill sets can form. It combines perspectives and techniques from security requirements engineering—appropriately placing it in a security risk context—with techniques for secure system development—including pattern-based and model-driven security. Secure software systems modelling, underpinned by a coherent security meta model, is the glue that ties it all together. In Matulevičius' framework, modelling serves to assess security in a wider organisational context, which hopefully also makes it easier for stakeholders from different domains of expertise to collaborate. Modelling is also used as a link from security issues to risk assessment, necessary for prioritising and selecting among security alternatives. Modelling even offers a bridge into secure software development and ICT operations, a bridge made even more streamlined by the use of domain-specific, pattern-based, and model-driven security modelling techniques.

Dr. Matulevičius' book gives a coherent account of the most important modelling-related security techniques today, and shows how to combine them. It describes an integrated set of systematic practices that can be used to deliver increased security to software projects already from the outset. It combines practical ways of working with practical ways of distilling, managing, and making security knowledge operational. Integrated organisation-level security approaches such as the ones presented here will become increasingly important components of corporate ICT security ecologies of the future. His book is well suited for educating the next generations of security experts. While being written primarily for students, it should also interest industrialists and researchers alike. It deserves a broad readership in both academia and industry.

Well done, Raimundas!

University of Bergen   Andreas L. Opdahl
Bergen, Norway
April 2017

Foreword by Nicolas Mayer

Digitalisation of classical industries (e.g., FinTech, Smart Cities, e-Health, etc.) as well as the growth of new data intensive sectors (e.g., robotics, Internet of Things, genomics, etc.) leads to the necessity of securing data and services. In his book about the industries of the future, the innovative technology leader Alec Ross reports that if any college student asked him what career would most assure 50 years of steady, well-paying employment, he would respond "Cybersecurity". Being 'only' $3.5 billion a dozen years ago, the size of the cybersecurity market is expected to be more than $100 billion by 2018.

While organisations and policy-makers being aware of the criticality but also of the cost of security, nowadays, a strong emphasis is put on the management of security risks. Modern day enterprises consider their risk management capabilities as an opportunity to drive their competitive advantage. From a security perspective, risk management supports enterprises to adopt cost-effective security measures because security threats are so numerous that it is impossible to act on all of them. In addition, enterprises are looking for a positive Return On Security Investment (ROSI). In this sense, security risk management plays an important role in alignment of a company's business with its IT strategy. The same paradigm is used by the policy-makers who propose security-related regulations. For example, in the telecommunications sector, the service providers have to comply with the EU Directive 2009/140/EC where the Article 13a speaks about security and integrity of networks and services. This means that the Member States must ensure that their providers would manage the security risks of the public communication networks and services.

A similar approach has been chosen in international security standards, like, for example, ISO/IEC 27001, which provides requirements for an information security management system (ISMS), or PCI DSS, which provides security requirements for organisations that handle credit cards. While being aware of these concerns, the first focus of the book by Dr. Raimundas Matulevičius places the particular interest on security risk management.

In collaboration with some colleagues, we have developed the TISRIM tool, which directly implements the ISSRM (Information System Security Risk Management) domain model depicted in this book. This tool has successfully been used in dozens of companies, going from SMEs of 5–10 employees to larger organisations, such as European institutions. It has especially been used in some of the initial ISO/IEC 27001 certifications in Luxembourg and has been selected as the reference tool for the national law about security measures, to be taken by the telecommunications service providers. This shows the relevance and soundness of the underlying domain model. However, based on the 10 year-experience while using this tool, also taking into account the feedback received from the risk assessment practitioners both from public and private organisations, the current approaches of security risk management suffer from a number of limitations. One of the most common ones concerns the product, which results from the different steps of the risk management process. The outcome is usually a huge matrix composed of hundreds of lines of risks. Today this result is no more sustainable while considering the complexity of current information systems, the extent number of threats, and the fast and continuous evolution of organisations over time. The introduction of modelling languages to deal with (specific parts of) risk management is daring. Additionally I consider that training of the current and future risk management professionals in model-based approaches is promising for the better consideration of security in companies. I am pleased that a large part of this book is dedicated to the accurate and insightful consideration of the relevant and innovative modelling approaches for the risk and security management.

In his book, Dr. Matulevičius introduces a fundamental set of knowledge for the advanced management of risk and security. While going from the conceptual aspects to the practical tools, this book gives a broad coverage of the field. The learning approach is based on the extensive use of examples and exercises; thus, it insures an efficient learning. The further readings guarantee that learners will be able to enhance his or her knowledge on some specific topics.

Congratulations, Raimundas, for this book that I will certainly use as a reference book at the Master-level courses and for professional training!

Luxembourg Institute of Science and Technology   Nicolas Mayer
Luxembourg
May 2017

Preface

Computer systems play an important role in everyday life. If we look around we see that everyone is using computers for editing documents, managing financial data, banking, communicating and other various activities that improve our way of living. However, this also means that we need to deal with the certain risks that affect data and information, such as bank account data, educational qualifications, health records and others. In many cases this data and information needs to be kept private, confidential, integral and available only for the intended audience. This means that the need to secure systems and software becomes a necessity rather than an option.

Although the importance of introducing security engineering practices early in the development cycle has been acknowledged, the current practices take security consideration only after implementing the software systems. However, on one hand, this makes security engineering costly. Even more, it might mean that some critical security risk potentially might be overlooked. On the other hand, early consideration of security allows analysts to envision security threats, their consequences and countermeasures. It also helps in considering system design alternatives and determining the ones, which do not offer a sufficient security level. Finally, early security consideration could contribute to the re-scoping or cancelling of the project if the security risks are estimated as too costly to handle. The **scope** of this book is:

- *security requirements engineering*, including security risk management, major activities, asset identification, security risk analysis and security requirements elicitation;
- *secure software system modelling*, including modelling of context and protected assets, security risks, and decisions of security risk treatment using various modelling languages;
- *secure system development*, including secure system development approaches, pattern-driven development, and model-driven security.

In this book, therefore, we analyse different secure software system engineering techniques with emphasis on security modelling. We emphasise security modelling including the determination and modelling of security requirements, which could be derived through systematic application of the principles for security risk management. Such requirements should be implemented in the security controls, which become assets in the protected software systems. In the book we illustrate how to combined different security modelling perspectives in order to complement generic secure software development.

Audience The reader of this book should be familiar with: (*i*) software system development, (*ii*) requirements engineering, and (*iii*) system modelling. The book could be used as a textbook in university-level courses, fully or partially supporting teaching of principles for secure software system modelling, engineering and development.

The primary target of this book, therefore, is *graduate students* (master and doctorate), who are studying cyber security, software engineering and system security engineering. Major benefits of the books are: (*i*) learning how to identify causes and consequences of (or the lack of) system and software security, (*ii*) learning how to master essential techniques to reduce and avoid system and software security problems, and (*iii*) learning how to introduce and to reason about security requirements, controls and the overall security solution.

The book might be interesting to *practitioners*, especially to the ones who wish to learn about the necessity to reason about decisions behind secure software systems. The book will consider (*i*) the importance of security engineering at early stages of software system development, (*ii*) the importance of the trade-off analysis, and (*iii*) the principles of model-driven security.

How to Read This Book The book consists of four parts and includes twelve chapters. In the introduction chapter (Chap. 1) we define what is meant by security engineering in software systems. Then the chapter provides overview of security and security risk management standards, security modelling approaches, domain-specific security languages and principles of model-driven security. Next, the chapter offers some insight into the multi-perspective secure system analysis. Finally, it presents the running example, which is use through the remainder of the book.

The first part of the book introduces the conceptual bases for security risk management. The part consists of three chapters. In Chap. 2, on *Domain Model for Information Systems Security Risk Management*, we discuss the ISSRM domain model, including definitions of asset-related, security risk-related, and security risk treatment-related concepts. This chapter also discusses concept relationships, multiplicities, processes as well as the metrics used to assess security risks.

In Chap. 3, on *Security Risk*, we define the major constituencies of the security risk. The discussion includes issues on asset harm using malicious software, common security error types and threats to distributed information systems. Next, the chapter discusses aspects of the threat agent profile and presents a number of techniques which could be used for threat model development. In Chap. 4, on *Security Requirements*, firstly, we differentiate between security problem, i.e., security criterion, and security solution, i.e., security requirements. Next, chapter

presents the taxonomy of security requirements and discusses the principles of
security requirements representation and specification.

The second part of the book focusses on security risk-oriented modelling
languages and their means to represent and specify security requirements as
well as to reason about why these security requirements should be introduced in
the considered software system. Security modelling helps developers to envision
potential security solutions before building the system. It can also be used to
discuss these solutions among the system stakeholders. Modelling could contribute
to the trade-off analysis, thus helping to discard ineffective security solutions. In
this part of the book we introduce four languages for security modelling. More
specifically and following the previous part of the book, we discuss how general-
purpose modelling languages are extended for security risk management. The part
consists of four chapters.

Chapter 5, on *Security Risk-Oriented BPMN*, discusses how the modelling
language of business process model and notation (a.k.a., BPMN) is extended with
security criteria, vulnerability, security requirements and other security risk management concepts. The outcome of this extension is the security risk-oriented BPMN.
Chapter 6, on *Security Risk-Aware Secure Tropos*, discusses the Secure Tropos
approach—a modelling language and method to deal with actor dependencies
and goals. The Secure Tropos language is mapped to the ISSRM domain model,
resulting in the security risk-aware Secure Tropos. Chapter 7, on *Security Risk-
Oriented Misuse Cases* introduces how use cases and misuse cases are aligned to
the ISSRM domain model. The chapter mainly focusses on the graphical language
extensions. However, it also briefly discusses the textual use/misuse case templates
and their means to support security risk management. Chapter 8, on *Mal-activities
for Security Risk Management*, introduces security risk management extensions to
mal-activity diagrams, another languages of the UML family. The chapter illustrates
how to analyse dynamic aspects of secure software system development.

The third part of this book is dedicated to the model-driven development of
secure software systems. The use of models could stimulate and support stakeholder
discussions, contribute to security requirements validation, guide software coding
and even automate the coding processes. Models could also be used for the
testing of the security solutions, or be used to reverse-engineer system design from
implementation. In this part we discuss few of these aspects. The part consists of
three chapters:

In Chap. 9, on *Transformations Between Security Risk-Oriented Modelling
Languages*, we discuss how modelling languages considered in the second part
of this book could be translated among themselves. Sets of transformation rules
and guidelines, based on language alignments to the ISSRM domain model, are
introduced and illustrated in four transformation cases. In Chap. 10, on *Role-
Based Access Control*, we discuss the principles of role-based access control. Two
security extensions of the generic UML language—SecureUML and UMLsec—are
considered to show various RBAC concerns and application principles. Based on
the RBAC domain, a set of transformation rules are defined to link both approaches
together and to support the static and dynamic RBAC perspectives. The chapter

ends with discussion on an RBAC model application to restrict access to data storage systems. In Chap. 11, on *Secure System Development Using Patterns*, secure software system development using security patterns is discussed. The chapter presents a taxonomy of the security patterns. Next it discusses how security risk-oriented patterns could be applied to extract security requirements from the business processes.

The last part consists of one chapter. In Chap. 12, *Secure System Development*, we present the three lifecycles of the secure software systems development. In the end, we shortly discuss how different security modelling techniques could be used in the various stages of secure software system development.

Acknowledgements I would like to thank my family: Sigita for her patience and encouragement, Mantvydas and Vygantas for their joyfulness and playfulness, which gave me minutes of thought and relaxation while preparing this book. I thank my parents for their continuous trust, love and support.

Moreover, I am thankful for the many colleagues at different places who gave me a lot of input through discussions, encouragement, joint contributions and active support. Firstly, I wish to thank Prof. Marlon Dumas (from University of Tartu, Estonia) for his continuous encouragement and supportive comments. Secondly, I am grateful to Prof. Patrick Heymans (University of Namur, Belgium), Prof. Eric Dubois (LIST, Luxembourg), Dr. Nicolas Mayer (LIST, Luxembourg), Prof. Guttorm Sindre (University of Science and Technology, Norway), Prof. Andreas Opdahl (University of Bergen, Norway), Prof. Haralambos Mouratidis (University of Brighton, UK), Prof. Kurt Sandkuhl (University of Rostock, Germany), and Prof. Mārīte Kirikova (Riga Technical University, Latvia) for the joint contributions, emphasising discussions and joint research, which contributed to different parts of this book.

I would like to thank to the students of the University of Tartu: Dr. Naved Ahmed, Morshed Chowdhury, Olga Altuhhova, Henri Lakk, Inam Soomro, Naiad Khan, Anastasiia Onchukova, Eduard Sing, Andrei Proskurin, Silver Jürimäe, Karl Kolk, Andrey Sergeev, and Silver Samarütel. Your research contributions and results are valuable inputs to the different parts of this book. I also thank all the participants of the Master-level courses on Principles of Secure Software Design. You have tested the different book chapters by providing your solutions to the exercises and discussing various aspects related to secure software systems modelling.

I would like to thank the company No Magic for its generous permit to use the MagicDraw modelling tool. This help a lot in modelling book's illustrative examples using the BPMN and UML modelling languages. The tool's flexibility and extensibility allowed visualising important principles of secure software systems modelling, model transformation, and technique application.

Last but not least I would like to thank Ralf Gerstner from Springer for his professional help in making this book a reality.

Tartu, Estonia   Raimundas Matulevičius
2017

Contents

Acronyms

ABAC   Attribute-Based Access Control
API   Application Programming Interface
AURUM   Automatic Risk and Utility Management
BPMN   Business Process Model and Notation
BSI   (*In German*) Bundesamt für Sicherheit in der Informationstechnik
CAPEC   Common Attack Pattern Enumeration and Classification
CC   Common Criteria
CCTA   Central Computer and Telecommunications Agency
CORAS   It is the name of the approach;
          "it is not, and has never been, an acronym" [122]
CRAMM   CCTA Risk Analysis and Management Method
CySeMol   Cyber Security Modelling language
CLASP   Comprehensive Lightweight Application Security Process
DAC   Discretionary Access Control
DITSCAP   Defence Information Technology Security Certification and Accreditation Process
DNS   Domain Name System
EBIOS   (*In French*) Expression des Besoins et Identification des Objectifs de Sécurité
ERIS   Electronic Registration Information System
FSR   Final Security Review
HTML   HyperText Markup Language
ICMP   Internet Control Message Protocol
IOI   Items of Interest
IS   Information System
ISO/IEC   International Organisation for Standardisation and the International Electrotechnical Commission
ISSRM   Information Systems Security Risk Management
$i*$ Intentional Distribution (Modelling Language)
KAOS   Knowledge Acquisition in autOmated Specification
MAC   Mandatory Access Control

MEHARi	(*In French*): Methode Harmonisée d'Analyse du Risque informatique
MEMO	Multi-Perspective Enterprise Modelling
MUCM	Misuse Case Maps
NIST	National Institute of Standards and Technology
OCL	Object Constraint Language
OCTAVE	Operationally Critical Threat, Asset, and Vulnerability Evaluation
OWASP	Open Web Application Security Project
RAdAC	Risk-Adaptive Access Control
RBAC	Role-Based Access Control
RE	Requirements Engineering
SEAM	Security Enhanced Actor Model
SEGM	Security Enhanced Goal Model
SQUARE	Security Quality Requirements Engineering
SREBP	Security Requirements Elicitation from Business Processes
SROMUC	Security Risk-Oriented Misuse Cases
SRP	Security Risk-Oriented Patterns
SSDL	Secure System Development Lifecycle
STRIDE	Spoofing, Tampering, Repudiation, Information Disclosure, Denial of Service, Elevation of privileges
TCP	Transmission Control Protocol
UCON	Usage CONtrol Model
UML	Unified Modelling Language
XACML	eXtensible Access Control Markup Language
XML	eXtensible Markup Language

Chapter 1
Introduction

Secure system development is not a trivial task. It comprises a number of activities, which need to be combined, analysed, and executed to produce a secure software system. In this section, after defining secure system engineering we give an overview of few existing security and security risk management standards. The chapter is followed by a survey of security modelling approaches, domain-specific languages for security modelling and principles of model-driven security. An important concern of the software system is the ability to capture multiple system perspectives. In this chapter we survey various modelling perspectives and argue for the importance of capturing these perspectives and complementing the system models using model transformation principles. This chapter also presents a running example and the structure of this book.

1.1 System and Security Engineering

In information system theory, a "*system* is a set of correlated phenomena, which itself is a phenomenon" [109]. However, in practical settings we could understand system [15] as (*i*) a product or component (e.g., personal computer, smartcard, a piece of software, etc.), (*ii*) infrastructure needed to combine the products or components (e.g., operating system, network, etc.), (*iii*) applications that are used to support everyday activities (e.g., browser, financial system, word processor, etc.), (*iv*), information technology staff who support the above-mentioned components, (*v*) internal users and management, who uses the technology to produce business products or services, and (*vi*) customers and other external users, who buy products and use services. In other words, *system* is everything, since all these elements (i.e., phenomena) correlate to each other. In addition, the system will not be a stand-alone element, but will interact with other systems; thus it will operate in the environment, making other systems on its own.

© Springer International Publishing AG 2017
R. Matulevičius, *Fundamentals of Secure System Modelling*,
DOI 10.1007/978-3-319-61717-6_1

"*Security engineering* is concerned with lowering the risk of intentional unauthorised harm to valuable assets to a level that is acceptable to the system's stakeholders by preventing and reacting to malicious harm, misuse, threats and security risks" [70]. Hence, security engineering is dealing with *intentional unauthorised risks* and it is different from *safety* engineering, where *unintentional* risk is considered. During security engineering process, analysts must understand what stakeholders' values (in terms of assets) are and how these values must be protected. It is not possible to reach "100 percent security" because there exist feasibility and acceptability boundaries defined during the engineering process. Finally, the definition highlights that security risk could be determined in different forms, including harm, misuse, and threat. Thus, the task of the security analyst is to recognise these forms and uncover the complete picture of the security risk.

Security engineering concentrates on tools, processes and methodologies that support analysing, designing and implementing new systems or adjusting an existing system according to the needs of its environment. The analysis of security should be performed through the whole software development process, starting from early requirements and going through later requirements, design, and implementation stages. An early consideration of security allows analysts and modellers to discover threats, understand their consequences and develop countermeasures to mitigate these threats. It also proposes security design alternatives, and could result in the decision of project cancellation if the security risks are too high.

1.2 Security and Security Risk Management Standards

There exist a number of standards to manage security or security risks. In [1] a short overview of these standards is presented. In this section we will recall it to explain the important security and security risk management principles.

Security standards define guidelines for information security management. For instance, the ISO/IEC 13335-1:2004 standard [93] defines security concepts and models fundamental for a basic understanding of information and communication technology security. It also addresses the general management issues that are essential to the successful planning, implementation and operation of information and communication technology security. The Common Criteria for information technology security evaluation [36] standard specifies security requirements and the desired security goals. The goal of evaluators is to determine whether the chosen security requirements help to achieve the defined security measures and to check whether they are implemented correctly.

The *security risk management standards* particularly focus on security risk management activities. Following [1, 133] we include a short overview of the ISO/IEC 2700x series [94, 95], a NIST special publication [154, 155], and the BSI standards 100 series for information technology [32–35].

The ISO/IEC 27001:2013 standard [95] defines the requirements to establish, implement, maintain, continuously improve and manage an information security management system. It presents requirements for managing an organisation's sensitive information by applying risk management, risk assessment and risk treatment means. The major parts of the standard include guidance on understanding context of organisation, leadership, planning, support, operation performance evaluation and improvement activities. It also provides a checklist of objectives and controls (although an organisation could also choose other controls according to its preferences). The objectives and controls could be combined to develop an organisation's treatment plan to respond to security risks. The ISO/IEC 27001 is supported by ISO/IEC 27005 [94], which introduces the security risk management process. The process consists of context establishment, risk assessment, risk treatment, risk acceptance, risk communication, consultation, risk monitoring and review. The process uses an iterative approach for risk assessment and/or risk treatment activities.

The National Institute of Standards and Technology (NIST) has published a set of standards addressing security and risk in information systems. For example, according to the NIST SP 800-39 standard [154], the risk management approach consists of four components: (1) frame risk; (2) assess risk; (3) respond to risk; and (4) monitor risk. The risk assessment components are addressed in NIST SP 800-30 [155]. This standard introduces a process consisting of risk assessment preparation, risk assessment conduction, risk assessment result communication, and risk assessment maintenance. In other words, the process guides the communication between the risk assessment and other organisational risk management processes.

An IT-Grundschutz is series of German standards for security management methods. It includes four standards for information security management systems [32], methodology [33], risk analysis [34], and business continuity management [35]. The standard on information security management systems [32] specifies the requirements of such systems. The methodology standard [33] defines successive steps to guide a management system for information security. It describes how to introduce and maintain an information security policy, how to select information security safeguards to implement the information security policy, and how to maintain and improve information security during its operation. The standard on risk analysis [34] highlights the risk analysis methodology in addition to the methodology defined in the second standard. A supplementary security analysis should be done for the particular assets (or target objects) determined in the methodology. The fourth standard on business continuity management [35] is based on the previous standards. It presents a method to detect the risks that can endanger the survival (i.e., economic existence) of an organisation, and to develop safeguards against such risks or even after incurring the risks. Overall, the BSI standards present a process for achieving and maintaining the required level of security, and the way to determine and achieve it.

The standards give an explanation of components to define the security and security risk management domain model. In Chap. 2 the domain model for security risk management is discussed. This model combines the principles of the above-mentioned standards to the systematic perspective and guidance for the security requirements definition and reasoning.

1.3   Security Development Approaches

There exist few literature surveys which present extensive overviews and comparisons of security requirements techniques, frameworks, processes and methodologies. For instance, in [63], Fabian et al. present a conceptual framework to compare and evaluate security requirements engineering approaches. In Chap. 4 a number of the security development approaches are summarised following the technique, framework, process and method classification suggested in [143].

In this book we will look at a few secure system modelling approaches especially ones related to system security risk management. For instance, we consider how business process model and notation can support security risk management. Next we illustrate extensions of Secure Tropos to security risk-aware analysis. To capture functional and behavioural properties of secure software systems, we apply misuse cases and mal-activities. UMLsec [100] and SecureUML [21, 119] will be considered to define access control authorisation constraints. Finally we illustrate the security requirements elicitation from business processes (SREBP), an approach to derive security requirements from the BPMN models [1, 4, 178].

1.4   Domain-Specific Languages for Security Modelling

Domain-specific modelling languages focus on particular a domain and help us find and visualise the targeted solution for problems of this domain. As in other domains, there exist a number of domain-specific languages for security modelling and engineering. For instance, approaches to model security using domain-specific languages are reported in [30]. Elsewhere in [122], the CORAS modelling language is dedicated to security and safety risk analysis. It suggests visual constructs to decompose and analyse threats, to reason and to introduce security countermeasures. In [195], the cyber security modelling language (CySeMoL) is introduced to express enterprise-level system architectures and to capture security attacks and reason about the countermeasures.

In this work we will consider extensions of traditional modelling approaches—BPMN [54, 159, 189], Tropos [29], misuse cases [158, 192], and mal-activity diagrams [158, 191]—and illustrate how they could be extended to the domain-specific modelling languages. This helps us manage security risks. We will also consider the domain of role-based access control and modelling languages—SecureUML [21, 119] and UMLsec [100]—dedicated to capturing principles of the role-based access control.

1.5 Model-Driven Security

Model-driven development is a development paradigm which uses models through the development cycle. Models could be used for the different purposes (see Fig. 1.1), including code visualisation, base modelling, roundtrip engineering, and model-centric development [197]. Models bring the abstraction of the real world to simplified viewpoints, and focus on certain concerns or phenomena. Models help transform code-based decisions to model-based decisions, without influencing the level of abstraction captured in the considered software system. Models also help separate classes of phenomena needed to implement the software system.

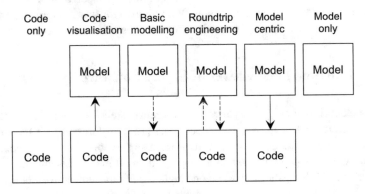

Fig. 1.1 Links between code and model, adapted from [197]

Models can be used for various reasons, but one of the principles of model-driven development concerns the means for model transformation. In [214] a taxonomy of transformation approaches is presented (see Fig. 1.2). Rule-based transformations are performed following predefined rules. Ontology-based transformations share vocabulary, where a common concepts are defined; hence the ontology acts as the intermediate level to transform models from one language representation to another based on the construct semantics. Identify-based transformations translate the source model to the target model without changing information: "the two models describe the same concepts but with different representation" [214]. The pattern-based transformation translates the source patterns (set of source elements) to target patterns (a set of target elements).

Model-driven security is an application of the model-driven technologies to develop secure software systems. In principle it defines the transformation-oriented approach to generate security constraints from the security requirements models. Principles of model-driven security could be used for various purposes. In this book we will discuss the use of models to elicit security requirements through security risk management. Next we will use models to represent various security requirements perspectives, including functional, behavioural, actor and role, goal and rule, and topological perspectives. We will apply rule-based and ontology-based trans-

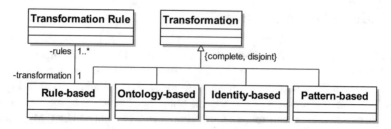

Fig. 1.2 Transformation taxonomy, adapted from [214]

formation methods to capture these different security perspectives of both security requirements and secure system design. We will also illustrate pattern-based transformation to capture security constraints from models of the secure software system.

1.6   Modelling Perspectives of Secure Software Systems

Software development typically involves different stakeholders with different goals, needs, requirements and system expectations [157]. Addressing all the different viewpoints and agreeing about them requires using various modelling techniques, estimating their dependencies, and managing them all in a consistent and coherent manner. In [109] Krogstie isolates among eight modelling perspectives: behavioural, functional, structural, goal and rule, object, communication, actor and role, and topological perspectives. The *behavioural perspective* deals with the phenomenon of states and transitions between them. The *functional perspective* defines a transformation as an activity, which transforms one set of phenomena to a different set of phenomena. The *structural perspective* concentrates on the static structure of the software system; it deals with entities, their relationships, their attributes and their values. The *goal and rule* perspective focusses on modelling goals (something that needs to be achieved) and rules (something that needs to be satisfied). The *object perspective* defines the main phenomena as objects, processes, and classes. The *communication perspective* is based on the language/action theory and on the premise of human collaboration through communication. The *actor and role perspective* originates from organisational modelling and deals with actors, agents, roles and their dependencies. Finally, the *topological perspective* deals with ordering between different perspectives.

Examples of Modelling Perspectives Although most of the modelling approaches cover several modelling perspectives at the same time, typically they acquire one primary perspective. For instance, business process model and notation (BPMN) [54, 159, 189] and UML activity diagrams [158] belong to the *functional perspective*. They both include the major construct groups such as flow objects, swimlanes, artefacts and connecting objects. However, BPMN is rather meant to model an organisation's workflows and business processes; in other words, BPMN is used to visualise *business* entities, their collaborations, and data flow and describe how the software system can be used to achieve business goals. The activity diagrams are dedicated to the dynamic aspects of the considered *software system*. In other words, activity diagrams are used to express the functional perspective of the software system and/or software system components.

UML use case diagrams are typically used to present the *behavioural perspective*. A use case represents "a declaration of an offered behaviour" [158], which is characterised by activities, interactions and states as well as pre-conditions and post-conditions.

Another modelling approach considered in this book is Tropos [29]. It originates form the *i** modelling language [213] used to capture social relationships between organisation's actors. Hence actor could be classified as agent, position or role. Agent could occupy position, position could cover role and agent could play the role. Naturally, the *i** and Tropos modelling approaches capture the *actor and role* modelling perspective, where the dependency relationships are defined between different agents (including the software system) in the organisation. Tropos also covers the *goal and rule* perspective, as one of the purposes of modelling using Tropos is to elicit and satisfy an actor's goal through the eligible performance of the plans and use of the available resources.

In the second part of this book we will consider how different modelling approaches (i.e., BPMN, Secure Tropos, UML use cases, and UML activity diagrams) can help in managing security risks using the language alignment to the domain model of the information systems security risk management [53, 133]. This alignment will illustrate the *topological perspective*, where different modelling constructs will be identified to address certain concepts of the security risk management domain.

Capturing Various Perspectives There were a few attempts to support a smooth transition between different the security modelling perspectives. For instance, [80] presents MEMO, a multi-perspective enterprise modelling. Its core components support multi-perspective development of secure systems. It concentrates on the technological, organisational and economic perspectives, takes into account the relevant contents, and provides integration of the perspectives. Hence the security risk management consists of four activities: (*i*) enterprise characterisation (i.e., asset identification, definition of goals and business structure, and others), (*ii*) security risk identification (i.e., identification of security threats and vulnerabilities), (*iii*) security risk evaluation (i.e., evaluation of threat likelihood and impact and determination of security risks), and (*iv*) security risk mitigation (i.e., risk prioritisation, control recommendation and implementation). Although MEMO suggests modelling notations to capture various perspectives and define their consistent representation and traceability, it still remains a domain-specific modelling approach that needs to be learnt by the stakeholders.

Another approach to linking secure system modelling perspectives is through the transformation of different models, as illustrated in Fig. 1.3. Such an approach has few advantages. Firstly, it helps capture the security concerns using different modelling languages, which still could (at least one or few representations) be familiar to the various stakeholders. Thus, the stakeholders would not need to learn new notations, but be familiar with the standard ones.

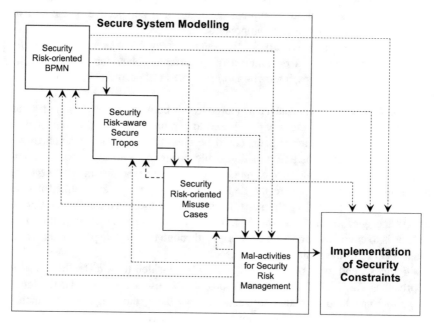

Fig. 1.3 Multiple modelling perspectives: approaches described in this book (*solid* arrows describe transformations discussed in this book, *dashed arrows* - other possible transformations)

Secondly, it helps ensure a systematic and consistent security engineering process through different development stages. This also helps maintain traceability between the security requirements, their implementation in the security controls and their transformation to the security constraints in the developed software application.

Thirdly, the transformations help to enhance the model of the considered system. As these modelling approaches, following the topological perspectives, would be aligned to the common ontology (in our case this is the domain model for security risk management [53, 133]), the model translations would be performed using ontology-based transformations.

As illustrated in the third part of the book, typically, the transformed model will not capture the same information that is defined in the original model. The modeller would complement the new model with additional details, bringing additional details and capturing the more complete description of the analysed system. Additionally, the transformed model would stimulate further system development with additional security concerns and help us see new emerging security risks and their countermeasures.

Finally, the security transformation could result in a transformed security code, which would help us capture security constraints of the software system. In the book, the principles of pattern-based transformation from security models (expressing the RBAC policy) to the security constraints will be illustrated.

1.7 Running Example

General Description In this book a *Football Federation case* is used as an example to show various principles of secure system modelling. This example was partially analysed in [107]; however, in this book a hypothetical case is developed to illustrate different principles of secure system modelling and design. Figure 1.4 provides some informal description of the system used in the *Football Federation case*. Like all organisations, Football Federation has a number of employees. For example, Football Federation Employee is carrying the typical business workflows in the organisation. To support his business activities he is using various systems. One of them is Electronic Registration Information System (ERIS), typically consisting of User Interface, Information Processing System, and Database, as illustrated in Fig. 1.4.

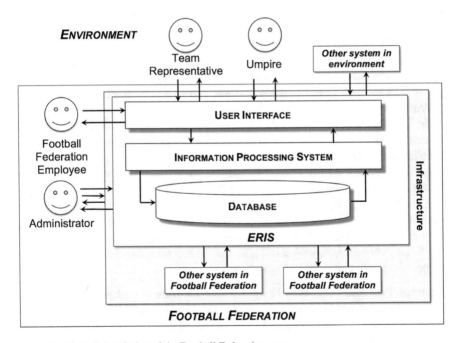

Fig. 1.4 Informal description of the Football Federation case

ERIS is not a standalone application, but is connected to Other systems used within the Football Federation organisation, and also Other systems existing in the environment. To maintain the Football Federation systems, a certain Infrastructure (including operating systems, networks, connection channels, etc.) should be established and constantly maintained. This is responsibility of an **Administrator**, who is an employee of the Football Federation.

Additionally there might exist *external users*, such as **Team Representative** and **Umpire**, who potentially might access the **ERIS** for one or another service or needed information. The Football Federation organisation is not isolated, and, as mentioned above, is connected to **Other systems** existing in the environment, which could request some services from ERIS or provide services by themselves.

Conceptual Model An extract of the conceptual model of the ERIS system is presented in Fig. 1.5 as a UML class diagram. It includes five concepts: **Game**, **Team**, **Player**, **Timetable** and **Umpire**.

Game represents games organised and administered by the Football Federation. Games are described by their information (i.e., attribute **gameInfo**), assigned umpired (i.e., attribute **umpire**), game report (i.e., attribute **gameReport**), and confirmation of the game report (i.e., attribute **confirmation**).

Team describes the football teams which are members of the Football Federation. Each team is characterised by its information (i.e., attribute **teamInfo**, which might include name, city, sponsor, etc.). Team has a team representative (i.e., attribute **teamRep**). Team makes a decision about participating in the tournaments (i.e., attribute **participationDecision**). Finally, if the participation decision is positive, the information about the team's region and league is added (i.e., attribute **regionAndLeague**).

Players are the members of the team. In this model, each player is described by his information (i.e., attribute **playerInfo**, which might include name, surname, position in the team, etc.) and his performance in a certain game (i.e., attribute **playerPerformance**).

In **Timetable**, a schedule of all games administered by the Football Federation is assembled. Timetable is described using timetable information (i.e., attribute **timeTableInfo**, list of including leagues, playing teams, place, etc.) and schedule of games (i.e., attribute **schedule**). In addition, each timetable should be confirmed by the league administrators (i.e., attribute **timeTableConfirmation**).

Finally, each game is assigned a certain number (typically 3, 4) of **Umpires**. Each umpire is described by his umpire info (i.e., attribute **umpireInfo** including umpire's name, surname, expertise, etc.). Umpire also receives special access to the ERIS (i.e., attribute **umpireAccess**), so that he can provide information about his games (described using the **assignedGames** attribute).

Business Processes The BPMN *value chain diagram* describes how an organisation's business functions are related to each other in order achieve the business goals [54, 159, 189]. In Fig. 1.6 an extract of the ERIS value chain is provided. The selected subprocesses are

- **Register team**—registering teams to the ERIS system;
- **Register player**—registering players and assigning them to the teams;
- **Register umpire**—registering umpires to the ERIS system;
- **Create leagues and divisions**—creating new leagues and preparing divisions;
- **Create timetable**—creating and preparing a timetable;

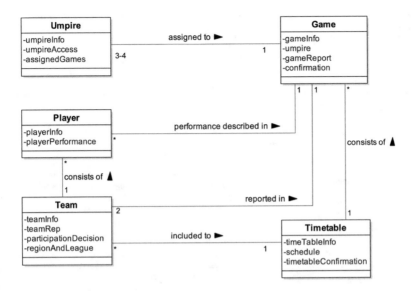

Fig. 1.5 Conceptual model

- Register game—registering games and their results.

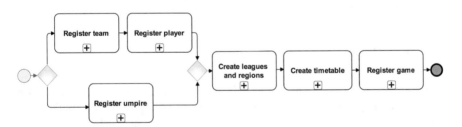

Fig. 1.6 Business process value chain

The latter subprocess—Register game report—is expanded in Fig. 1.7. Here the Football Federation Employee decides to enter a new game (see task Enter new game) and thus submits the game information (see task Submit game info); once the initial game information is received, the entry is created in the game storage (see task Create game). The Football Federation Employee also assigns the umpire (see task Assign umpire). After the game the Umpire submits a game report (see task Submit game report). After the game report is updated (see task Update game report) it needs to be confirmed by the Football Federation Employee (see task Confirm game report).

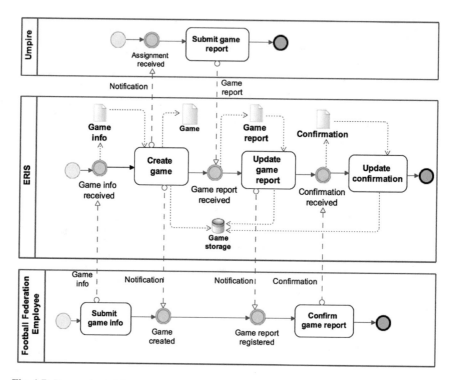

Fig. 1.7 Process to register game report

1.8   Exercises

Exercise 1.1 Describe what "system" is in the *Football Federation case*. What or who are the products/components of the system, its infrastructure applications, information technology staff, internal users and management, customers and other external users? To support your answer, fill in Table 1.1.

Table 1.1 Template to support answer of Exercise 1.1

System components	Football Federation case
Products / Components	
Infrastructure	
Applications	
Information technology staff	
Internal users and management	
Customers and external users	
Environment	

Exercise 1.2 Compare the components and processes of different security risk management standardisation initiatives:

- ISO/IEC 2700x vs. NIST;
- NIST vs. BSI;
- BSI vs. ISO/IEC 2700x.

Exercise 1.3 Discuss what techniques, frameworks, processes and methods for secure software system development are familiar to you from your previous practices and courses. What were your bad and good experiences?

Exercise 1.4 What are modelling perspectives? How do different modelling perspectives influence development of secure software systems?

Exercise 1.5 Discuss advantages and disadvantages of the transformation-driven approaches to developing secure software systems?

Exercise 1.6 How could different Football Federation subprocesses (see Fig. 1.6) be expanded? Model **Register team**, **Register player**, and **Create leagues and regions** subprocesses using business model and notation, BPMN (or any other modelling language of your preference).

Part I
Security Risk Management

Chapter 2
Domain Model for Information Systems Security Risk Management

One important task during secure systems development is to understand what assets need to be protected against which risks, and how these risks could be mitigated by proposed security countermeasures. However, the problem is that the domain terminology needs to be understood in the same way by the people working on the problem. To solve this problem, some domain model should be introduced to guide these activities.

A domain model for information systems security risk management (ISSRM) is developed through a survey of security-related standards, security risk management standards, and security risk management methods. This domain model is presented in [53, 133]. In this chapter we present the concepts of the ISSRM domain model, risk management process and security risk metrics. We will complete the chapter with the illustrative example and some overview of the related approaches for the security risk management.

2.1 Domain Model

The ISSRM domain model [53, 133] consists of three major groups of concepts: asset-related concepts (see Sect. 2.1.1), risk-related concepts (see Sect. 2.1.2), and risk treatment-related concepts (see Sect. 2.1.3). In Fig. 2.1, the domain model is presented as a UML class diagram and a glossary where concept definitions are provided. In this section we will briefly present these definitions.

2.1.1 Asset-Related Concepts

Asset-related concepts describe which of an organisation's assets are important to protect and what criteria guarantee a certain level of asset security. An *asset* is anything that is valuable and plays a role accomplishing the organisation's

© Springer International Publishing AG 2017
R. Matulevičius, *Fundamentals of Secure System Modelling*,
DOI 10.1007/978-3-319-61717-6_2

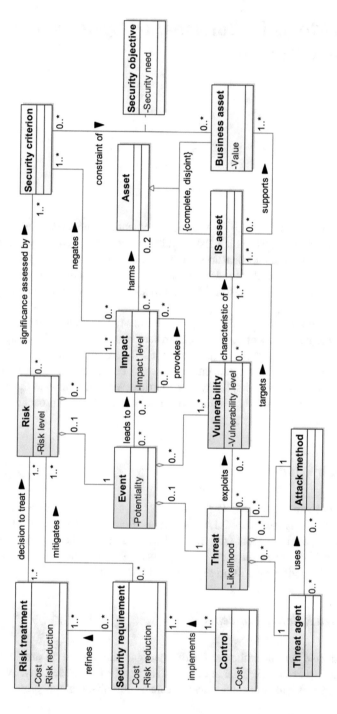

Fig. 2.1 The ISSRM domain model, adapted from [53, 133]

objectives. Assets can be classified as business assets or organisational assets. A *business asset* describes the information, processes, capabilities and skills essential to the business and its core mission. Typically, business assets are immaterial. An *IS asset* is a component or part of an information system, valuable to the organisation since it supports business assets. An IS asset[1] can be a component of the information technology system (e.g., hardware, software or network), but also person or a facility that plays a role in the system and, therefore, in its security. The IS assets (with the exception of software) are material. A *security criterion* (also called *security property*) characterises a security need and is a property or constraint on business assets. The security objectives are defined using security criteria on business assets. Thus, the security criteria describe the security needs, which are, typically, expressed as confidentiality, integrity and availability of business assets.

2.1.2 Risk-Related Concepts

Risk-related concepts introduce definitions of risk itself and its immediate components. A *risk* is a combination of a threat with one or more vulnerabilities leading to a negative impact on two or more assets[2] by harming them. The combination of threat and vulnerabilities represents a risk event and impact is the consequence of this risk.

An *impact* is the potential negative consequence of a risk that negates the security criterion defined for business assets and harms these assets when a threat (or an event) is accomplished. The impact can also be described at the level of IS assets (e.g., data destruction, failure of a component, etc.) or at the level of business assets, where it negates security criteria (e.g., loss of information confidentiality, loss of process integrity, loss of data availability). In addition, one impact can provoke a chain reaction of impacts (or indirect impacts), for example, a loss of confidentiality of sensitive information leads to a loss of customer confidence.

A risk *event* is an aggregation of a threat and one or more vulnerabilities. A *vulnerability* is the characteristic of an IS asset or group of IS assets that exposes a weakness or flaw in terms of security. A *threat* is an incident initiated by a threat agent using an attack method to target one or more IS assets by exploiting their vulnerabilities. A *threat agent* is an agent that has the means to intentionally harm IS assets. A threat agent triggers a threat and, thus, is the source of a risk. The threat agent is characterised by expertise, its available resources, and motivation. An *attack method* describes a standard means by which a threat agent executes a threat.

---

[1]Later in the book we will refer to the *IS asset* as a *system asset*, indicating the generosity of different IS components in supporting the business assets.

[2]The domain model assumes that if there is a business asset, it is supported by at least one IS asset. Thus, the impact harms at least one business asset and at least one IS asset.

2.1.3 Risk Treatment-Related Concepts

Risk-treatment related concepts describe the concepts to treat risk. A *risk treatment decision* is a decision to treat the identified risk. A treatment satisfies a security need, expressed in generic and functional terms and refined to security requirements. There are four categories of risk treatment decisions possible:

- *Risk avoidance* is a decision not to become involved with or to withdraw from a risk. The system's functionality is modified or discarded for avoiding the risk;
- *Risk reduction* includes actions to lessen the probability, negative consequence, or both associated with a risk. Security requirements are, typically, selected for reducing the risks;
- *Risk transfer* defines how risk parties could share the burden of loss from a risk. A third party is related to the (or part of the) system. This also means that some security requirements could be defined regarding the third party;
- *Risk retention* constitutes acceptance of the burden of loss from a risk. No design decision is necessary in this case.

A *security requirement* is a condition on the phenomena of the environment that we wish to make true by installing the information system, in order to mitigate risks. A security requirement is the refinement of a risk treatment decision to mitigate the risks. On the one hand risk reduction decisions lead to security requirements. But sometimes, risk transfer decisions need to improve some security requirements on third parties. Avoiding risk and retaining risk do not need any security requirement. On the other hand, each security requirement contributes to cover one or more risk treatments for the target system.

A *control* (*countermeasure* or *safeguard*) is a designed means to improve the security by implementing the security requirements. Security controls can be processes, policies, devices, practices or other actions or components of the IS and its organisation that act to reduce risks.

2.2 Relationships and Multiplicities

In [133], relationships and multiplicities between the ISSRM concepts are discussed. They are presented in Fig. 2.1 and discussed in this section.

Relationships of Asset-Related Concepts Assets can be *specialised* as two different kinds: business assets and IS assets. The specialisation is *disjoint* and complete. An information system asset can *support* one or more business assets, but a business asset can have no support in the system (e.g., the selling skills of the sales department are an asset of the company, but they are not part of the system). However, a usual situation is that a business asset *is supported by several* IS assets. Each business asset can *be constrained* from zero (e.g., if the business asset has no support in the IS) to several security criteria. A security criterion can *be a constraint of* several different business assets, or not constrain any of them.

One or several security criteria can be taken into account to *assess the significance of* a risk. But a security criterion can *be concerned* by none of the risks in the case where there is no relevant impact for this criterion found.

Relationships of Risk-Related Concepts A risk is *composed of* an event and one or more impacts. The same impact can be part of several risks, but an event identifies a given risk. A given event *leads to* zero (if no relevant impact is found; in this case the event does not produce a risk) or to several impacts. An impact can *be caused by* many different events. One or several impacts *can provoke* some other (indirect) impacts.

Impacts *harm* assets, both at the business and at the system levels. An asset can *be harmed* by zero (if no impact is considered as relevant) or several impacts, and an impact *harms* at least one system asset and at least one business asset. At the level of business assets, an impact *negates* one or more security criteria, and a given security criterion can *be negated by* zero (if no relevant impact is concerned with this security criterion) or several impacts.

The risk event *is composed* of a threat and one or more vulnerabilities. A given threat can only be related to a given event. The threat *exploits* zero to several vulnerabilities. If a threat is identified, but has no relevant associated vulnerability, it will be neither part of an event nor a risk. A given vulnerability can *be exploited by* many different threats and, therefore, related to many different events, or *not be exploited by* any of them, if no relevant threat is found.

A vulnerability is a *characteristic of* a system asset or group of them. An IS asset can have from zero to several vulnerabilities. A threat *targets* one or more system assets and this asset can be targeted by zero to several threats.

A threat is *defined in terms* of a threat agent that *uses* an attack method. Each threat agent (respectively, attack method) identified as relevant can be involved in several threats, or sometimes in none of them if no relevant corresponding attack method (respectively threat agent) is found. A given threat agent *uses* from zero to several attack methods, and an attack method can *be used by* zero or more threat agents.

Relationships of Risk Treatment-Related Concepts A risk treatment *expresses* the decision to treat one or more risks. Each identified risk *has a risk treatment* and sometimes several of them can be combined (they are not mutually exclusive). A risk treatment decision *is refined to* one or more security requirements. However, the risk treatments of acceptance and avoidance *are refined to* none security requirement. Each security requirement *refines* one or many risk treatments.

A security requirement *mitigates* one or more risks. A given risk *cannot be mitigated* by any security requirement (e.g., when the risk is accepted), but can be *mitigated by* several security requirements if they are necessary to reach an acceptable level of risk. Finally, a control *implements* one or more security requirements, and the same security requirement may *be implemented by* one or several controls.

2.3 Metrics

The ISSRM security metrics are defined in [135] and included in the visual domain model representation, in Fig. 2.1. The value of business assets is measured using the *Value* metric. This value metric is used to estimate the security need of each business asset in terms of confidentiality, integrity and availability. A metric to assess *Security need* expresses the importance of the security criterion with respect to the business asset. This metric is introduced as an attribute of the security objective concept.

Risk is estimated using the *Risk level* metric. The risk level depends on the event *Potentiality* and the *Impact level*, these two concepts composing the one of risk. Since an event is composed of threat and vulnerability, an event's *Potentiality* is estimated through threat *Likelihood* and *Vulnerability level*. It is necessary to note that threat agent and attack method do not have their own metric representing their level. Some characteristics of threat agents and attack methods can be identified independently, like the motivation and the competence of the threat agent and the kind of attack method (natural, human, etc.). But they can be used as indicators to well estimate the risk-related concepts and mainly the likelihood of a threat.

In risk treatment-related concepts, risk treatment and security requirements are estimated in terms of *Risk reduction* performed and *Cost* incurred. Controls can be only estimated in terms of *Cost*.

The proposed metrics are rather abstract. Their implementation could result in qualitative, quantitative, or combined (i.e., qualitative and quantitative) approaches. *Quantitative risk analysis* typically employs a set of methods or principles for assessing risks, based on the use of precise numbers [135]. It tries to assign hard financial values to assets, expected losses, and cost of controls. This method gives the most accurate data, but quantitative risk analysis requires significant amount of information and time.

Qualitative risk analysis typically employs a set of methods or principles based on non-numerical categories or levels (e.g., very low, low, moderate, high, very high) [135]. The basic process for risk assessment of a qualitative approach is similar to what happens in the quantitative approach. However, the main difference is in the relative calculation values; these do not require a lot of time or staff to calculate precise financial numbers for asset valuation, possible impact from a risk being realised or the cost of implementing controls. The drawback of a qualitative approach is that the results are vague and imprecise because of the relative values.

2.4 Process

The ISSRM domain model is focussed around a process, describing activities to perform in order to manage security risks. In [133] this process (see Fig. 2.2) is reported as the result of the analysis of the security and security risk management standards (see Chap. 1).

The process begins with (a) a study of the organisation's context and the identification of its assets. In this step, the organisation, its environment and the system(s) used in this organisation are described. Then, based on the level of protection required for the assets, one needs to determine the (b) security objectives. Security objectives are defined in terms of confidentiality, integrity and availability of the business assets. The next step of the process is (c) risk analysis, where security risks which harm assets and threaten security objectives are elicited and assessed. Once risk assessment is finished, decisions about (d) risk treatment are taken (e.g., avoiding, reducing, transferring or accepting the risk). The next step (e)) is the elicitation of security requirements to mitigate the identified risks. Finally, security requirements are implemented as security controls (f), i.e., system-specific countermeasures that are implemented within the organisation.

The ISSRM process is iterative. Several iterations need to be performed, until we reach an acceptable level for each risk. Figure 2.2 presents only few the major iteration points. Even after reaching an acceptable level for all risks, the ISSRM process should be regularly reviewed. Risks are obviously not static and should be monitored either automatically or manually by the risk analyst in an organisation. Each modification in the organisation's business, in its context and/or in its system can produce modifications on risks and their levels. In an ideal way, the ISSRM process should in fact be continuously performed, in order to keep the organisation's business and its associated security needs aligned with the taken measures, thus ensuing the required security level.

2.5 ISSRM Application Example

The example of the application of the ISSRM domain model is taken from the *Football Federation case*, described in Sect. 1.7. We will illustrate how the example could be developed using the ISSRM concepts (see Table 2.1 for the asset-oriented concepts).

Let's assume that the Umpire submits the Game report data to the ERIS system. Thus, here the Game report corresponds to the *business asset*, which is supported at least by two *system assets—input interface* (e.g., frame to Submit game report), used by the Umpire to submit the data, and *database* (e.g., Game storage), where the ERIS data are stored. We extend this context with one additional *system asset*—Transmission medium, used to transfer submitted Game report from the *input interface* to the *database*. The example content is illustrated in Fig. 2.3. Security criteria in our example are Confidentiality of the game report and Integrity of the game report.

There might exist several security risks in this context. In this example (see Table 2.2) we present a few risks related to the transmission medium. Let's say there exists a *threat agent*, i.e., an attacker with means to intercept the transmission medium by acting as a proxy between the input interface and the database. Thus, using his expertise and available means, this attacker is able to perform

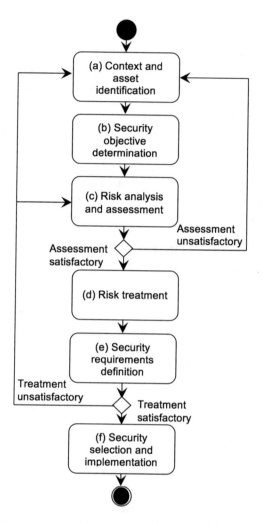

Fig. 2.2 The ISSRM process, adapted from [133]

the *attack method*: firstly, he intercepts the transmission medium between the input interface and the database; secondly, he manipulates data. Data manipulation could be done in two ways (thus characterising two different security risks): (*i*) capturing, modifying and passing data to the database, or (*ii*) capturing, reading, and keeping data for the later use). These security risks are possible because there exists the potential weakness of the transmission medium, which can be intercepted (i.e., *vulnerability* that defines Characteristics of transmission medium to be intercepted) and because there exists no functionality to hide data (i.e., the *vulnerability* that there is a Lack of crypto-functionality at the input interface and database).

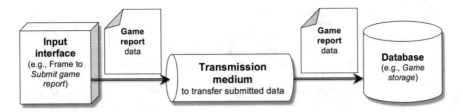

Fig. 2.3 Illustrative example

Table 2.1 Example of the asset-related concepts

Asset-related Concepts		
Assets	Business assets	Game report data submitted at the frame to *Submit game report* and stored in the Game storage
	System assets	(*i*) Frame to Submit game report used by umpire, (*ii*)Transmission medium that transfers game report, and (*iii*) Game storage to store ERIS data
Security criteria		(*i*) Confidentiality of game report and (*ii*) Integrity of game report

If the *threat agent* succeeds in executing the *attack method* because of the existing *vulnerabilities*, this will lead to the risk *impact*; i.e., loss of Game report confidentiality or loss of Game report integrity. Additionally, such a risk *event* will also harm both the *IS asset* and the *business asset*: (i) the Game report will not be securely submitted and stored; (ii) the reliability of the transmission medium will be lost.

As compiled in Table 2.2, concepts *threat*, *event*, and *risk* are identified as the composed elements using *threat agent*, *attack method*, *vulnerability*, and *impact*.

We identify (at least) two potential risk treatment decisions (see Table 2.3): risk avoidance and risk reduction. It is important to note that both decisions would mitigate the two previously identified risks (see Table 2.2). In the treatment of *risk avoidance* it is possible to change the transmission medium so that there would be no possibility to intercept it. For example, instead of using the computer means, the user could physically (himself or using postal service) deliver the printed documents; then the receiver would manually enter the Game report in the Game storage.

In the case of the *risk reduction* decision, *security requirements* could be defined to lower the potentiality of a risk event happening. For example, if one makes Game report unreadable to attackers (i.e., cryptography algorithm is implemented as the *security control*), this would mitigate the significance of security risk assessed by the Game report confidentiality. If one defines how to verify the received Game report with the originally sent data (i.e., checksum algorithm is implemented as the *security control*), this would mitigate the significance of security risk assessed by the Game report confidentiality.

Table 2.2 Example of risk-related concepts

Risk-related Concepts		
Risk	An attacker intercepts the transmission medium, and captures, modifies and passes Game report due to the transmission medium characteristic to be intercepted and due to the lack of crypto-functionality at the frame to Submit game report and Game storage, leading to loss of Game report integrity.	An attacker intercepts the transmission medium and captures, reads and keeps the Game report due to the transmission medium characteristic to be intercepted and due to the lack of crypto-functionality at the frame to Submit game report and Game storage, leading to loss of Game report confidentiality.
Impact	• Loss of Game report integrity; • Game report is not securely submitted and stored; • Loss of transmission medium reliability.	• Loss of Game report confidentiality; • Game report is not securely submitted and stored; • Loss of transmission medium reliability.
Event	An attacker intercepts the transmission medium due to its characteristics to be intercepted, captures Game report due to the lack of crypto-functionality at the frame to Submit game report, and modifies and passes data to Game storage due to the lack of crypto-functionality at the Game storage.	An attacker intercepts the transmission medium due to its characteristics to be intercepted, captures Game report due to the lack of crypto-functionality at the frame to Submit game report, and reads and keeps data for later use.
Vulnerability	• Characteristics of transmission medium to be intercepted. • Lack of crypto-functionality at the frame to Submit game report and Game storage.	• Characteristics of transmission medium to be intercepted. • Lack of crypto-functionality at the frame to Submit game report (and Game storage).
Threat	An attacker intercepts the transmission medium, and captures, modifies and passes Game report to Game storage.	An attacker intercepts the transmission medium, and captures, reads and keeps Game report for the later use.
Threat agent	An attacker with means to intercept transmission medium by acting as a proxy.	An attacker with means to intercept transmission medium by acting as a proxy.
Attack method	1. Intercept the transmission medium between the frame to Submit game report and Game storage. 2. Capture, modify and pass data to the Game storage.	1. Intercept the transmission medium between the frame to Submit game report and Game storage. 2. Capture, read and keep Game report for the later use.

Table 2.3 Example of the risk treatment-related concepts

Risk Treatment-related Concepts		
Risk treatment decision	Risk avoidance	Risk reduction
Security requirement	• Change the transmission medium that does not have the ability to be intercepted	• Make Game report unreadable to attackers (mitigates risk to Game report confidentiality) • Verify the received Game report with the original (mitigates risk to Game report integrity)
Control	• Physically delivers the Game report to the football federation. • Game report saved to Game storage by entering it manually	• Cryptographic algorithm • Checksum algorithm

2.6   Further Reading

In general, *security risk management* is an analytical procedure that helps us identify system valuable assets, stakeholders and operations, as well as risk levels of undesirable events. It also provides logic and guidance to find and implement appropriate solutions for specific situations and mitigation strategies. Typically it introduces measures, defined in order to lower the risk level and reduce the likelihood of undesired events. To achieve these goals many different methodologies were developed.

In this section we will survey a few of these security risk management methods. They are useful for understanding the major security risk analysis concepts and principles and how they could be used in various domains. However, this overview is not complete since there exist a large number of approaches[3] to security risk management and different teams might prefer different ways of problem solving.

AURUM (Automated Risk and Utility Management) is a prototype-tool [59] to support decision making according to organisational needs with respect to selection of security measures. AURUM provides different modules regarding the general information security domain. For instance, tools support system characterisation, threat determination, and calculation of risk levels for different organisational assets. The AURUM-supported method consists of a number of steps, where the Bayesian

---

[3]For example, a recent survey [98] identified *sixteen* security risk management methods.

network method is used to support the activities of risk management. Firstly, it concentrates on the system boundary definition. Secondly, it supports identification of system threats and their sources. The main objective of the third step is to identify managerial, operational and technical vulnerabilities. Next, it introduces controls to mitigate identified risks, to analyse security impact and to support the overall decision making process.

CORAS is a model-driven approach [122], which includes systematic guidance for security risk analysis. The CORAS method includes a language (based on the UML profile and realised by the CORAS tool) and proposes means for documentation, analysis and representation of security risks. The CORAS guidelines include eight steps consisting of a number targeted sub-steps. The main steps are preparation for the analysis, customer presentation of the targets, refining of the target description using asset diagrams, approval of the target description, risk identification using threat diagrams, risk estimation using threat diagrams, risk evaluation using risk diagrams and risk treatment using treatment diagrams. In [170] it is discussed that the CORAS method could be considered as a relevant means to manage cyber-security risks.

CRAMM (CCTA Risk Analysis and Management Method) describes a process-oriented method [212] to analyse risks and to manage those risks through countermeasures. This method is composed of three stages. Firstly, one needs to identify assets and evaluate them. This includes physical assets evaluation from their replacement cost and data and software assets evaluation from the impact of breaches of any of the security objectives (i.e., unavailable, destroyed, disclosed, or modified). Secondly, one needs to assess threats and vulnerabilities from the predefined mappings between threats and assets as well as between threats and their impact. Thirdly, based on the previous steps one needs to define sets of countermeasures that contain necessary information (ranging from high-level security objectives to technical solutions) to manage identified risks.

The *EBIOS* (*French*: Expression des Besoinset Identification des Objectifs de Sécurité) method [50] is used for assessment and treatment of risks relating to information systems security (ISS). It can also be used for communicating this information within the organisation and to its partners. The method's major steps include identification of essential organisation's essential components, determination of security needs and objectives, mapping of security needs to the identified threats, and selection of security requirements to satisfy security needs.

The *MEHARI* (*French*: Methode Harmoniséed' Analyse du Risque Informatique) method [44] is aligned closely with the ISO/IEC 2700x standard family [94, 95]. The method focusses on risk assessment and risk management techniques. It consists of different modules including security stake analysis and classification by identifying and evaluating potential risks and their consequences. The evaluation is guided by security services for assessing the level of system security and by focussing on the main system vulnerabilities. After the risk analysis is performed, the method guides the description of security requirements.

OCTAVE (Operationally Critical Threat, Asset, and Vulnerability Evaluation) is a process-driven approach [8] to identify priorities and manage information security risks. It consists of three stages: first for building asset-based threat profiles from different levels of organisation; second for identifying the key components and critical assets and evaluating their technological vulnerabilities; and third for risk evaluation, risk profile development and identification of security strategy and risk mitigation plans. There few instantiations of the OCTAVE approach: OCTAVE-S, designed for a small organisation, relies on individuals' knowledge of security and information systems. OCTAVE Allegro proposes a process specifically targeted to the information assets, their usage, storage, transport, and processing, their threats, vulnerabilities, and disruptions.

In this chapter we have presented the ISSRM domain model, its concepts, relationships, metrics and risk management process. In [134] this domain model was developed after analysing security and security risk management standards (see Sect. 1.2), some security modelling and analysis approaches (see Sect. 4.6) and several security risk management methods.

2.7 Exercises

Exercise 2.1 Define what is:

- business asset;
- IS/system asset;
- security criterion;
- threat agent;
- attack method;
- threat;
- vulnerability;
- event;
- impact;
- risk;
- risk treatment (decision);
- security requirement;
- control.

Exercise 2.2 Identify some context in the *Football Federation case*. What are the *business assets* and their *security criteria*? How are these business assets supported by the *system assets*? To structure your answer, fill in Table 2.4.

Table 2.4 Template to support answer of Exercise 2.2

Security context	Football Federation case
Business assets	
System assets	
Security criteria	

Exercise 2.3 For the security context defined in Exercise 2.2, identify at least one *security risk*. Consider the following questions: Who are the *threat agents*? How are the assets *attacked*? What are the *weaknesses/vulnerabilities* of the *system assets*? What is the *impact* of the event on the *system assets* and *business assets*. How does this risk *negate security criteria*? To structure your answer, fill in Table 2.5.

Table 2.5 Template to support answer of Exercise 2.3

Risk constituencies	Football Federation case
Risk	
Impact	
Event	
Vulnerability	
Threat	
Threat agent	
Attack method	

Exercise 2.4 For the security risk identified in Exercise 2.3, what are the possible security *risk treatment decisions*? What are the *security requirements* and how could they be implemented? To structure your answer, fill in Table 2.6.

Table 2.6 Template to support answer of Exercise 2.4

Security risk treatment	Football Federation case
Risk treatment decision	
Security requirements	
Controls	

Exercise 2.5 Following the solutions of Exercises 2.2, 2.3, and 2.4, brainstorm and calculate the *values* of security risk metrics (i.e., business asset value, threat likelihood, vulnerability level, event potentiality, impact level, risk level, security cost, risk reduction level).

Exercise 2.6 How could security risk metrics could be used to perform security trade-off analysis? The answer could be based on examples of risk management given in Sect. 2.5 and elicited in Exercises 2.2–2.5.

Exercise 2.7 Compare different approaches for security risk management to the ISSRM domain model. The comparison could be performed following approach concepts, process steps and changes, assessment metrics and/or other criteria.

Chapter 3
Security Risk

Before introducing security countermeasures to the system, it is important to explain
what the most important risks are, what their constituencies are and how they
could harm the valuable system assets. As discussed in Chap. 2, security risk harms
valuable *assets*. Both business assets and system assets are *harmed* by *security
impact*. In terms of security, the system assets could be *characterised* by their
vulnerabilities. Finally, the system assets are *targeted* by security *threats*. As it is
important to understand what the system assets are, this chapter starts with a quick
comprehensive overview of the major groups of system asset components. Then
the chapter proposes a set of guidelines for the determination of the security risks
and their constituencies. The chapter continues with the potential appearance of the
impact and then "visits seven pernicious kingdoms" to understand the nature of the
system *vulnerabilities*. Then, the discussion continues on *threat agents* and their
attack methods, which both are major components of a security *threat*. The chapter
ends with a number of references to security risk modelling approaches.

3.1 System Assets

System assets are defined as assets that support *business assets*. In other words,
system assets include everything that is needed to support ordinary business
transactions, information gathering, storage and maintenance, and other business
asset-related functions. Further, in many cases system assets should also be considered human beings who actually deal with the business data or processes, and
therefore are vulnerable regarding security (e.g., social engineering) threats.

Information Processing Functions In [12], Alter discusses how using information technologies, one could basically perform six major *information processing
functions*: (*i*) capturing information (e.g., using keyboard, bar code reader, digital camera, etc.), (*ii*) transmitting information (e.g., wired or wireless phones,

© Springer International Publishing AG 2017
R. Matulevičius, *Fundamentals of Secure System Modelling*,
DOI 10.1007/978-3-319-61717-6_3

Internet etc.), (*iii*) storing information (e.g., hard disk, memory card, databases, Internet cloud etc.), (*iv*) retrieving information (e.g., from any physical device), (*v*) manipulating information (e.g., calculations, combinations, statistics, etc.), and (*vi*) displaying information (e.g., monitor, printer, etc.). This means that all these six operations are used to support typical business assets expressed as data, information, or in some cases business operations and processes.

Functionality Decomposition Layers Another classification of functional components in distributed systems is provided in [205]. Here, the authors define six system decomposition layers: (*i*) user interaction, (*ii*) data/storage management, (*iii*) resource management, (*iv*) distribution management, (*v*) communication, and (*vi*) addressing.

User interaction deals with interfacing and/or interacting with users. It includes *input ports*, i.e., components which can receive user inputs, and *output ports*, where system users can obtain information from an application.

Data/storage management concerns storing and managing information used in the system/application. From the application point of view, data are defined using *data structures*, can be stored in objects or encapsulated in some other abstractions (e.g., files). Data management also includes the organisation of *database systems* or *file systems*, typically managed by operating systems.

Resource management covers resource allocation, global scheduling, process migration, and dynamic configuration of active software components. *Resources* are any components that are created, deployed, controlled, etc., for use by other components. These include components for process scheduling, data storing, and other services. Resource management is defined through *algorithms* for solving deadlocks, organising data replication, configuring data and others.

Distribution management deals with component collaboration, coordination of local/remote execution, and synchronisation/concurrency control. Components are interconnected among themselves using *interfaces* (e.g., programmatic functions, APIs, etc.). Each component can perform certain operations at a different level of abstraction (e.g., sharing business workload, executing object methods, or performing system administration calls). Thus, it results in mapping of the concrete software units to objects, beans, applets, etc. This also involves coordination of the operation system's *processes*, where abstraction levels potentially will be different from the ones defined at the business level.

Communication addresses all concerns related to communication between software systems' components. *Messages* are the units of data in collaboration. They may include function calls, parameters, documents and others. Messages are transmitted using communication channels, such as network links, publish/subscribe interfaces, phones, etc. The actual message transmission is performed using a protocol (e.g., TCP/IP protocol, SSL protocol, etc.), which defines the sequence of actions, needed to transfer a message. Finally, the *networking infrastructure* needs to be defined and it includes introduction of routes, switches, hubs and other networking components.

Addressing encompasses all aspects linked to address, identifier and/or name allocation, distribution and discovery/lookup. For components to be reachable, their entities are assigned identifier, addresses, names, etc. using targeted protocols/algorithms. The data, related to the component address or identifiers, is then often stored in tables either at the application level or in the network infrastructure.

Table 3.1 presents a link between the functionality decomposition layers [205] and the information processing functions [12]. As one observes they both are closely intertwined. This makes it an important and rather challenging task to define the system assets, clarify their support for the business assets, and determine their vulnerabilities during the risk management process.

Table 3.1 A link between functional decomposition layers and information processing functions

Functionality decomposition layers	Information processing functions
User interaction	*Capturing information* through input ports, *Displaying information* through output ports
Data / storage management	*Storing information* using data structures, database systems, file systems. *Retrieving information* using data structures, database systems, file systems.
Resource management	*Manipulating information* using needed and allocated resources, avoiding deadlocks, having correct data configurations, etc.
Distribution management	*Manipulating information* through defined interfaces between different components at different levels of abstraction.
Communication	*Transmitting information* using messages, protocols, and network infrastructures.
Addressing	*Manipulating information* through identifiable and reachable components.

3.2 Risk Analysis

As already discussed in Chap. 2, a *security risk* is the combination of a threat with one or more vulnerabilities (representing the event), leading to a negative impact harming on two or more assets by harming them. *Risk analysis and assessment* is the third step in the security risk management process, as shown in Fig. 2.2. The main goal of this step is to understand and explicitly clarify the major constituencies of the security risk. Hence, a few guidelines on how to perform risk analysis are listed:

- *Identify explicitly what system assets are targeted.* Understanding of the system assets is an important activity since then it becomes possible to judge the possible system vulnerabilities and look for security threats which could exploit these vulnerabilities, thus targeting system assets. A possible analysis of system assets is discussed in Sect. 3.1.
- *Use existing knowledge* (e.g., vulnerability catalogs) and (previous) expertise to characterise potential vulnerabilities of the considered system assets. In

Sect. 3.4 a taxonomy of software errors, which typically open the gate for system vulnerabilities, is surveyed.

- *Security analysts should impersonate the threat agent* and consider all the available means, knowledge and expertise to target the considered system assets. We analyse the important characteristics of the threat agent in Sect. 3.6, where he or she is defined by the motive, capabilities, means and opportunities.
- *The attack method should be explicitly stated including its major steps* (their sequence) and explain how these steps are targeting the considered system assets and are exploiting their vulnerabilities;
- *Elicit and state explicitly what the impact of the defined risk event is.* To define impact one needs to specify (*i*) how security criteria are negated, (*ii*) what harm is to one or more business assets, and (*iii*) what harm is to one or more system assets which support the considered business asset(s). In Sect. 3.3 a list of malicious software is surveyed. Such software in fact could bring harm to the system and business assets, thus negating the security criteria.
- *Once all the major risk constituencies* (i.e., threat agent, attack method, vulnerabilities, and impact) *are defined, state explicitly what the identified security risk is* as it follows from the definition of security risk [53, 133].

Finally, it is important to understand that risk analysis is highly iterative. The major reasons for iteration potentially include discovery of new data or vulnerabilities of system assets, uncovering of new threat agents, necessity for additional information and others.

3.3   Harm: Malicious Software

Security impact is a negative consequence that negates security criterion and harms assets. Impact appears once the security event has happened. This means that some threat agent was able to use the attack method and exploit system vulnerabilities. Typically, the impact on the system assets becomes visible from system misbehaviour (e.g., increased processor usage, network connection problems, deletion or modification files, emails being sent automatically, and other). The software which causes the harm to the system assets is called *malicious software*, or *malware* [120]. This software is used to steal data, break access control policies and compromise software systems in different ways in order to negate confidentiality, availability and/or integrity of the business assets.

Typical malware types are defined in [120] and listed in Table 3.2. *Adware* is advertising-supported software, which automatically delivers advertisements. *Spyware* is software, whose main functions include spying on user activity without the user's knowledge. *Bot* is an assembly of programs created to automatically perform specific operations. *Bug* is a flaw, which typically exists in the source code or program compiler. This can result is the unwanted program execution. *Ransomware* holds a computer system captive until some ransom is payed.

Rootkit remotely accesses or controls a computer without being detected by users or security programs. *Virus* copies itself and spreads to other computers. *Worm* is different from the virus in the way that it can self-replicate and spread independently without human's activity. *Trojan horse* looks like a normal program. This way it tricks users, who download and install it. *Spam* is an electronic transmission (e.g., emails, message, text, blogs, and other) of mass unsolicited messages.

Table 3.2 Malware types, adapted from [120]

Malware type	Harm to assets
Adware	Pop-up ads on websites, advertisements, could be used to deliver spyware. Used to slow down the business workflow, track user activities, steal information
Spyware	Collecting keystrokes, user activity monitoring, data (account information, logins, financial data) harvesting and stealing
Bot	Collections of computers controlled by third parties for, e.g., DDoS attacks, rendering advertisements, scraping server
Bug	Open system vulnerabilities, cause software crashing or freezing, allows threat agents to bypass user authentication, override access privileges, steal data
Ransomware	Encrypt files on the hard drive, lock down the system, restrict user access, this way becoming business assets unavailable
Rootkit	Threat agent can remotely execute files, access, control computer system as part of botnet, install concealed malware. Used to access/steal information, modify system configuration or business data
Virus	Spread by attaching themselves to programs (executing code, script, documents) when user launches the infected program. Used to steal information, harm host computers and networks, create botnets, steal money, render advertisements
Worm	Spread over computer networks by exploiting operating system vulnerabilities (e.g., spread by sending mass emails with infected attachments to users contacts). Consume bandwidth and overload web servers, could be used to bring payloads
Trojan Horse	Provide remote access to an infected system. Used to steal data (credentials, financial data and other), to install other malware, to change files, monitor user activity, to use the computer in botnets
Spam	Could bring different malware. Spam could be send by malware existing in the harmed system

There are few simple "best practices" that systems should follow to prevent malware infections [120]. For instance, nowadays antivirus programs can detect, quarantine and remove multiple types of malware (i.e., viruses, worms, spyware, adware, and Trojans). The antivirus programs can also ensure that the incoming and existing data are scanned for malware and that malware is removed once detected. Another standard recommendation includes keeping the software and operating systems up to date with current vulnerability patches. Finally, downloading of files and attachments should be done only from recognised and acknowledged sources.

3.4   Taxonomy of Security Errors

There exist a number of the vulnerability databases[1] that we could use when
developing and protecting software systems. However, in this section we will
survey a taxonomy of software system errors (i.e., bugs) that result in system
security flaws. This taxonomy is suggested in [202] and gives a classification of the
code and configuration errors that are typical open vulnerabilities in the software
systems. Taxonomy includes (*i*) input validation and representation, (*ii*) application
programming interface (API) abuse, (*iii*) security features, (*iv*) time and state, (*v*)
error handling, (*vi*) code quality, and (*vii*) encapsulation errors. In addition, the
taxonomy mentions errors related to the environment.

Input validation and representation problems (in terms of meta-characters,
encodings, and numeric representations) result from trusting input through the
system's interfaces. The problem appears if the provided input is not validated. The
resulting problems include *buffer overflow, command injection, cross-site scripting,
illegal pointer value, string termination error* and others.

API abuse is caused by the *caller* to respect its end of the contract with the
callee. For instance, if "some program fails to call chdir() after calling chroot(), it
violates the contract that specifies how to change the active root directory in a secure
way" [202]. Resulting errors of this class include *dangerous functions, often misused
exception handling, unchecked return value, directory restriction* and others.

Security features are described by security requirements, such as authentication,
access control, confidentiality, cryptography, and privilege management. Incorrect
implementation of these requirements could lead to *insecure randomness, missing
access control, password management* (plain text, hard-coded, password in config
files, weak cryptography), and *privacy violation* problems.

Time and state errors refer to distributed computation. When different software
components communicate, they share space—and this takes time. Overlooking the
ways in which memory states should be shared could cause problems like *deadlock,
failure to begin a new session upon authentication, insecure temporary file, file
access race condition, signal handling race condition* and others.

Errors related to error handling are related to *API abuse*, but because of
their frequency, they are defined as a separate class. Programming languages
include a lot of exception handling mechanisms, however poor error handling or
fixing introduces other error-related vulnerabilities. Examples of them are *catch
NullPointerException, empty catch block, overly-broad catch block, overly broad
throw declaration,* and *unchecked return value.*

Code quality plays an important role during software system development.
Poor quality is recognised from a lack of code compliance with design, buggy
code, poor code readability, residual old code pieces. Thus the attacker observes

---

[1]For example, common vulnerabilities and exposure https://cve.mitre.org/cve/index.html,
national vulnerability database—https://nvd.nist.gov/, OWASP vulnerability database—https://
www.owasp.org/index.php/Vulnerability.

the opportunity to find the system's vulnerabilities and exploit such errors as *inconsistent implementation, memory leak, obsolete code, underfined behaviour, uninitalised variable, unreleased resource, use after free cases* and others.

Encapsulation is about determining strict boundaries. The problems appear when these boundaries are neglected—for example, between the WebApps and system resources, or between validated and unvalidated data, or between classes with different methods. The examples of encapsulation problems are *data leaking between users,trust boundary violation,comparing of classes by name, leftover debug code*, and others [202].

Finally, *Environment* problems include everything that is not directly related to the code [202]. The software system is running on a computer (or any other hardware device), with an operating system and other systems connected to other devices through networks. This complexity opens the gates for problems such as *misconfiguration issues, insecure compiler optimisation* and similar, which are not related to the system code.

3.5 Security Threats

Security threat targets a system asset by exploiting its vulnerabilities. The *STRIDE* approach [188] is recommended practice to understand the security risk threats when developing systems using Microsoft's secure system development lifecycle. *Spoofing* is pretending to be someone or something other than the intended entity. Spoofing threats includes spoofing a process on the same machine, spoofing files, spoofing a person, and spoofing a role. *Tampering* threats involve modifying something on a disk (e.g., file), on a network, or in memory. *Repudiation* threats include claiming that someone or something didn't do something, or was not responsible for it. Repudiation can be honest or false, thus the key question is to gather evidence of the true happening. *Information disclosure* is providing information to someone not authorised to see it. Information disclosure threats could be carried on against processes, data stores, and/or data flows. *Denial of service* includes absorbing resources needed to provide services (i.e, in terms of process, data store and/or data flow). Finally, *elevation of privileges* means allowing someone or something to do something he or she or it is not authorised to do. These threats include elevation of privileges against a process by corrupting it, elevation through missed authorised checks, elevation through buggy authorisation checks, and elevation through data tampering.

Completeness and correctness of the STRIDE approach were assessed in the empirical settings in [179]. The study showed that the application of STRIDE has the potential to produce a big number of threats especially in the categories of tampering, information disclosure and denial of service. It was also observed that the taxonomy is relatively easy to use. It helped to find the threats and to document them using the misuse cases (see language description in Chap. 7). Finally, it was noted that the application of the STRIDE method contributes with a relatively high number of overlooked threats but also it results in relatively high number of correctly determined security threats.

In [205], Uzunov and Fernandez present a security *threat taxonomy for distributed systems*. The important characteristic of this taxonomy is that it distinguishes between (1) *the system threats* and (2) *the threats to the security infrastructure of the system*.

The *system threats* consist of eight classes: (*i*) identify attacks, (*ii*) network communication attacks, (*iii*) network protocol attacks, (*iv*) passing illegal data attacks, (*v*) stored data attacks, (*vi*) remote information inference, (*vii*) loss of accountability, and (*viii*) uncontrolled operations. When carrying out *identify attacks* (e.g., identity spoofing and advantageous identity allocation), the threat agent attempts to fabricate or misuse identities in a system. *Network communication attacks* includes threats to communication between distributed components. There exist a wide range of these threats, such as message secrecy violation, message integrity violation, message authenticity violation, traffic analysis, protocol sniffing, covert network channel, session hijacking, session state poisoning, route poisoning, and message flooding. *Network protocol attacks* describe threats to the protocols used in network communication. Examples of these threats include message replay, message reuse, protocol field modification, use of abnormal packet size, use of abnormal package sequencing, and use of reserved protocol packet. During the threat of *passing illegal data*, the attacker tends to manipulate input data for some malicious purpose. This type of threat could be illustrated by an injection threat. *Stored data attacks* (e.g., corruption) describe threats on storage data. *Remote information inference* threats concern extraction of information from the system or its components using remote means. The known threats of this group are scanning (i.e., information gathering), probing (i.e., vulnerability checking), output information disclosure, and data inference. *Loss of accountability* threats (e.g., track erasing and repudiation) impact accountability attributes. Finally, the threat class of *uncontrolled operations* includes threats that target system functionality in ways that would not normally be allowed (e.g., race condition, access to data and others). Typical threats of this class include unauthorised access, invoking unauthorized operations, spoofing privileged processes, unsafe code execution, exploitation of tight component coupling, process overflow attack, exploiting concurrency flaws, resource exhaustion, and targeted process crashing. The system threats and their corresponding functionality decomposition levels (see Sect. 3.1) are compiled in Table 3.3.

The *threats to the security infrastructure of the system* cover four threat classes [205]: (*i*) cryptography attacks, (*ii*) countermeasure attacks, (*iii*) configuration/administration attacks, and (*iv*) network protocol attacks. *Cryptography attacks* characterise threats to countermeasures that use cryptography. Examples of these threats are forging cryptographic credentials, abuse of weak algorithm, exploiting vulnerable security protocol, and password attacks (e.g., guessing, brute force, rainbow tables). *Countermeasure attacks* threaten the design of certain countermeasures (e.g., use of default credentials, bypassing controls and leveraging authorisation model). *Configuration/administration attacks* describe threats (e.g., exploiting bad policies and unauthorised modification of rights) to the configuration and adminis-

Table 3.3 Threats to distributed system components, adapted from [205]

Threat	Functional Decomposition Layers
Identity attacks	User interaction, Distribution control
Network communication attacks	Communication, Addressing
Network protocol attacks	Communication, Addressing
Illegal data attacks	User interaction, Data/storage management, Distribution control
Stored data attacks	Data/storage management
Remote information inference	User interaction, Data/storage management, Distribution control
Loss of accountability	User interaction, Communication, Addressing
Uncontrolled operations	User interaction, Data/storage management, Resource management, Distribution control

tration of the security infrastructure. Finally, the class of *network protocol attacks*, also characterised as threats to the system, cover the threats applicable to *secure protocol design*.

3.6   Threat Agent

A threat agent is an agent that could cause harm to IS assets [53]. It triggers a threat and is thus the source of the risk. A threat agent is typically characterised by *motivation*, *expertise* and *available resources* (or *means*, which include skills, knowledge and tools). In Fig. 3.1 this definition is extended with *capability* and *opportunity* concepts [163].

Capability is the threat agent's ability to access or use a set of system resources to exercise the threat, that is the ability to use appropriate means and opportunities to cause the threat by exploiting related vulnerabilities. *Opportunity* is time to perform a successful attack method. The means that a threat agent could use to cause a threat depend on the capabilities that it has. In Table 3.4 some examples of threat agent's capabilities with respect to the system assets are compiled.

Table 3.4 Threat agent capabilities *wrt* system assets, adapted from [163]

Object type	Capability examples
Hardware device	Physical access.
Software component	Local access (e.g., copying); Communicate with the component from within the local domain; Communicate with the component from outside the local domain.
Database	Query the database and modify the data files.
Communication link	Intercept messages and modify messages, or remove messages.

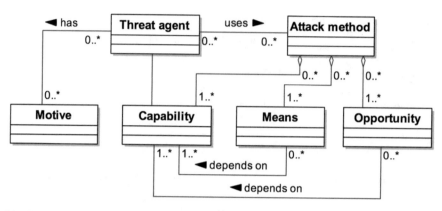

Fig. 3.1 Threat agent definition, adapted from [163]

In [188] four motivation types that drive a threat agent's behaviour are described. These are curiosity, personal fame, personal gain, and national interest. *Curiosity* characterises a threat agent's wish to experiment and try out things, potentially performing some vandalism along the way. *Personal fame* describes a threat agent's wish to be recognised among friends. Such threat agents leave their signs for others to see, so they build their notoriety. *Personal gain*-motivated threat agents could range from spammers to those who create financial threats. Their major purpose is their personal financial gain.

The main goals of threat agents motivated by *national interest* could be either legitimate or illegitimate. A *legitimate* threat agent protects a country's national interests; for instance, it might crack into a terrorist's computer or discover a planned security risk. An *illegitimate* threat agent seeks to undermine the country's national interest, for example, by attacking a flight registration system to learnt about the passengers' details and misuse them later.

Threat agents may also vary regarding their level of expertise and skills [188]. For example, some threat agents (e.g., characterised as *script kiddy*) could have rather little real system or programming knowledge and experience; however, they are able to follow instructions and apply tools in order to exploit system's vulnerabilities. Another type of threat agent—*undergraduates*—could perform some modifications (e.g., tailoring, or slightly altering the data); however, they lack expertise to harm a system by changing its settings. *Experts* are rather advance threat agents that are able to write worms and viruses and exploit network weaknesses. Finally, *specialists* are able to develop extremely specialised abilities. They tend to work carefully and are careful not to leave traces of their performance.

3.7 Further Reading

The major goal of this chapter was to give an overview of the constituencies of the security risk. The chapter did not consider security modelling techniques, but further readings we would like to survey a few of them. Following the classifications suggested in [22, 63], approaches such as Secure Tropos, KAOS, Abuse frames and a few others (e.g., attack trees) support the security risk and more specifically security threat analysis. The Secure Tropos approach is discussed in Sect. 6.

KAOS is a goal-oriented approach [113] to refine top-level goals to lower-level goals until they (requirements) are assigned to the software agents or (expectations) to the environment agents. In [112] the KAOS approach is extended with the notions of anti-goals and anti-requirements, expressed in the anti-models. Hence anti-requirements are refined until the vulnerability (defined as the domain property) is found and anti-goals (anti-requirements/anti-expectations) are assigned to the threat agent. Security requirements are then introduced to mitigate these anti-goals. The KAOS extension to security is aligned with the ISSRM domain model in [133].

Abuse frames [117] extend the problem frames with anti-requirements that the threat agent have to fulfil. Like misuse cases, abuse frames consider threats to a system from the viewpoint of a malicious user. But following the principles of problem frames [96], the *anti-requirements* concept is introduced to define requirements with malicious intent. The main goal, however, remains to use these representations to structure and to bound the scope of the security problem. *Attack trees* is a modelling technique [181] that could help us understand a potential attack method and its alternatives and estimate what means a threat agent should have to achieve its goals. It also could be used to reason about security solutions and guide us through the trade-off analysis.

3.8 Exercises

Exercise 3.1 Give examples of different information processing functions in the *Football Federation* case.

Exercise 3.2 Give examples of the functional decomposition layers of the *Football Federation* system (e.g., of ERIS, from Fig. 1.4).

Exercise 3.3 Describe what system assets are in the *Football Federation* case. What business assets do they support? How could malware harm Football Federation? To structure your answer, fill in Table 3.5.

Exercise 3.4 Following Exercise 3.2, describe different security threats regarding functional decomposition layers.

Table 3.5 Template to support answer of Exercise 3.3

Malware type	Football Federation system asset	Football Federation business assets supported by system asset
Adware		
Spyware		
Bot		
Bug		
Ransomware		
Rootkit		
Virus		
Worm		
Trojan Horse		
Spam		

Exercise 3.5 What capabilities should the threat agent have to break a target system's assets at different functional decomposition layers (and/or regarding different information processing functions).

Exercise 3.6 Apply the guidelines given in Sect. 3.2 and define security risk constituencies elicited in Exercises 3.1–2.5.

Chapter 4
Security Requirements

When considering security problems, it is important to separate the problem and solution spaces. In this chapter, at first we will discuss the differences between the security criteria (problem space) and security requirements (solution space). Then we will concentrate on the security requirements and present some schemes for their classification. In the second part of the chapter we will discuss means for security requirements representation and specification.

4.1 Security Criterion

A security criterion is a constraint on a business asset [53, 133]. It is expressed through confidentiality, availability and integrity:

- *Confidentiality* describes the property of not being made available or disclosed to unauthorised individuals, entities or processes [53, 133]. In other words, it deals with preserving authorized restrictions on information access and disclosure, including mcans for protecting personal privacy and proprietary information [106]. Examples: Confidentiality of game report, Confidentiality of game info.
- *Availability* describes the property of being accessible and usable upon demand by an authorised entity [53, 133]. So it means ensuring timely and reliable access to and use of information [106]. Examples: Availability of game report, Availability of game info.
- *Integrity* is the property of guarding the accuracy and completeness of business assets. Accuracy could be threatened by unauthorised or undesirable updates or tampering. Completeness could be threatened be altering or deletion [53, 133]. In other words, integrity is guarding against improper information modification or destruction, and includes ensuring information non-repudiation and authenticity [106]. Examples: Integrity of game report, Integrity of game info.

© Springer International Publishing AG 2017
R. Matulevičius, *Fundamentals of Secure System Modelling*,
DOI 10.1007/978-3-319-61717-6_4

The security need is defined using a security criterion on a business asset. To understand the security need, one has to estimate the need of confidentiality, integrity and availability of the considered business asset.

4.2   Requirements Definition

"Requirements Engineering (RE) is a set of activities concerned with identifying and communicating the purpose of a software-intensive system, and the contexts in which it will be used. Hence, RE acts as the bridge between the real-world needs of users, customers, and other constituencies affected by a software system, and the capabilities and opportunities afforded by software-intensive technologies" [58]. This definition implies application domain and machine domain (where machine is the thing which is to be built) [96], as illustrated in Fig. 4.1. The real world is described through the *application domain*. The application domain constitutes the purpose of the machine, and this means that requirements for the new software system are determined in the application domain.The *machine domain* is the set of phenomena that the machine has access to—for example, data structures it can manipulate, algorithms it can run, devices it can control, and others. The application domain is the real world where the machine will be introduced and used. The application domain and machine domain are connected via *shared phenomena* [58], i.e., things that are both in the machine and in the application domain. Examples of shared phenomena include real-world events sensed by the machine (e.g., buttons pressed, sensor capturing) and real-world actions caused by the machine (e.g., photos on a screen).

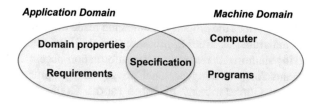

Fig. 4.1 Application domain and machine domain, adapted from [58, 96]

To define the "bridge", i.e., to specify the shared phenomena between the application and machine domains, an analyst has to elicit two aspects of the application domain [58]: (*i*) the *requirements*—things that the machine is required to make true (e.g., prevent access to unauthorized personnel) and (*ii*) the *domain properties*—things that are true about the application domain irrespective of whether we build the machine or not (e.g. only a manager can assign access authority). Using these, the requirements analyst writes a specification for the machine, in terms of phenomena that are observable at its interface with the world (e.g. when the user enters a valid password, the computer will display the software system's interface). The program, then, needs to be designed to run on a computer to meet the requirements specification.

4.3 Security Requirements Classification

As defined in Chap. 2, a *security requirement* is a condition over the phenomena of the environment that we wish to make true by installing the system, in order to mitigate risks [53, 133]. This also means that one needs to find out the domain properties which must be respected, so that security requirements could be fulfilled in order to define the expected level of security with respect to the identified security risks.

Security requirements have a number of conditions to fulfil to mitigate the risks and secure both system and business assets [68]. For instance, they are used to ensure and manage the identify of system users (and service applications). Security requirements help ensure that the system user (and service applications) can access data and system services for which they have been authorised, and detect unauthorised users (and their applications), thus keeping the system secure from infection by malware. Security requirements should also be used to define what to do to secure communication and data from intentional corruption and to ensure that interactions with system components would not be repudiated. Security requirements also deal with the privacy of confidential information as well as with the auditing of the system and security control mechanisms. Security requirements define what actions need to be performed to survive security attacks, to protect assets against destruction, theft, damage, etc. Finally they should ensure that system maintenance is performed properly and does not cause negation of already used security controls. This broad list of conditions indicates that there exist security requirements of different types [68]. Some of them are analysed in this section.

Identification requirement is any security requirement that specifies the extent to which a system[1] shall identify its externals (i.e., stakeholders and other systems) before interacting with them [68]. For example:

- The ERIS shall identify Football Federation Employees before allowing them to use its functions.
- The ERIS shall identify Team Representatives before allowing them to use its functions.
- The Football Federation shall identify Football Federation Employees before allowing them to enter.

Authentication requirement is any security requirement that specifies the extent to which a system shall verify the identity of its externals (i.e., stakeholders and

---

[1]In [68] security requirements are introduced for *business*, *application*, and/or *components*. In this discussion we follow our previous terminology and present security requirements regarding *system* and *system assets*.

other systems) before interacting with them [68]. The objectives of an authentication requirement are to ensure that externals are actually who or what they claim to be. For example:

- The ERIS shall verify the identity of Football Federation Employees before allowing them to use its functions.
- The ERIS shall verify the identity of Team Representatives before allowing them to use its functions.
- The Football Federation shall verify the identity of Football Federation Employees before permitting them to enter.

Authorisation requirement is any security requirement that specifies the access and usage privileges of authenticated users (individual persons, other internal and external systems, and groups of related persons or systems) [68]. For example:

- The ERIS shall allow each Football Federation Employee to obtain access to his personal account information.
- The ERIS shall not allow Team Representative to *change* the Game reports.
- The ERIS shall not allow other external systems to *change* data.
- The ERIS shall not allow internal systems to *change* data.

Authorisation requirements specify that persons who have been appointed on behalf of the organisation that owns and controls the system, are able to authorise specific authenticated users to access specific systems' functions and data. They also require that authenticated users be able to access an application's functions and data if and only if they have been explicitly authorised to do so. Or in other words, the authorisation requirements prevent unauthorised users from obtaining access to confidential data and using the restricted system's functions.

Immunity requirement is any security requirement that specifies the extent to which a system shall protect itself from infection by unauthorised undesirable programs [68] (e.g., malware). Immunity requirements specify what to do to prevent them from destroying or damaging data or the system itself. For example:

- The ERIS shall protect itself from infection by scanning the entered or downloaded data;
- The ERIS shall notify the Administrator if malware is detected during a scan.

Integrity requirement is any security requirement that specifies the extent to which a system shall ensure that its data and communications are not intentionally corrupted via unauthorised creation, modification, or deletion [68]. These requirements specify that the communication and data be trustworthy. For example:

- The ERIS shall prevent unauthorised corruption of emails sent to Team Representatives.
- The ERIS shall prevent unauthorised corruption of data collected from Team Representatives.

Intrusion detection requirement is any security requirement that specifies the extent to which a system shall detect and record attempted access or modification by unauthorised individuals [68] (or other systems). These requirements should specify what to do to detect unauthorised attempts to access the system, to record data about the unauthorised access attempts, and to notify security personnel so that it would become possible to handle these attempts. For example:

- The ERIS shall detect attempted accesses that fail identification requirements.
- The ERIS shall detect attempted accesses that fail authentication requirements.
- The ERIS shall detect attempted accesses that fail authorisation requirements.
- The ERIS shall notify the Administrator of all failed attempted accesses during the previous 24 h.

Nonrepudiation requirement is any security requirement that specifies the extent to which a system shall prevent a party to one of its interactions (e.g., message, transaction) from denying having participated in all or part of the interaction [68]. The nonrepudiation requirements specify that adequate tamper-proof records be kept to prevent parties to interactions from denying that they have taken place. They also describe what to do to minimise any potential future legal and liability problems that might result from someone disputing one of their interactions. For example:

- The ERIS shall store tamper-proof records of the following information about each game: *game information*, *umpires*, *game report*, and *confirmation*.

Nonrepudiation requirements typically involve the storage of a significant amount of information about each interaction, including the identity of all parties involved in the transaction, timestamp of the interaction, and information passed during the interaction.

Privacy requirement is any security requirement that specifies the extent to which a system shall keep its sensitive data and communications private from unauthorised individuals and programs [68]. Privacy requirements specify that unauthorised individuals and programs not gain access to sensitive data and communication. For example:

- The ERIS shall not store personal information about the Football Federation Employee.
- The ERIS shall not allow unauthorised individuals access to communications.
- The ERIS shall not allow unauthorised programs access to communications.
- The ERIS shall not allow unauthorised individuals access to Player data.
- The ERIS shall not allow unauthorised programs access to Player data.

The first requirement illustrates the case of *anonymity*, the second and the third *communication privacy*. The last two requirements specify *data storage* privacy.

Security auditing requirement is any security requirement that specifies the extent to which a system shall enable security personnel to audit the status and use of its security mechanisms [68]. Security auditing requirements define what the system collects, analyses, and reports with regard to information about the status (e.g., enabled vs. disabled, updated versions) and use of its security mechanisms (e.g., access and modification by security personnel). For example:

- The ERIS shall collect the status of its security mechanisms every Friday at 18:00 h.
- The ERIS shall organize the status of its security mechanisms every Saturday at 18:00 h.
- The ERIS shall summarise the status of its security mechanisms every Sunday at 12:00 h.
- The ERIS shall report the status of its security mechanisms every Sunday at 18:00 h.

Here *security mechanisms* are understood as controls to fulfil *identification, authentication, authorisation, immunity, privacy, intrusion,* and *detection* requirements.

Survivability requirement is any security requirement that specifies the extent to which a system shall survive the intentional loss or destruction of its component [68]. Survivability requirements ensure that the system fails gracefully or else continues to function in a degraded mode, even though certain components have been intentionally damaged or destroyed. For example:

- The ERIS shall not have a single point of failure.

Physical protection requirement is any security requirement that specifies the extent to which a system shall protect itself from physical assault [68]. Physical protection requirements define what to do to protect a system from physical damage, destruction, theft, or replacement of hardware, software, or personnel due to vandalism, sabotage, or terrorism. For example:

- The Football Federation shall protect its hardware components from physical damage.
- The Football Federation shall protect its hardware components from theft.
- The Football Federation shall protect its hardware components from surreptitious replacement.
- The Football Federation shall protect its personnel from death.
- The Football Federation shall protect its personnel from injury.
- The Football Federation shall protect its personnel from kidnapping.

System maintenance security requirement is any security requirement that specifies the extent to which a system shall prevent authorised modifications (e.g., defect fixes, enhancements, updates) from accidentally defeating its security mechanisms [68]. System maintenance security requirements define what to do to maintain the levels of security specified in the security requirements during the usage phase. For example:

- The ERIS shall not violate its security requirements as a result of updating data.
- The ERIS shall not violate its security requirements as a result of updating hardware.
- The ERIS shall not violate its security requirements as a result of the updating of a software component.

- The ERIS shall not violate its security requirements as a result of replacement of data.
- The ERIS shall not violate its security requirements as a result of replacement of hardware.
- The ERIS shall not violate its security requirements as a result of replacement of a software component.

Security requirements relationships are presented in Fig. 4.2. *Identification requirements* are prerequisites for *authentication requirements*. *Authentication requirements* are typically insufficient by themselves, but they are necessary prerequisites for *authorisation requirements*. Authorisation depends on both identification and authentication. *Intrusion detection requirements* depend on *identification, authentication,* and *authorisation requirements*. *Nonrepudiation requirements* are related to, but potentially more restrictive than, *security auditing requirements*. *Privacy requirements* must be consistent with *security auditing requirements, identification requirements,* and *nonrepudiation requirements,* which require users to be identified and information about their interactions to be stored. *Physical protection requirements* are related to *survivability requirements*. *Survivability requirements* specify continued functioning after an attack, whereas *physical protection requirements* specify the protection of components. *Physical protection requirements* are typically prerequisites for *survivability requirements*.

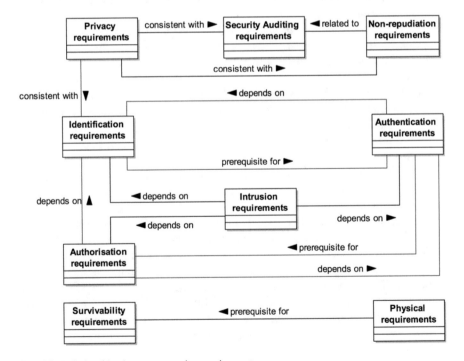

Fig. 4.2 Relationships between security requirements

4.4 How to Specify Security Requirements

In [49], Davis et al. present a list of quality characteristics that a good requirements specification should respect. It says that a requirements specification should be unambiguous, complete, correct, understandable, verifiable, consistent, achievable, concise, design-independent, traceable, modifiable, electronically stored, executable, annotated, not redundant, at the right level of details, precise, reusable, organised, and cross-referenced. This also means that individual requirement needs to be specified in a way which contributes to the high quality of the overall requirements specification. In this section we shortly review what are the typical errors of requirements and what are the best practices for specifying good requirements [11].

Bad Requirements There exist a number of practices which must be avoided when specifying (security) requirements [11]. For instance, requirements should be specified without such keywords as:

- *or* (to avoid ambiguity). Example: The same subsystem shall also be able to generate visible or audible caution or warning signal for the attention of security or business analyst.
- *and*, *or*, *with*, and *also* (to avoid specification of multiple requirements). Example: The warning indicator shall light up when an ERIS intrusion is detected and the current Football Federation Employees workspace or Game report data shall be saved.
- *if*, *when*, *except*, *unless*, *although*, and *always*: not to define left-out clauses. Example: The fire alarm shall always be sounded when the smoke in Football Federation building is detected, unless the alarm is being tested when the antivirus is deployed.
- *usually*, *generally*, *often normally*, *typically* and similar—to avoid speculation. Example: Umpires and Team Representatives normally require early indication of intrusion into ERIS.
- *user-friendly*, *versatile*, *approximately*, *as possible*, *efficient*, *improved*, *high-performance*, *modern* and similar—not to include vague, undefinable terms. Examples: (*i*) Security-related messages should be versatile and user-friendly; (*ii*) The OK status indicator shall be illuminated as soon as possible after ERIS security self-check is completed.
- Requirements should not be specified with long ***rumpling sentences***. Example: Provided that the designated Game report input signals from the specified mobile devices are received in the correct order by the way which the ERIS is able to differentiate the designators, the security solution should comply with the required framework to indicate the desired security states.
- Requirements should not support wishful thinking, like ***100 percent reliable/safe/secure, handle all unexpected failures, please all users, run on all platforms, never fail, upgrade to all future situations*** and similar.

By definition, requirements are representing *what* software system has to do in order to help system stakeholders to achieve their goals. The same applies to the security requirements—*what* to do in order to achieve a necessary level of security and to mitigate the security risks. This also means that when specifying the security requirements, one should avoid describing *how* software systems needs to behave; one should avoid specifying system design in terms of ***names of components***, ***materials***, ***software objects/procedures***, ***database fields***, etc. In other words, security requirements should not be specified in terms of design or architecture (i.e., in terms of security controls) which is used to implement them. Table 4.1 presents the typical system design and architecture elements, which should be avoided when specifying the security requirements.

Table 4.1 System design elements to be avoided when specifying security requirements, adapted from [68]

Security requirements	Should **NOT** be specified in terms of
Identification requirements	(*i*) Who You Say You Are (e.g., name, user identifier, or national identifier, e.g., social security number), (*ii*) What You Have (digital certificate, employee ID card, a hardware key, and other), (*iii*) Who You Are (fingerprint, hand print, face recognition, voice pattern, signature style, keystrokes, and other)
Authentication requirements	(*i*) Who You Say You Are (e.g., name, user identifier, or national identifier, e.g., social security number), (*ii*) What You Have (digital certificate, employee ID card, a hardware key, and others), (*iii*) Who You Are (finger print, hand print, face recognition, voice pattern, signature style, keystrokes, and others)
Authorisation requirements	Authorization lists or databases; person vs. role-based vs. group-based authorisation; physical access controls, etc.
Immunity requirements	Antivirus programs, firewalls, programming languages, or/and standards
Integrity requirements	Cryptography and/or hash codes
Intrusion detection requirements	Alarms, event reporting, use of a specific commercial-off-the-shelf (COTS), intrusion detection system (IDS), intrusion prevention system (IPS) and others
Nonrepudiation requirements	Digital signatures (to identify the parties), timestamps (to capture dates and times), encryption and decryption (to protect the information), hash functions (to ensure that the information has not been changed)
Security auditing requirements	Audit trails and event logs
Survivability requirements	Hardware redundancy, data centre redundancy, and/or failover software
Physical protection requirements	Locked doors, security guards, and/or rapid access to police
System maintenance security requirements	Maintenance and enhancement procedures, associated training, and/or security regression testing

Good requirements should answer the question about *what* the new software system should do (and not *how it should do it*). They also avoid premature design or implementation. They are understandable, clear (not ambiguous), and cohesive (one thing per requirement).

Good requirements are also testable (somehow possible to test or validate that the requirement has been met). This means that there should be clearly defined quantifiable acceptance criteria. For example:

- The response time of button press should be max 2 s.
- The security of function F should be at least 99.9%

Guidelines for writing good requirements [11] include (*i*) usage of simple direct sentences, (*ii*) usage of limited vocabulary, (*iii*) explicit identification of type of user who wants this (each) requirement, (*iv*) focus on stating result, and (*v*) definition of verifiable criteria. For example:

- (*i*) Security analyst should be able to view ERIS status.
- (*ii*) Security analyst should be able to change the infected ERIS component in less than 12 h; or (*ii*) Security analyst should be able to reconfigure the infected ERIS component in less than 12 h
- (*iii*) The Football Federation Employee shall be able to (*iv*) view game reports (*v*) after 2 h after the game.

4.5 Related (to Security) Requirements

In addition to these few requirement types, a number of dependability requirements, such as *reliability*, *robustness*, *survivability*, *trust* and *trustworthiness*, etc., could be taken into account when considering security of the developed system. In this section we consider a few groups of requirements related to the security requirements. More specifically, we look into the *safety requirements*, which also consider harm to the assets but focus on accidental risk, and the *privacy requirements*, which sometimes could be considered as part of the security requirements (see Sect. 4.3), but sometimes could contradict them.

Safety Requirements and Safety Risk Management Both *security* and *safety* harm or damage the system assets. However, security is understood as _intentional_ act towards the system, while safety is characterised as _unintentional_ happening [71]. Figure 4.3 presents the main concepts of safety risk management. Here *asset* is anything (i.e., business asset, system asset or the environment) of value that should be protected from accidental harm. *Safety risk* is the potential harm to an asset due to accidents (based on the vulnerabilities). Similarly to security risk, safety risk is a decomposition of the accident and harm, as illustrated in Fig. 4.3. *Harm* is damage to or a negative impact (i.e., negative outcome) on an asset due to an incident. An *accident* is "an unplanned and unintended (but not necessarily unexpected) event or series of related events resulting in harm to an asset" [66]. Hence an accident could be to health, property or the environment. Similarly to security, *vulnerability* is a weakness in the system that increases the likelihood that an accident will occur and cause harm. This weakness may be in the system's architecture, design, implementation, integration, deployment, or configuration. *Hazard* defines "a situation that increases likelihood of one or more related accidents" [66]. Two types of hazards could be identified—*potential hazard*, which is recognised early in the system design, and *actual hazard*, which is identified in the running system.

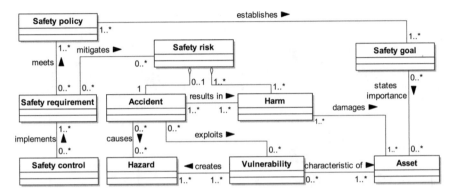

Fig. 4.3 Domain model for safety risk management

Safety goals state the importance of achieving a target level of safety or one of its subfactors. *Safety policy* is a quality policy that mandates a system-specific quality criterion for safety or one of its subfactors. Finally, *safety requirement* is specified in terms of a system-specific criterion and a minimum mandatory level of an associated quality metric that is necessary to meet safety policies and to mitigate the safety risks. Based on the specific context, safety requirements could be classified as [69]: asset harm requirements, safety accident requirements, hazard requirements, safety risk requirements, protection of vulnerable assets requirements, detection of safety incidents requirements, reaction to safety incidents requirements, and adaptation to safety incidents requirements. Safety requirements, similarly to security, are implemented by *safety controls*.

Privacy by Data Minimisation   Privacy by data minimisation is expressed in terms of anonymity, unlinkability, unobservability, and pseudonymity [168]. The typical settings are illustrated in Fig. 4.4. Here, *sender* sends *messages* to *recipients* using a *communication network*. Messages are sent and received through stations using a communication channel.

The interest of an *attacker* includes (*i*) monitoring of occurring communications, (*ii*) monitoring of existing communication patterns, and (*iii*) manipulating the communication. Let's assume that the attacker uses all information available to him to infer (probabilities of) his items of interest (IOIs), i.e., *who* did *send* or *who* did *receive* which *messages*.

Anonymity of a sender or recipient (called subject) means that he is not identifiable within a set of the anonymity set, i.e., all subjects [168]. From an attacker's point of view it means that the attacker is not able to identify the subject within a set of subjects. *Unlinkability* only has meaning when anonymity properties has been defined and the attacker has been characterised. From an attacker's point of view unlinkability of two or more items of interest (e.g., actions, subjects, messages, and other) means that the attacker cannot sufficiently distinguish whether they are related or not [168].

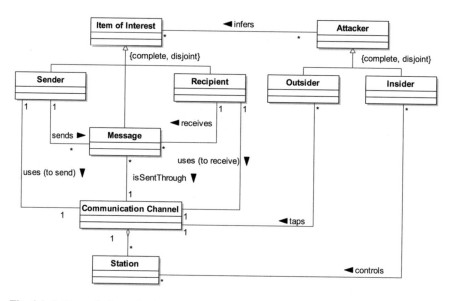

Fig. 4.4 Settings of privacy for data minimisation

Undetectability of an item of interest means that the attacker is not able to distinguish between whether the item of interest exists or not [168]. For example, if some message is defined as an item of interest, then this messages is not sufficiently differentiated from "random noise". *Unobservability* of an item of interest consists of *undetectability* and *anonymity* [168]. Sender or receiver unobservability means that it is sufficiently undetectable whether any receiver/sender receives/receives. Unobservability of a relationship means that the attacker is not able to detect if within the relationship unobservability set of all possible sender-recipients pairs, a message is delivered in any relationship.

Pseudonymity is the use of pseudonyms as identifiers [168]. A pseudonym is an identifier of a subject (i.e., sender or recipient) other than one of his real names. A sender or recipient is pseudonymous if a pseudonym is used as the identifier instead of a real name.

Identifiability, from the attacker's perspective, means that the attacker can sufficiently identify the subject within a set of subjects [168]. An *identity* is any subset of attribute values of a person which sufficiently identifies this person within any set of persons. Attribute values or even attributes themselves change over time. If the attacker has no access to the change history, the fact if a particular subset of attribute values of a person is an identity or not may change over time, too [168]. But if the attacker has access to the change history of each attribute, any subset forming an identity will make an identity from the attacker's point of view irrespective of how attribute values change. Identity management deals with defining identity attributes, developing and choosing pseudonyms and partial identities in the considered context [168].

Differential Privacy The proposal on differential privacy is gaining attention. It is a technique which focusses on privacy analysis in *honest-but-curious* adversary cases. Let's assume a scenario [56] where some *sensitive data* are stored in a *statistical database*. The required statistics could be computed from a sample of the sensitive data. A trusted and trustworthy *curator* gathers the sensitive data from a larger number of respondents (the sample), with the goal of learning (and releasing) statistical facts. The problem is releasing these *statistical facts* without compromising the privacy of the individual *respondents*. Two types of settings are typically considered: non-interactive and interactive.

In the non-interactive setting the *curator* prepares some sort of summary (or synthesis of synthetic database) to respond known queries of a particular type [56]. This means that the curator releases a "sanitised" (also known as "anonymisation" and "de-identification") response [57]. Sanitisation means employ such techniques as perturbation and sub-sampling, as well as removing well-known identifiers (e.g., names, birthdates, and social security numbers). It may include releasing various types of synopses and statistics. In the non-interactive scenario, since the data will never be used again, the curator can destroy the data (and himself) once the statistics have been released [56].

In the interactive setting the *curator* provides an interface, through which *users* may pose queries about the *sensitive data* and get (possibly noisy) *responses* [57]. In other words, *queries* posed by the *user* and/or the *responses* to these queries, may be modified by the *curator* in order to protect the privacy of the *respondents*. Hence, the *curator* is situated between the *user* and the *sensitive data* [55, 56]. In the malicious scenario such a user could be treated as an *adversary*, using his *auxiliary information*, that is, information available to the adversary other than from access to the database. In the interactive setting the data cannot be destroyed and the curator must remain present throughout the lifetime of the database. Also note that any interactive scenario could become a non-interactive one if the queries are known in advance—in this case the curator prepares the response to the known queries and releases the resulting statistics.

Concepts of the interactive setting are summarised in Fig. 4.5. Here the *user* poses a *query* which could be modified by the *curator*. The *query* is posed on *sensitive data*, possibly consisting of an *identifier* (e.g., name, surname, etc.), a *quasi-identifier* (e.g., ZIP code, gender, age, etc.) and *sensitive* attributes (e.g., diagnosis, rented adult movies, etc.) [115]. The *response* is extracted from the *sensitive data* and released to the *user*. *Response* potentially can also be modified by the *curator*.

Interested readers should check existing privacy surveys. For instance, in [76] the authors present ontologies for privacy requirements engineering. Elsewhere, in [73], methods for privacy-preserving data are considered. In [48, 186] an overview of privacy enhancing technologies is provided.

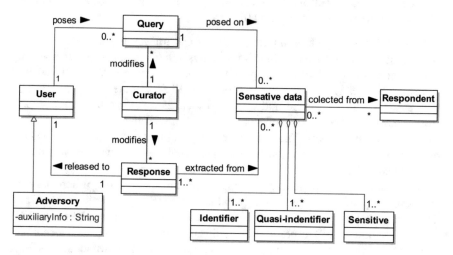

Fig. 4.5 Concepts of interactive setting

4.6 Further Reading

Fabian et al. present a conceptual framework to compare and evaluate security requirements engineering approaches [63]. Elsewhere, in [143], a systematic review is done to classify security-related approaches to techniques, frameworks, processes and methods. We will recall this review to give a short overview of existing security requirements engineering approaches.

Techniques Security modelling techniques could be understood as extensions of standard languages of the UML family [158]. For example, misuse cases [192] are extensions of use cases and mal-activity diagrams are extensions of activity diagrams, both modelling of threat-oriented scenarios. Capturing the abuser stories is also considered in the technique for agile security requirements engineering [167].

UMLsec [100] is an extension of UML using stereotypes, associated tags and values; it helps in capturing a range of the security constraints (e.g., fair exchange, RBAC, data security and others) at the software system design stage. Another extension—SecureUML [21, 119] shows how UML could be used to model role-based access control policies.

Frameworks In [92], a framework for intrusion detection in component-based systems is presented. The framework consists of four development stages which include both (*i*) development of system services and components, and (*ii*) security intrusion identification, modelling, signature implementation and deployment. The framework is addressed through the UMLintr modelling language, an extension of UML for intrusion modelling.

Based on the defence information technology security certification and accreditation process (DITSCAP), Lee et al. present the requirements and risk domain model [114]. It defines the risk components, such as threats and vulnerabilities of the assets, and countermeasures to mitigate or reduce these vulnerabilities. The risks and their component definitions are adapted from the Common Criteria model [36]. Another security ontology-centric framework is suggested in [203, 204]. Here security ontology is "an ontology that elaborates on the security aspects of an information system" [203]. This ontology includes major security concepts, such as asset, stakeholder, vulnerability, countermeasure and threat. It illustrates that every information asset is associated with certain threats, which are then mitigated by a set of security countermeasures. The ontology is used to define the ontology-centric security framework, which provides guidelines for (*i*) security ontology instantiation of the targeted problem, (*ii*) security requirements collection, (*iii*) security action definition and (*iv*) security action deployment and monitoring.

In [206] a framework to derive security requirements using the CLASP method [82] is presented. The framework supports formulation of the security requirement in four steps: (*i*) identification of roles and resources, (*ii*) categorisation of resources into abstractions, (*iii*) identification of resource interactions, and (*iv*) specification of mechanisms for each core security service. Since CLASP already contains the list of security countermeasures, the framework basically guides their allocation to the targeted resources of the considered system. A framework for security requirements engineering [84, 146] separates security goals, security requirements and the architecture which implements these requirements. Four core activities of the framework application are (*i*) identification of functional requirements, (*ii*) identification of security goals, (*iii*) identification of security requirements and (*iv*) construction of satisfaction criteria.

Processes Common Criteria (CC) provide the standard for assessing information security [36]. Based on CC, a maturity model is used to evaluate the level of organisational maturity. Another CC application is discussed in [141, 142], where authors propose a security requirements engineering process (SREP). The approach integrates other modelling techniques, such as UMLsec [100], misuse cases [192], and others.

A process to capture security requirements using the abuse frames is discussed in [61]. Following the principles of the problem frames [96], the approach includes system modelling, asset identification, threat and vulnerability identification, and security requirements elicitation and evaluation. This helps authors develop the threat and security requirements catalogs following the traditional classifications suggested in, for example, the STRIDE [188] classification. In [215–217] a holistic security management framework is suggested. It defines a workflow for business modelling, project planning, security analysis and design, implementation and maintenance. The framework also takes into account human relation and business foundation concerns. A threat modelling process as a base to define security requirements is presented in [152]. After identifying the system contents and assets, the authors use the STRIDE classification [188] to find security threats and propose countermeasures. Elsewhere in [187], a separation between the application requirements and security requirements modelling is suggested. The approach applies use cases and class diagrams to extract requirements from the system component and connector architecture.

Methods The security quality requirements engineering (SQUARE) method [139, 140] consists of nine steps and facilitates the use of different techniques for artefact development, risk management and assessment, security requirements elicitation and filtering. The goal of the first step is to agree on definitions for the process. The second step is deciding upon the initial security goals. Step three involves developing or collecting artefacts of the system being worked on. Artefacts could be defined in misuse diagrams, goals, attack trees and other relevant models. They are important as the security requirements elicitation will be based on them. In the fourth step, one is performing risk assessment; this includes assessment of the vulnerabilities and the classification of threats. The fifth step covers the selection of security elicitation techniques. During step six, developers are deriving security requirements based on the outcome of the previous steps. The next two steps include the security requirements categorisation and prioritisation. The last step is security requirements inspection. The requirements, which have been produced through the previous SQUARE steps, will be scrutinised to ensure that each requirement is valid and verifiable. Each of the requirements should be financially feasible for implementation, too.

Knowledge Acquisition in Automated Specification (KAOS) [112], Secure i* [18], and Secure Tropos [18, 77, 78, 147, 148, 150] facilitate the requirements elicitation and specification by providing the rationale for a particular requirement. The introduction of goal analysis and specification removes ambiguity and conflicts from the requirements, and bring transparency and traceability through secure system requirements specification, design and implementation.

4.7 Exercises

Exercise 4.1 What are the differences between "security criterion" and "security requirements"?

Exercise 4.2 Define "requirement", "security engineering" and "security requirement".

Exercise 4.3 Which requirement is not correct? Read the following questions and select correct answer.

Q1. Which *identification requirement* is not correct?

1. ERIS shall identify Football Federation Employees and Team Representatives before allowing them to use its capabilities
2. ERIS shall not require a Football Federation Employee to identify himself/herself multiple times during a single session
3. ERIS shall identify other applications (both internal and external) before allowing them to use its capabilities
4. ERIS should identify Football Federation employees by scanning her or his employee card data

Q2. Which authentication requirement is not correct?

1. ERIS shall verify the identity of Football Federation Employee before allowing her or him to update her or his user information
2. ERIS shall verify the identity of Team Representative before allowing him/her to use ERIS capabilities
3. ERIS shall verify the identity of Football Federation Employee by checking the entered social security number before allowing her or him to change her or his password
4. ERIS shall verify the identity of other external systems before allowing them to use ERIS capabilities

Q3. Which authorisation requirement is not correct?

1. ERIS shall allow other external systems to automatically email a Team Representative's password to that Team Representative's email address
2. ERIS shall not allow Team Representatives to successfully use a denial of service (DoS) attack to flood ERIS with legitimate requests of service
3. ERIS shall allow Football Federation Employee to obtain access to all of her or his own personal account information
4. ERIS shall not allow any Football Federation Employee to access any account information of any other Football Federation Employee or Team Representative

Q4. Which immunity requirement is not correct?

1. ERIS shall protect itself from infection by scanning all entered and downloaded data and software for known computer viruses, worms, Trojan horses, and other similar harmful programs
2. ERIS shall disinfect all files found to contain a harmful program if disinfection is possible
3. ERIS shall use the Kaspar antivirus program to detect and disinfect all known viruses and Trojan horses
4. ERIS shall notify the Administrator if it detects a harmful program during a scan

Exercise 4.4 Correct the following requirements:

Req.4.3.1: The same ERIS subsystem shall also be able to generate a visible or audible caution or warning signal for the attention of a security or ERIS business analyst.

Req.4.3.2: The warning signal shall light up when an ERIS intrusion is detected and the current workspace or input shall be saved.

Req.4.3.3: The Team Representative shall be able to view the current selected channel number, which shall be displayed in 14 pt Swiss type on an LCD panel tested to standard 657–89 and mounted with shockproof rubber washers.

Req.4.3.4: Administrator normally require early indication of intrusion into the ERIS.

Req.4.3.5: Security-related messages should be versatile and user-friendly.

Req.4.3.6: The ERIS network shall handle all unexpected errors without crashing.

Exercise 4.5 Following the guidelines of "good requirements", elicit security requirements of different types for the *Football Federation* system ERIS:

- identification requirements;
- authentication requirements;
- authorisation requirements;
- immunity requirements;
- integrity requirements;
- intrusion detection requirements;
- nonrepudiation requirements;
- security auditing requirements;
- survivability requirements;
- physical protection requirements;
- system maintenance security requirements.

Exercise 4.6 What is the difference between *security*, *safety* and *privacy* engineering?

Part II
Modelling Languages for Security Risk Management

Chapter 5
Security Risk-Oriented BPMN

Business process management is an instrument to manage an organisation's activities in a holistic manner and to guarantee business outcomes that add value both to the organisation and the customers [54]. Thus understanding what business values (in terms of the data, processes, policies, etc.) should be protected against security risks becomes rather necessity than an option.

Business Process Model and Notation (BPMN), a multi-vendor standard controlled by the Object Management Group,[1] is a language for constructing business process models. BPMN is considered business-friendly, because it is based on notions familiar from traditional flowcharting in business process management. At the same time, the language is linked to a semantic model, which means that each shape used in the notation has a specific meaning, with defined rules of connections between objects. A systematic introduction of the BPMN modelling language and guidelines could be found in [54, 189]. In this chapter we will discuss some major constructs and then we will illustrate how BPMN is aligned to the ISSRM domain model and, thus, could be used for security risk management.

5.1 Business Process Model and Notation

Figure 5.1 illustrates some major graphical BPMN constructs [54, 189]. Figure 1.7 (see Chap. 1) displays a simple BPMN diagram from the *Football Federation case*. A *Pool* (e.g., Umpire, ERIS and Football Federation Employee) is a container for a *process*. A *Lane* is used for subdivision of the process, which is described using flow objects (i.e., Sub-processes, Tasks, Events and Gateways). *Task* (e.g., Create game, Register umpire, etc.) is an atomic activity, meaning an activity that has no internal subparts defined by the model. *Sub-process* is a compound activity which can be represented as a process.

---

[1] URL: http://www.bpmn.org.

© Springer International Publishing AG 2017
R. Matulevičius, *Fundamentals of Secure System Modelling*,
DOI 10.1007/978-3-319-61717-6_5

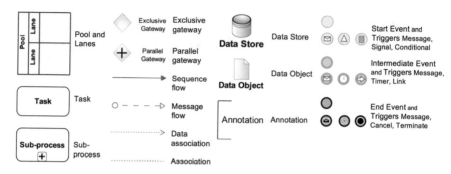

Fig. 5.1 BPMN concrete syntax for descriptive modelling

A *Start Event* indicates the start of the process. An *Intermediate Event* represents a signal that something has happened during a process. An *End Event* indicates the end of a path in a process. Triggers (e.g., *Message, Signal, Timer, Cancel, Terminate* and etc.), used with events, characterise a certain condition when the event could start, end or result in an intermediate happening.

A *Sequence flow* is used to connect activities, gateways, and events within a single pool. A *Message flow* is used to send messages between two pools.

A gateway represents a control point in the process. An *Exclusive gateway* (i.e., exclusive decision) means that only one of the outputs is to be followed based on some condition. A *Parallel gateway* (i.e., parallel split) means that all of the outgoing sequence flows are to be followed in parallel unconditionally.

Data Objects (e.g., Game, Game info, etc.; see Fig. 1.7) are used to represent data or document flows between process activities and events. *Data Stores* (e.g., Game storage) are used to represent files, databases or business applications that store data. Both data objects and data stores are associated to the tasks using a *Data association* relationship. Arbitrary text could be inserted and linked to another object with *Annotation* and *Association* relationships [189].

As discussed in [189], the BPMN application is divided into three usage levels: descriptive, analytical (describes the activity flow) and executable (targeted to system development) modelling. In this work our scope is *descriptive modelling*, which concentrates on the business process by documenting the major business flows.

5.2 Security Risk Management Using BPMN

The BPMN language is specifically dedicated not to security modelling but to business process modelling. However, its application domain could be extended to deal with security problems. In [14], Altuhhova et al. discussed how BPMN could be aligned to the ISSRM domain model; thus it could be used for security risk management.

On one hand, the major version of the language should not lose its original purpose, and it should remain relatively simple. On the other hand BPMN provides the major set of constructs that help describe important business assets, their security risks, and potential security requirements. Below, we view over the BPMN correspondence to ISSRM, discuss its semantic alignment and abstract and concrete syntax.

5.2.1   Semantics

Asset-Related Concepts In the first place, the BPMN approach is meant for describing business processes within an organisation. As observed in [14], BPMN constructs such as *task*, *gateway*, *event* and their connecting link, i.e., *sequence flow*, help describe valuable processes (i.e., ISSRM *business assets*). The *flow objects* (such as *task*, *gateway* and *event*) are defined in BPMN as *containers*; i.e., *pools* and *lanes*. In other words, the *container* constructs support definition and execution of the business processes. In terms of ISSRM, the *pool* and *lane* constructs are aligned to the ISSRM *IS assets*. The BPMN *data object*, which describes the required or produced data, is aligned to the ISSRM *business asset*, and the BPMN *data store* is defined as the ISSRM *IS asset*.

Risk-Related Concepts BPMN does not contain the direct means to model security risks. However, in [14]) BPMN is applied to model negative and harmful processes. Then the BPMN *pool*, when it represents a negative/not intended actor, could be characterised as the ISSRM *threat agent*. Thus, the means (e.g., BPMN *tasks*, *flow* and *data association flow*) that the *threat agent* is capable of using are considered as the ISSRM *attack method*. There were no explicit BPMN constructs to model the ISSRM *risk*, *impact*, *event*, or *vulnerability*. But some of these concerns could be understood implicitly from the analysed problem. For instance, it is possible to define the ISSRM *threat* as a combination of the *threat agent* and *attack method*.

Risk Treatment-Related Concepts The ISSRM *security requirements* are presented using the BPMN *task*, *gateway*, and *event* constructs connected using *sequence flow* links. However, there is no BPMN construct to express the ISSRM *controls*. It was also noted that in late system development stages the combination of the BPMN *task*, *gateway*, and *event* constructs might result in different security control modules (however, not modelled using BPMN at level of the descriptive modelling).

5.2.2   Abstract Syntax

BPMN uses four major classes of constructs at the level of *descriptive modelling*: these are *FlowObjects*, *Containers*, *Flows* and *Artefacts* (see Fig.5.2). *FlowObjects* represent atomic units of a process, which can consist of *Events*, *Tasks*, and

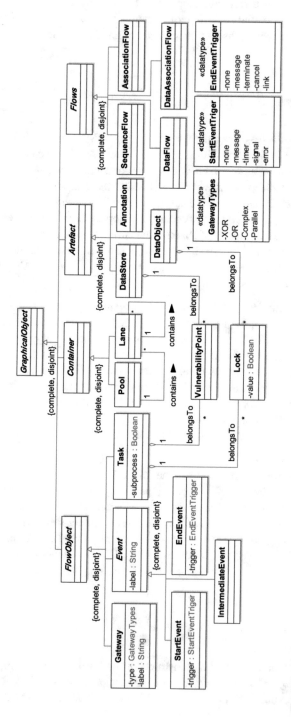

Fig. 5.2 Abstract syntax of the security risk-aware BPMN: concept classification; adapted from [14]

Gateways. An *event* indicates *start* or *end* of a process path; it can be *triggered* or *non-triggered*. A *task* is an atomic activity that has no internal sub-parts defined by the model. In some cases, the *task* can also represent sub-process, a compound activity with sub-parts. The control of the divergence and convergence of sequence flows is realised by the *gateways*.

Containers could be used for different object holders. These include a *pool* and a *lane*. The *pool* represents a participant of the process as independent units, showing the *message flows* between them. The *pool* can contain some number of *lanes*, each representing a different part of a working system, e.g., a performer role on the organizational unit.

The *artefacts* are represented by *data store*, *data object*, and *annotation*. *Data objects* describe resource that travel within the process flow, i.e., data can be produced by one activity and, then, used as an input by another. To demonstrate how the data can be stored, the *data store* is used. *Annotations* are applied to give any additional textual information to the process or its components.

We propose two additional abstract concepts at the abstract syntax level. In Fig. 5.2 the *Vulnerability point* is introduced as a property of a task or a data store and indicates the place of a system weakness. The *lock* concept is defined to express a constraint on valuable business with respect to a security objective (e.g., *integrity*, *confidentiality* and *availability*). *Lock* has a value attribute, which indicates whether the security criteria is maintained (see *security objective* in Fig. 5.5) or negated (see *impact* in Fig. 5.6).

Relationships (Fig. 5.3)[2] between different BPMN constructs are defined using *flows*, which include *sequence flows*, *data flows*, and *data association flows*. For instance, the *sequence flows* link together the BPMN activities, gateways, and events within a single pool. The *data flows* show the input/output between pools. The *data association flows* link together the BPMN tasks and artefacts (i.e., data objects, data stores, and annotations).

As illustrated in Fig. 5.4, the vulnerability point and lock are associated to annotations. This means, for example, that the vulnerability point indicates the place where the weakness of the system (i.e., IS asset) exists, and then, using annotations, one is able to define the actual vulnerability of the IS asset (see the visual presentation in Fig. 5.5). Similarly, the exact security criterion is defined in annotations and associated to the security objective expressed using a security objective, i.e., locks (see Fig. 5.6).

---

[2]Here we do not define the explicit integrity constraints of the abstract syntax. But these exist, especially, to strengthen the flow relationships. For instance, the data association flow could only be defined between the artefacts and a task; the data flow could only be defined between a pool and task/event; and others.

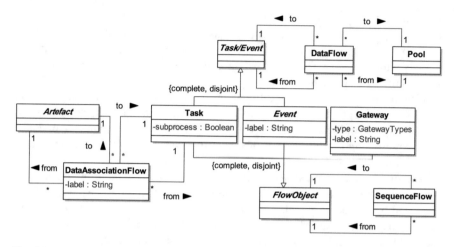

Fig. 5.3 Abstract syntax of the security risk-aware BPMN: relationships (1); adapted from [14]

5.2.3 Concrete Syntax

In this section we present the concrete syntax of the BPMN security risk-aware
extensions in Figs. 5.5, 5.6, and 5.7. Here **C** means language *concept* and **R** means
relationship. As discussed in Sect. 5.2.1, some BPMN visual constructs (e.g., *task*,
pool, etc.) could be used to express different risk management concepts (e.g., *task*
could be used to model *business asset*, *system asset*, *attack method*, and *security
requirement*). Therefore it is important to find a way to differentiate between
these different semantical constructs in the model. A possible solution is to use
different colours to differentiate between the meanings: (*i*) **black** for the asset-
related constructs; (*ii*) **red** for the risk-related constructs; and (*iii*) **blue** for the risk
treatment-related constructs.

Asset-Related Constructs Figure 5.5 lists the BPMN constructs for the asset-
related constructs [14]. The BPMN *task* could be used to express both the ISSRM
business assets and the *system assets*. In order to separate this we introduce
two icons—(B) for *business assets* and (S) for system assets—as illustrated in
Fig.5.5. Additionally we also present a visual element—*lock*—to express the
ISSRM *security objective*. The *lock* is placed (as a *constraint of*) on the business
asset, representing its security needs. The *security criterion* is defined, then, in the
annotation associated to the *lock* construct.

Risk-Related Concepts Concepts to express the risk-related constructs [14] are
presented in Fig.5.6. The ISSRM *threat agent* could be expressed using the BPMN
containers, i.e., *pools* and *lanes*, and the ISSRM *attack method* is defined as a
combination of *flow objects* (i.e., *event*, *gateway*, and *task*) using *sequence flows*.
   Figure 5.6 shows that vulnerability could be defined using *annotations*, which are
assigned to the *vulnerability point*. This point is defined as the *characteristic* of the

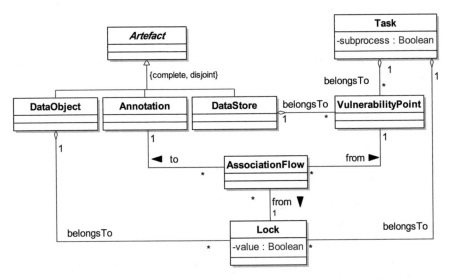

Fig. 5.4 Abstract syntax of the security risk-aware BPMN: relationships (2); adapted from [14]

IS asset (see Fig. 5.5). Further, we also introduce the notion of the ISSRM *impact* through the *unlock* symbol. If the security criterion is negated then the *security objective* (defined using *lock* as presented in Fig. 5.5) is broken. The appropriate BPMN relationships (see Fig. 5.6, *leads* to relationships) are used to define how risk harms the *business assets* and *system assets*.

Following the domain model, the ISSRM *threat* is defined as a combination of the BPMN constructs used to model *threat agent* and *attach method*; the ISSRM *event* is expressed through a combination of constructs for *threat* and *vulnerability*. The ISSRM *risk* is modelled using the BPMN constructs for *event* and *impact*.

Risk Treatment-Related Concepts Figure 5.7 presents the BPMN constructs used to express the ISSRM risk treatment-related constructs. In principle it introduces the combination of *flow objects* (i.e., *event*, *gateway*, and *task*) used to model the ISSRM *security requirements* and the *mitigation* relationship. Other ISSRM constructs are not explicitly expressed because (*i*) the *risk treatment* is rather a mental decision taken for the mitigation of the identified risk, and (*ii*) security *control* is a part of the system implementation stage (but not analysis, where BPMN is typically applied).

5.3 Example

In this section we will present an example where the security risk-oriented BPMN is applied to an extract of the Football Federation case. The risk analysis example is provided in Chap. 2. It will be illustrated how this risk management could be performed using security risk-oriented BPMN.

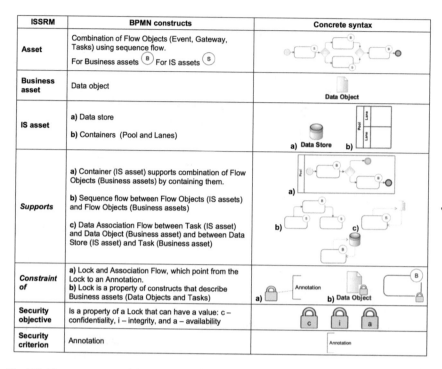

ISSRM	BPMN constructs	Concrete syntax
Asset	Combination of Flow Objects (Event, Gateway, Tasks) using sequence flow. For Business assets ⓑ For IS assets ⓢ	
Business asset	Data object	Data Object
IS asset	a) Data store b) Containers (Pool and Lanes)	a) Data Store b)
Supports	a) Container (IS asset) supports combination of Flow Objects (Business assets) by containing them. b) Sequence flow between Flow Objects (IS assets) and Flow Objects (Business assets) c) Data Association Flow between Task (IS asset) and Data Object (Business asset) and between Data Store (IS asset) and Task (Business asset)	a) b) c)
Constraint of	a) Lock and Association Flow, which point from the Lock to an Annotation. b) Lock is a property of constructs that describe Business assets (Data Objects and Tasks)	a) Annotation b) Data Object
Security objective	Is a property of a Lock that can have a value: c – confidentiality, i – integrity, and a – availability	c i a
Security criterion	Annotation	Annotation

Fig. 5.5 Concrete syntax of the security risk-aware BPMN: asset-related concepts; adapted from [14]

Context and Asset Identification Figure 5.8 presents the case, where the Umpire is sending the Game report to ERIS. Here, Game report (represented as *data object*) is the business asset and contributes with value to the Football Federation. The means to support the business asset, such as *task* Register game report, *datastore* Game storage, and *lane* ERIS, are the system assets. In the current illustration, *tasks* Submit game report and Update game report are considered as business assets; however, it is important to note that with the potential emphasis on these tasks to the support processing of the Game report, they could also be treated as the system assets.

Security Objective Determination In this example we consider *confidentiality* and *integrity* of the Game report as indicated by the constructs in Fig. 5.8. Additionally we will address *integrity* of the *task* Update game report.

Risk Analysis and Assessment Figure 5.9 presents the security risk analysis. Let's assume that there exists a Violator (i.e., red-coloured *lane*) who is able to intercept the Transmission channel (another system asset used to transfer data from Umpire to ERIS) due to the weak Transmission channel characteristics. If this happens, the Violator is able to read and keep game report for later use or Modify game report and pass to ERIS. In this way the Violator harms the Game report and negates its *integrity* and/or *confidentiality*. If the Game report is passed to the

ISSRM	BPMN constructs	Concrete syntax
Risk	Combination of Event and Impact	
Event	Combination of constructs for Threat and Vulnerability	
Targets / leads to *(harm of IS assets)*	a) Sequence Flow from Flow Objects (Attack method) to Flow Objects (IS assets). b) Data Association Flow from Task (Attack method) to Data Store (IS asset).	
Leads to harm of Business assets	a) Sequence Flow from Flow Objects (Attack method) to Flow Objects (Business assets). b) Data Association Flow from Task (Attack method) to Data Object (Business asset).	
Impact/ negates/ harms	a) Unlock b) Unlock is a property of constructs that describe the Business assets	
Threat	Combination of construct for Threat Agent and Attack method	
Vulnerability	Annotation	
Characteristics of	a) Vulnerability point and Association Flow that points to Annotation. b) Vulnerability point is a property of constructs that describe IS assets, i.e. Data Object and Task	
Threat agent	Pool and Lane (Containers)	
Attack method	Combination of Flow Objects (Event, Gateway, Task) using Sequence Flow and Data Flows	
Uses	Data Flow	

Fig. 5.6 Concrete syntax of the security risk-aware BPMN: risk-related concepts; adapted from [14]

ERIS, it could also negate *integrity* of task **Update game report** (e.g., it is modified with the malicious scripts).

ISSRM	BPMN constructs	Concrete syntax
Risk treatment	-	-
Decision to threat	-	-
Leads to	-	-
Security requirements and Mitigates	Combination of Flow Objects using Sequence Flow	
Implements	-	-
Controls	-	-

Fig. 5.7 Concrete syntax of the security risk-aware BPMN: risk treatment-related concepts; adapted from [14]

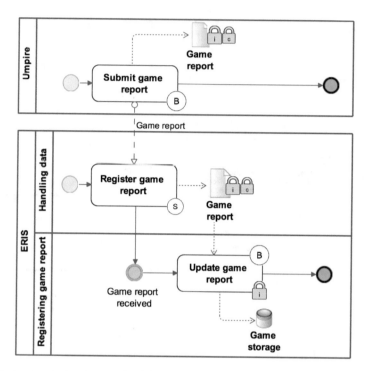

Fig. 5.8 Asset analysis using security risk-aware BPMN

Risk Treatment In this scenario we will illustrate how the *risk reduction* solution is implemented (see Table 2.3).

Security Requirements Definition In Fig. 5.10, security requirements are introduced as blue-coloured *tasks*. Tasks Make game report unreadable and Make game report readable could contribute to the *confidentiality* of the Game report. They would result in the Cryptographic algorithm implementation. The other two tasks, Calculate checksum of game report and Verify integrity of game report, could contribute to the *integrity* of the Game report. Their implementation would result in the Check sum algorithm.

Control Selection and Implementation Security risk-oriented BPMN does not contain the means to deal with control selection and implementation. This should be done using other techniques.

5.4   Further Reading

Extending BPMN towards domain-specific needs is an important research direction. In [27] Braun et al. highlight the basic extension attributes, checking whether the extensions are performed at the concrete, abstract syntax and semantic levels. The

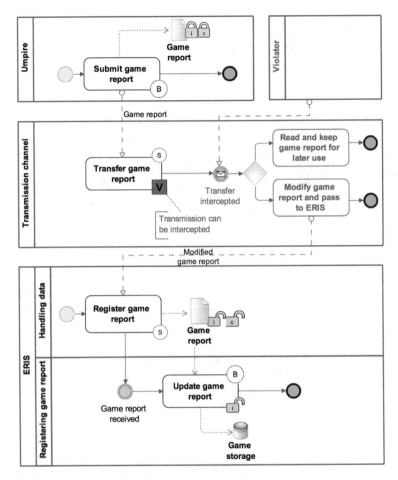

Fig. 5.9 Security risk analysis using security risk-aware BPMN

work also investigates how these extensions correspond to the BPMN standard as well as what the methodology is to support language application. The authors discuss and classify 30 domain-specific BPMN extensions, including security engineering, compliance and assurance management domains. Few of these BPMN extensions, especially the ones related to the risk management, compliance and security domains, are viewed over below in this section.

In [124] Marcinkowski and Kuciapski consider how BPMN could help in handling risk. Here, the *risk* concepts are associated with the BPMN constructs (at the level of the abstract syntax) and equipped with the targeted additional properties. For example, the concept of *risk factor* is implemented as a child element of *Artefact* and supplemented with additional properties *occurrence probability* and *impact*. Similar extensions are proposed regarding the *risk type* and *risk handler* concepts.

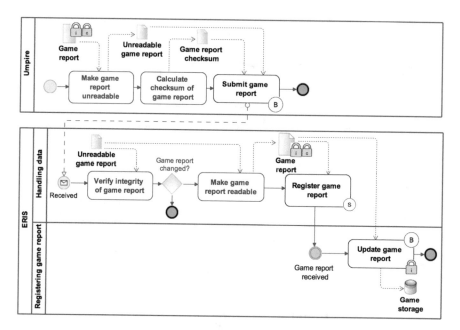

Fig. 5.10 Security risk treatment using security risk-aware BPMN

The BPMN extensions for modelling secure business processes through understanding security requirements are proposed in [171]. Here, business analysts are supposed to understand the necessary security concerns. BPMN extensions are suggested both at the abstract syntax level (by introducing *non-reputation, attack harm detection, integrity, privacy, access control, security role,* and *security permission* constructs) and at the concrete syntax level by proposing stereotype-based extensions of the BPMN visual constructs. Elsewhere in [151], based on some security vocabulary, the BMPN security constraints and security-specific user involvement are defined. Here security units are represented as structured text annotations tied to a particular set of BPMN constructs (e.g., tasks, lanes, message flows, etc.). The study discusses that such approach could support a smooth transformation of the security-annotated business process models to the executable processes.

Menzel et al. have proposed BPMN enhancements towards trust modelling [144]. Their proposal includes annotating the business process models with security intentions and ratings. The enterprise assets are presented using BPMN tasks, data objects, and communication links between tasks and participants. In addition, the authors define how to enable trustworthy interactions, organisational trust, and security intensions through BPMN. Cherdantseva et al. enrich BPMN with information assurance and security modelling capabilities [38]. This enrichment is performed by mapping the BPMN constructs to the concepts of information assurance and security domain model, designed by the authors, and followed with the abstract and concrete syntax extensions. Schleicher et al. define the concept of *compliance scope* used to restrict certain areas of a business process to avoid the modifications that would result in a non-compliant business process [180]. The study presents a method to impose the compliance constraints on the business processes expressed in BPMN. Elsewhere, in [31], BPMN is extended to support the security and compliance requirements by defining *access control*, *separation of duty*, *binding of duty* and *need to know* principles. The authors also suggest the method and support to enforcing defined requirements during the process runtime.

5.5 Exercises

Exercise 5.1 Discuss what major extensions of security risk management are introduced to the business process model and notations (BPMN).

Exercise 5.2 What are the *business assets*, *system assets* and security criteria modelled in Fig. 5.8? To structure your answer, fill in Table 5.1.

Table 5.1 Template to support answer of Exercise 5.2

Security context	Football Federation case
Business assets	
System assets	
Security criteria	

Exercise 5.3 What risk and its constituencies are modelled in Fig. 5.9? To structure your answer, fill in Table 5.2.

Table 5.2 Template to support answer of Exercise 5.3

Risk constituencies	Football Federation case
Risk	
Impact	
Event	
Vulnerability	
Threat	
Threat agent	
Attack method	

Exercise 5.4 What are the security risk treatment decision, security requirements and controls modelled in Fig. 5.10? To structure your answer, fill in Table 5.3.

Table 5.3 Template to support answer of Exercise 5.4

Security risk treatment	Football Federation case
Risk treatment decision	
Security requirements	
Controls	

Exercise 5.5 Develop an example of how Security risk-aware BPMN could be used to define security risk on the asset *availability* (e.g., availability of the game report, availability of update game report activity, etc.) in the *Football Federation* case.

Chapter 6
Security Risk-Aware Secure Tropos

Understanding the key actors and their strategic dependencies could help us estimate the security needs, determine unsecured connections, and mitigate untrusted social relationships. This especially becomes important when the social-technical systems are developed.

This chapter considers Secure Tropos, an approach introduced by Mouratidis et al. in [147, 148, 150]. It is an extension of the agent-oriented methodology Tropos [29], which supports a social-technical system developed starting with early and late requirements definitions, continuing with architecture and detailed design and finishing with system implementation. Specifically, a brief and comprehensive summary of the security risk-aware Secure Tropos [131, 132], which is the alignment of the Secure Tropos approach to the ISSRM domain model, is presented. We discuss the major constructs and their relationships to express the security risk management concepts, and consider how security risk-aware Secure Tropos supports separate steps of the security risk management process.

6.1 Tropos and Secure Tropos

The Tropos approach supports the system development through four phases: early and late requirements and architectural and detailed design. *Early requirements* analysis helps us define a problem by studying its organisational setting. *Late requirements* analysis defines the system-to-be in the context of its operational environment. *Architectural design* deals with the definition of system architecture. *Detailed design* specifies each architectural component in terms of inputs, outputs, controls and other relevant information. In this paper, we focus on the early stages (i.e., *early* and *late* requirements) of the system development.

Secure Tropos [147, 148, 150] is based on the Tropos methodology [29], with the scope to define security during system development. The major aspects are: (*i*) social issues of security are analysed during the early requirements; (*ii*) security

© Springer International Publishing AG 2017
R. Matulevičius, *Fundamentals of Secure System Modelling*,
DOI 10.1007/978-3-319-61717-6_6

is considered simultaneously with the other requirements of the system-to-be; (*iii*)
security is addressed in depth during the system design phases.

Secure Tropos separates security analysis to a number of models. The language
constructs are shown in Fig. 6.1. The *actor model*[1] identifies environment actors,
system actors and their dependency relationships. Here, an *Actor* describes an entity
that has strategic goals and intentions within the system or within the organisational
setting [29]. To deal with the security issues, *security constraints* are introduced
to place a restriction related to security that the system must have and actors must
respect [147, 148, 150].

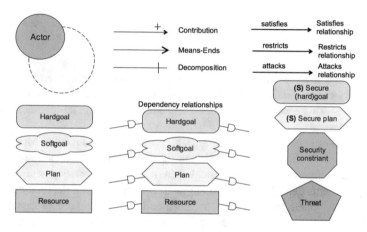

Fig. 6.1 Secure Tropos (major) constructs

Dependency between two actors indicates that one actor (the depender) depends
for some reason (dependum) on another actor (the dependee) [29]. *Secure depen-*
dency introduces one or more security constraints that must be respected by actors
for the dependency to be satisfied [147, 148, 150]. This means that the depender
expects from dependee to satisfy the security constraints and to make an effort to
deliver the dependum by satisfying the security constraint(s).

The *goal model*[2] supports a deeper understanding of how the actors reason about
goals to be fulfilled, plans to be performed and availability of resources [29]. A
Hardgoal, hereafter, represents an actor's strategic interest. A *Softgoal*, unlike a
hardgoal, does not have clear criteria for deciding whether it is satisfied or not and,
therefore, it is subject to interpretation (goals are said to be satisfied while softgoals
are said to be satisficed). A *Plan* represents a way of doing things. A *Resource*
represents an informational or physical entity. Elements are linked by the *Means-*
ends, *Decomposition* and *Contribution* relationships.

A *Secure Goal* represents the strategic interest of an actor with respect to security.
Secure goals are introduced to achieve possible security constraints that are imposed

---

[1]In [131, 132] this model is called Security Enhanced Actor Model (SEAM).
[2]In [131, 132] this model is called Security Enhanced Goal Model (SEGM).

on an actor or exist in the system [147, 148, 150]. How secure goals are achieved
is described by a *Secure Task*. In *security reference diagrams*, the threats represent
circumstances that can put in danger the security features of the system. An actual
attack is defined with the aid of a security attack scenario. Developers can identify
the goals of the possible attacker and through these identify a set of possible attacks
to the system. The *Attacks* relationship points to the target of an attacker's plan.

6.2   Security Risk Management Using Secure Tropos

Security risk-aware Secure Tropos [132] is an alignment of the Secure Tropos
approach [147, 148, 150] to the concepts of the ISSRM domain model [53, 133].
In this section we discuss the semantics and concrete syntax of the Secure Tropos
asset-related (see Fig. 6.2), risk-related (see, Figs. 6.3 and 6.4) and risk treatment-
related (see Fig. 6.5) concepts. Next, we view over the abstract syntax of the security
risk-aware Secure Tropos.

6.2.1   Semantics and Concrete Syntax

Asset-Related Concepts   The ISSRM assets (see Fig. 6.2) are defined using *actor*,
hardgoal, *plan*, *resource*, and *softgoal* constructs and *dependency*, *means-ends*,
contribution, and *decomposition* relationships. The ISSRM *supports* relationship
is expressed using the different Secure Tropos relationships. The ISSRM *security
criterion* is modelled through *softgoal* and/or *security constraint*. *Softgoal* represents high-level security criteria and *security constraint* is used for its refinements.
The ISSRM relationship *constraint of* is addressed both implicitly and explicitly in
Secure Tropos. An implicit restriction is placed on the dependum (i.e., *hardgoal*,
task or *resource*) in the *dependency* relationship. In the *goal model*, the ISSRM
constraint of relationship is modelled explicitly by *restricting* the actual goal, plan
or resource using the *security constraint*.

Risk-Related Concepts   Secure Tropos constructs can be used to express risk-
related concerns. But to avoid ambiguities, in [118], using black shadows to capture
malicious concerns is suggested. For instance, more solid (darker) colours for the
Secure Tropos construct background are proposed as shown in Fig. 6.3.

   We represent *threat agent* as an *actor*, *attack method* as a *plan*, and *threat* as
a *hardgoal* and/or *plan*. Following [62], a *vulnerability* point is used to represent
the ISSRM *vulnerability*. The Secure Tropos *attacks* relationship represents the
targets relationship of ISSRM. In order to be compliant with ISSRM, the *exploits*
relationship is introduced to define a link between a *plan* (ISSRM *threat*) and an
asset with the *vulnerability point*.

   Threat agent, *attack method*, and *vulnerability* can be combine to represent the
event of the risk (see Fig. 6.3). To generalise, one can apply the Secure Tropos *threat*

ISSRM	Secure Tropos constructs	Concrete syntax
Assets **IS assets**	1) Actor, Hardgoal, Plan, Resource, Secure Goal	
Business assets	2) Composition of the construct (1) using Dependency, Means-ends, Contribution and Decomposition relationships	
supports	Relationships: *Dependency, Means-ends, Contribution* and *Decomposition*	
Security criterion	*Softgoal, Security constraint, Contribution, Security constraint decomposition*	
constraint of	Implicitly: In the *Secure Dependency* link *Security constraint* restricts (is a constraint on) a dependum	
	Explicitly: *Restricts* link between *Security* constraint and *Plan, Resource,* and *Goal*	

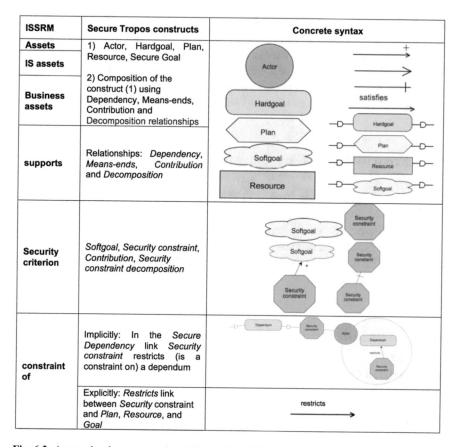

Fig. 6.2 Asset-related concepts, adapted from [131, 132]

constructs (see Fig. 6.4). A *risk* is understood as the combination of the risk *event* (represented as the Secure Tropos *threat*) and *impact* (represented using the *impacts* relationship).

Risk Treatment-Related Concepts To differentiate between ISSRM concepts, the visual syntax of risk treatment-related concepts needs to be updated, too. Constructs like *actor, hardgoal, plan, softgoal,* and *security constraint* (and/or their combinations), used to represent *security requirements* and/or *controls*, need to carry a dotted background pattern (see Fig. 6.5). *Security requirement mitigates* the identified risk. To represent this, we introduce the *mitigates* relationship. It is defined as a link between constructs representing the ISSRM *security requirement* concept and the *threat* (i.e., ISSRM *event*).

ISSRM	Secure Tropos constructs	Concrete syntax
Threat agent	*Agent*	
Attack method	*Plan*	
uses	*Agent* executes *Plan*	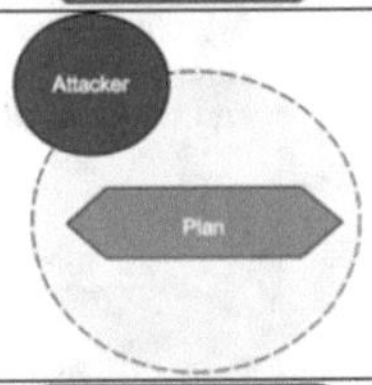
Threat	*Goal*, *Plan*	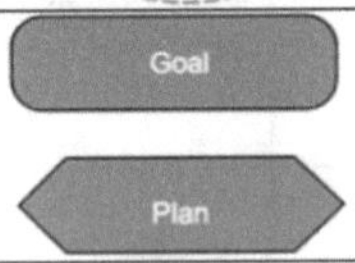
Vulne-rability	Vulnerability is not modelled, but *vulnerability points* can be identified by the attributes of the assets	
exploits	*Exploits*	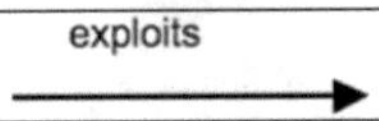 exploits
characte-ristic of	An attribute of the vulnerable asset (presented as *Hardgoal, Plan, Resource*)	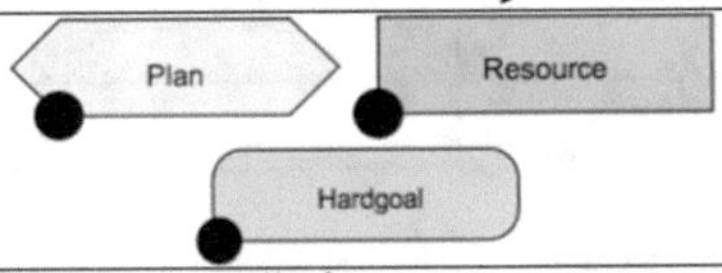
targets	*Attacks*	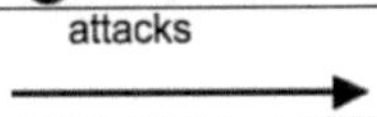 attacks

Fig. 6.3   Risk-related concepts – 1, adapted from [131, 132]

6.2.2   Abstract Syntax

To understand how graphical language constructs could be combined together, it is important to introduce the abstract syntax of the security risk-aware Secure Tropos. This section shortly presents it.

Actor Model   As illustrated in Fig. 6.6, the major element in this model is an *Actor*. He might be a *depender* or *dependee*. A *Security Constraint* is imposed on an *Actor* that represents a restriction on the *Hardgoal(s)*, *Plan(s)* and/or *Resource(s)* on an *Actor* related to security issues [148]. A *Security Constraint* enhances the language by defining the notion of *Secure Dependency*.

A *Secure Dependency* introduces one or more *Security Constraints* that must be fulfilled for the dependency to be valid [148]. Three types of secure dependency are distinguished: *dependee secure dependency*, *depender secure dependency*, and *double secure dependency*. Dependee secure dependency is defined when *Dependee SC* is defined (*Security Constraint.Dependee* equals 1). Depender secure depen-

ISSRM	Secure Tropos constructs	Concrete syntax
Event	1) Composition of an *Actor*, *Goal*, *Plan*, *Targets*, *Exploits*, and *Vulnerability point* 2) *Threat*	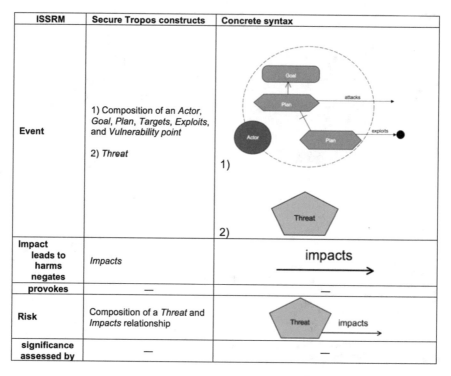
Impact leads to harms negates provokes	*Impacts*	impacts
	—	—
Risk	Composition of a *Threat* and *Impacts* relationship	
significance assessed by	—	—

Fig. 6.4 Risk-related concepts – 2, adapted from [131, 132]

dency is received when *Depender SC* is defined (*Security Constraint.Dependee* equals 1). Double secure dependency is represented when both *Depender SC* and *Dependee SC* are defined [132].

Goal Model Figure 6.7 presents an *Actor* that executes *Plans*, uses *Resources*, and has *Goals*. Plans can be *and/or decomposed* to other *Plans*, *Resources*, or *Hardgoals*. *Hardgoals* (and *Secure goals*) are achieved through *and/or Means-ends* relationship by satisfying other *Hardgoals*, executing *Plans* or making *Resources* available. To satisfice *Softgoals*, a sufficient degree of contribution should be defined with other *Softgoals*, *Security constraints*, *Hardgoals*, *Plans*, and *Resources*.

Security constraint is imposed on Actor. It *Restricts* (see Fig. 6.7) execution of *Plans*, availability of *Resources* and achievement of *Hardgoals* held by this *Actor*. A *secure goal* defines the strategic interest of an *Actor*. *Secure goals* contribute to the satisfaction of *Security Constraints* by defining a *Satisfies* relationship (see Fig. 6.7). A *secure plan* is defined as a *Plan* (by managing *isSecure* attribute). It defines how a *secure goal* is satisfied. A *secure resource* is defined as an entity that is security-critical for the system under development [132].

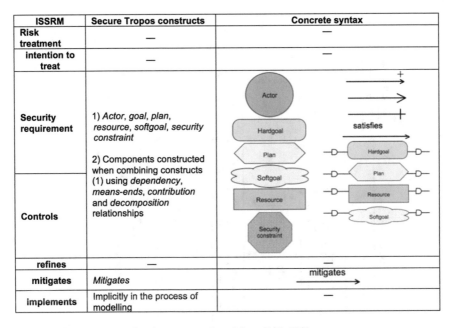

Fig. 6.5 Risk Treatment-related concepts, adapted from [131, 132]

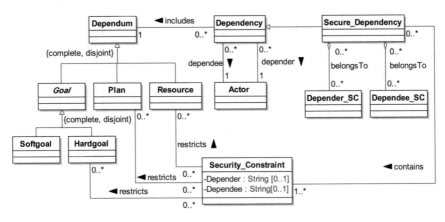

Fig. 6.6 Abstract syntax of security risk-aware Secure Tropos: actor model, adapted from [131, 132]

Security Constraint Relationships It is important to define how *Security constraint* is satisfied [132]. This will help us illustrate how it can *mitigate a Threat.*, so to lower its the *Impact* to *Plans*, *Resources* and *Hardgoals*. In Fig. 6.8, *Security Constraint* has a number of relationships with other language constructs. Generally, the *Security Constraint* restricts *Plan*, *Resource* and *Hardgoal* in the goal model.

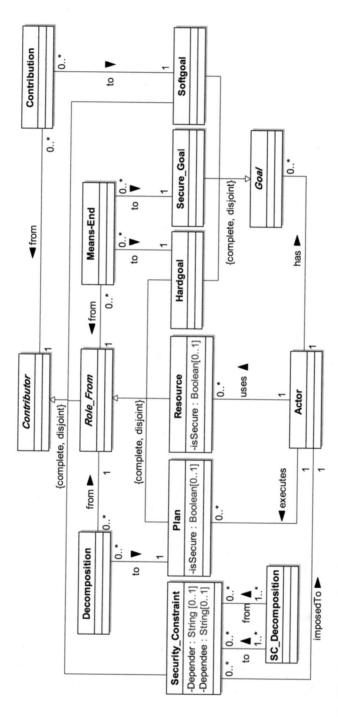

Fig. 6.7 Abstract syntax of security risk-aware Secure Tropos: goal model, adapted from[131, 132]

In the actor model *Security Constraint* places restrictions on the *Secure Dependency* fulfilment.

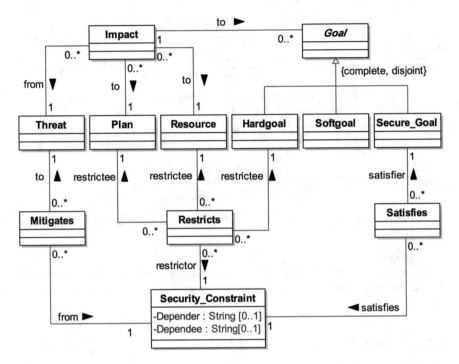

Fig. 6.8 Abstract syntax of security risk-aware Secure Tropos: relationships to security constraint, adapted from [131, 132]

Security Attack Scenario Figure 6.9 presents the abstract syntax used when defining the *security attack* scenarios. In security attack scenarios, two conceptually different sets of constructs are used: asset- and risk-related constructs to address the corresponding ISSRM concepts [132]. Thus, they both obey the same syntax rules (presented in Figs. 6.6 and 6.7) when combined within this conceptual boundary. The difficulty arises when one wants to show the relationship between them.

To distinguish malicious actors (*attackers*) from system actors (*assets*), an attribute is defined to the class *Actor* (see Fig. 6.9). Next, an integrity constraint is defined: Actor **A**, who executes a *Plan exploiting/attacking* other elements in the diagram, and Actor **B**, who holds *exploited/attacked* elements, are different. For actor **A**, we set an attribute *attacker true*, meaning a malicious actor. Actor B's attribute is set to *false*, meaning that this actor represents attacked assets. Graphical representation of both constructs is given in Fig. 6.13.

The *Exploits* relationship defines how a *Plan* executed by an attacker exploits *Hardgoal, Resource,* or *Plan*. It points to the vulnerability point (see attribute

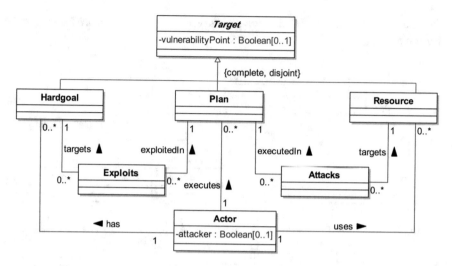

Fig. 6.9 Abstract syntax of security risk-aware Secure Tropos: relationships in attack scenario, adapted from [131, 132]

vulnerabilityPoint) of the target. The *Attacks* relationship shows a link between a *Plan* executed by a *malicious actor* and the *Resource* used by an attacked actor.

6.3   Examples

In this section we will present an extract of the Football Federation example. We will show how using the security risk-aware Secure Tropos to secure *Game report* against a *Brute force attack*. Application of Security Risk-aware Secure Tropos consists of three stages: (*i*) asset identification and determination of security objectives, (*ii*) risk analysis and assessment, and (*iii*) security requirements definition.

Asset Identification and Determination of Security Objectives   At the first stage, use of Security Risk-aware Secure Tropos does not differ from that of the language usage described in [147, 148, 150]. One needs to make a separation between the *business assets* and the *system assets*. In Fig. 6.10, there is no information on how the ERIS supports business processes, since only Umpire (name) received and Game report received related to business artefacts and activities are introduced.

In Fig. 6.11 it is illustrated what is needed to support business assets. One important task here is Manage game storage. This diagram also shows what the security criterion is and how it is used to put a constraint on the business asset. In Secure Tropos, it is possible to identify security objectives using softgoals (e.g., Integrity of game report), which are then refined using security constraints (i.e., Only if access is granted). Such a strategy could be understood as a *top-down* approach. However, in Secure Tropos, it is more natural to define implicit security

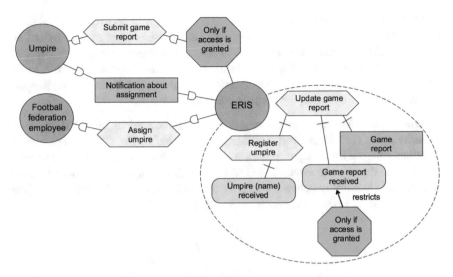

Fig. 6.10 Business asset modelling

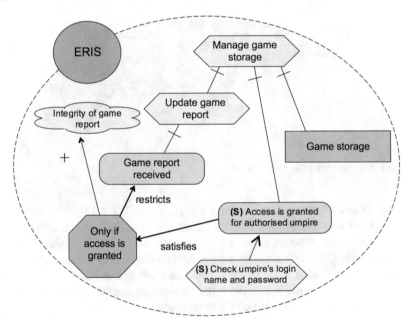

Fig. 6.11 Refinement of assets and security criterion

objectives using secure dependencies (see Fig. 6.10) and then refine them in the goal diagram (i.e., Fig. 6.11).

When defining system assets it is important to discover what *plans* have to be performed, what *resources* should be available, and what *goals* need to be fulfilled in order to support business assets [131, 132]. Satisfying security constraints is performed through *secure goals*, which are also considered as system assets. In Fig. 6.11, Only if access is granted is satisfied if the *secure goal* Access is granted for authorised umpire is fulfilled. The *plan* Check umpire's login name and password satisfies the *security goal*, thus contributing to the support of business assets by satisfying security constraints.

Risk Analysis At the second stage, a risk is introduced to the ERIS system. Security event (i.e., Brute force attack) is presented in Fig. 6.12. It describes a situation where a threat agent passes itself off as a trusted actor in order to fake identity and damage the assets. The Brute force attack *impacts* Integrity of game report. The traceability between Integrity of game report and Game report (see Figs. 6.10 and 6.11) shows the *harm* at the business level.

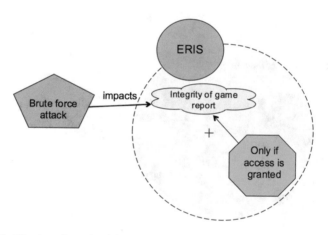

Fig. 6.12 Identification of security risk

Detailed analysis of the identified risk is presented in Fig. 6.13, which displays a security attack scenario. Here, a Violator has a *threat* (i.e., Collect info and change game report) to Game storage, which supports *business asset* Game report. Violator *attacks* Game storage by exploiting the vulnerability identified in Check umpire's login name and password. Thus, the *exploits* link shows a relationship between an *attack method* (i.e., Check game storage access repeatedly) and a *vulnerable asset* (i.e., Check umpire's login name and password).

Security Requirements Definition In order to mitigate the identified risk Brute force attack, a *risk reduction* decision is made. In this example, the plan Check umpire's login name and password is substituted with *plan* Check umpire's ID card (see Fig. 6.14). Note that the new plan has a dotted background pattern, thus, identifying that it represents security requirements. In this situation, Only if access is granted also becomes a security requirement, mitigating the risk.

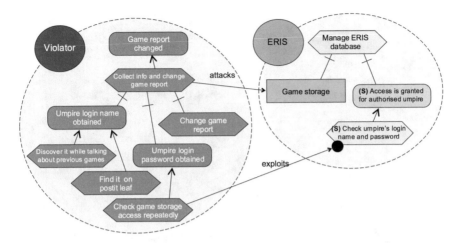

Fig. 6.13 Potential attack scenario

The ISSRM process is iterative. After identifying security requirements, one needs to test the system again against new possible risk events. For example, one can now identify **ID card authorisation attack**. This means that new vulnerabilities need to be analysed and new countermeasures defined. Thus, a risk analysis should be performed again.

6.4   Further Reading

The Tropos approach is a rather popular approach to model security concerns. There exist several proposals to use Tropos for security analysis.[3] For instance, an extension of Tropos towards security (also called Secure Tropos) is suggested in [77, 78]. The authors refine dependency relationships between actors with concepts (and visual constructs) of *trust, delegation, provisioning*, and *ownership*. The *ownership* concept means that the owner of the service has full authority to access and dispose of this service. *Provisioning* describes who is allowed to provide the service, whereas the relationship of *delegation* characterises a formal transmission of authority over some service (e.g., from the owner to the provider). The *trust* relations have their intuitive meaning among actors, thus also distinguishing between trust in managing permissions and trust in managing executions. Recently the approach has been extended to socio-technical system development [46].

Goal risk-driven assessment is a method [18] in software engineering to manage security risks. The method is addressed at three conceptual layers: asset, event and treatment. The *asset layer* introduces system-valuable assets and strategic interests

---

[3]In this discussion we exclude security extensions of the *i** modelling language [213], which stands as the base for the Tropos approach.

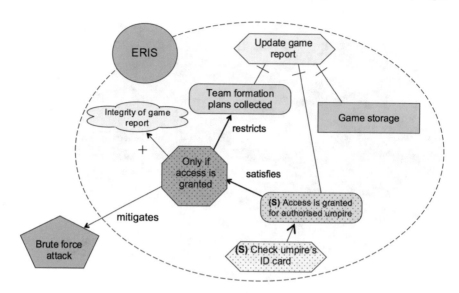

Fig. 6.14 Security requirements definition

of stakeholders, and interrelations between them. The *event layer* characterises events, concentrating on their likelihood and severity. Likelihood is defined as a property of an event and can hold qualitative values (e.g., likely, occasional, rare or unlikely). Severity is addressed as a sign of an impact relation. Severity can be the following: strong positive, positive, negative or strong negative. The *treatment layer* focusses on risk treatment, mitigation and countermeasures. There are two variants of how the treatment impacts the risk: it can reduce its likelihood or smooth its severity. Treatment methods are divided into following categories: removal or avoidance, prevention, attenuation and retention. The choice of how to elicit treatment depends on how it mitigates the risk on the event layer.

In [116], a *three-layer security analysis framework* for socio-technical systems involving business processes, applications and physical infrastructure is proposed. The *business process* layer highlights social dependencies, trusts, and business processes. At the *application* layer, software applications and their related IT infrastructures are considered. The *physical infrastructure* layer focusses on deployments of software applications and placements of devices. Using this framework, security requirements are continuously refined from the general ones to the specific ones, which are later implemented as security controls in the social-technical system.

6.5 Exercises

Exercise 6.1 How do the three stages of a security risk-aware Secure Tropos application (see Sect. 6.3) correspond to the security management process (see Fig. 2.2)?

Exercise 6.2 What context, asset-related, risk-related and risk treatment-related concepts are visualised in Figs. 6.10, 6.11, 6.12, 6.13, and 6.14? To structure your answer, fill in Table 6.1.

Table 6.1 Template to support answer of Exercise 6.2

ISSRM concepts	Football Federation case
Business assets	
System assets	
Security criteria	
Risk	
Impact	
Event	
Vulnerability	
Threat	
Threat agent	
Attack method	
Risk treatment decision	
Security requirements	
Controls	

Exercise 6.3 Figure 6.14 introduces security countermeasures. Let's assume that the threat agent has motives and capabilities to perform an attack on the umpire's ID card. Prepare Security Risk-aware Secure Tropos diagrams which would illustrate:

1. How *the attack on the umpire's ID card* could be performed.
2. What and how *security countermeasures* should be introduced to mitigate this attack.

Exercise 6.4 Perform a trade-off analysis between the two security countermeasures—Check umpire's login name and password (see Fig. 6.11) and Check umpire's ID card (see Fig. 6.14)—illustrated in the Football Federation case in Sect. 6.3.

Chapter 7
Security Risk-Oriented Misuse Cases

System functional requirements define what actually the system under consideration should do. Here, security requirements play a vital role, since their implementation contributes to system efficiency and reliability. Typically, implementation of functional and security requirements go in parallel during the project. However, the systematic understanding and assessment of the impact of security requirements on system functionality should happen before any implementation activity.

This chapter considers how misuse cases [192], a security-oriented extension of standard UML use cases, could be applied to understand security risks and introduce security requirements. An extension of misuse cases [130, 196] at both the semantic and the syntactic levels, is presented in order to enable the language to deal with security risk management.

7.1 Use and Misuse Cases

An *actor* specifies a role played by a user or any system that interacts with the subject [158]. A *use case* is the specification of a set of actions performed by a system, which yields an observable result that is of value for one or more actors or stakeholders of the system. An *include* relationship defines that a use case contains the behaviour defined in another use case. An *extends* relationship specifies extension of the behaviour of the targeted use case.

In [192] Sindre and Opdahl have extended misuse cases the standard UML use cases [158] to model security concerns. A *misuse case* defines a list or sequence of steps that cause harm to the system. A *misuser* is an actor that is willing to use the system with unfavourable intents. The *threaten* relationship targets a use case that a misuse case wants to harm. The *mitigate* relationship describes how a security use case lowers impact of the misuse case.

In [67] the concept is further extended to model *security use cases*, which are introduced as functions to secure system assets from the identified risks. In

© Springer International Publishing AG 2017
R. Matulevičius, *Fundamentals of Secure System Modelling*,
DOI 10.1007/978-3-319-61717-6_7

[174], the concept of *vulnerability* (i.e., weakness of the system) was added to the graphical misuse case diagrams. The graphical notations of the aforementioned use and misuse case constructs are illustrated in Fig. 7.1.

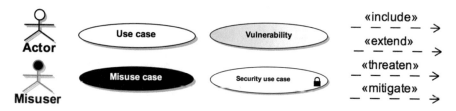

Fig. 7.1 Graphical misuse case constructs

Misuse case application process consists of five steps [192]: (1) critical asset identification, (2) definition of security goals, (3) threat identification, (4) identification and analysis of risks, and (5) definition of security requirements.

7.2   Security Risk Management Using Misuse Cases

7.2.1   Semantics and Concrete Syntax

As illustrated in [130, 196], misuse cases could help us to express security risk management concepts. Basically the extensions are performed using UML stereotypes. Firstly, this section presents semantic language alignment and graphical constructs. Next, the abstract syntax of security risk-oriented misuse cases (SROMUC) will be discussed.

Asset-Related Concepts Figure 7.2 introduces concrete syntax constructs to represent the ISSRM asset-related concepts. Assets correspond to *Actor* and *Use case*. The business asset and the system asset are modelled as a *use case*. Additionally, the system asset could be expressed using the misuse case *system boundary*, since business assets (i.e., *use cases*, which represent business assets) are within the boundary of the analysed content. The ISSRM *supports* relationship is expressed using *extends* and *includes* relationships. The ISSRM security criterion is expressed as the use case with the *security criterion* stereotype. It is linked to the business asset use case using the *constraint of* relationship (stereotyped *include*).

Risk-Related Concepts Figure 7.3 presents the concrete syntax to represent the ISSRM risk-related concepts. Here a *threat agent* is represented as a *misuser*; *attack method* as a *misuse case*; and *vulnerability* as a *use case* with the *vulnerability* stereotype. A *threat* then is modelled as a combination of *misuser* and *misuse case* (i.e., misuser communicates with misuse cases). The ISSRM *targets* relationship is represented as the misuse case *threatens* link. Another stereotype is used to express the ISSRM *impact* concept.

ISSRM	Misuse case constructs	Concrete syntax
Asset	*Actor*	Actor
System asset	(IS) *use case* *System boundary*	Use case System boundary
Business asset	(Business) *use case*	Use case
supports	Explicitly: *includes* and *extends*	«include» ----→ «extend» ----→
	Implicitly: business asset constructs that are under the system boundary	
Security criterion	*Security criterion* *(use case with stereotype* *<<security criterion>>)*	«security criterion» Security criterion
constraint of	*constraint of*	«constraint of» ------→

Fig. 7.2 Asset-related concepts, adapted from [130, 196]

In order to be compliant with the ISSRM domain model, stereotypes to the *include* link are defined to model *exploits*, *leads to*, *harms* and *negates* relationships. The *exploits* link defines a relationship between *misuse case* and *vulnerability*, whereas the *leads to* link defines a relationship between *misuse case* and *impact*. The *harms* link connects an impact and a *business use case*, whereas the *negates* link defines a relationship between *impact* and *security criterion*. The constructs of *threat agent*, *attack method*, *vulnerability*, and *impact* are combined to represent an *event*, whereas a *risk* is understood as a combination of *event* and *impact*.

Risk Treatment-Related Concepts Figure 7.4 presents the concrete syntax for the risk treatment-related concepts. To express the ISSRM *security requirement*, the *security use case* is extended with the *security requirement* stereotype (also leaving the padlock icon). The *mitigates* relationship is modelled with the *mitigates* link from a *security use case* to a *misuse case*, representing the *attack method*).

7.2.2   Abstract Syntax

The abstract syntax of the security risk-oriented misuse cases (SROMUC) is presented in Fig. 7.5. Two main language constructs are *Actor OR Misuser* and *Use OR Misuse Case*. *Actor OR Misuser* initiates *Communication* to interact with *Use OR Misuse Case*. Their cardinality shows that an *Actor OR Misuser* can

ISSRM	Misuse case constructs	Concrete syntax
Risk	A combination of constructs used to express event and impact	
Impact	*Impacts* *(use case with stereotype <<impact>>)*	
Event	A combination of constructs used to express threat and vulnerability	
Attack method	*Misuse cases*	
Vulnerability	*Vulnerability (use case with stereotype* *<<vulnerability>>)*	
Threat agent	*Misuser*	
Threat	A combination of misuser and misuse case using communication link	
targets	*threaten link*	«threaten»
exploits	*exploit link*	«exploit»
negates	*negate link*	«negate»
harms	*harm link*	«harm»
lead to	*lead to link*	«lead to»
characteristic of	*include links*	«include» «extend»
uses	*communication link*	

Fig. 7.3 Risk-related concepts, adapted from [130, 196]

ISSRM	Misuse case constructs	Concrete syntax
Risk treatment	–	–
Security requirement	(Security) *use case* *(use case with stereotype <<security* *requirement>>)*	
Control	–	–
refines	–	–
mitigate	*mitigate link*	«mitigate»
implements	–	–

Fig. 7.4 Risk treatment-related concepts, adapted from [130, 196]

communicate with one or more *Use OR Misuser Case*. *Actor* and *Misuser* are specialisations of *Actor OR Misuser*.

  Use OR Misuse Case can *include* or *extend* another *Use OR Misuse Case*. *Use Case*, *Vulnerability* and *Misuse Case* are the specialisations of *Use OR Misuse Case*. *Use Case* includes one or more *Vulnerabilities* that can be exploited by one or more misuse cases. A *Misuse Case threatens* one or more use cases. A *Misuse Case Leads*

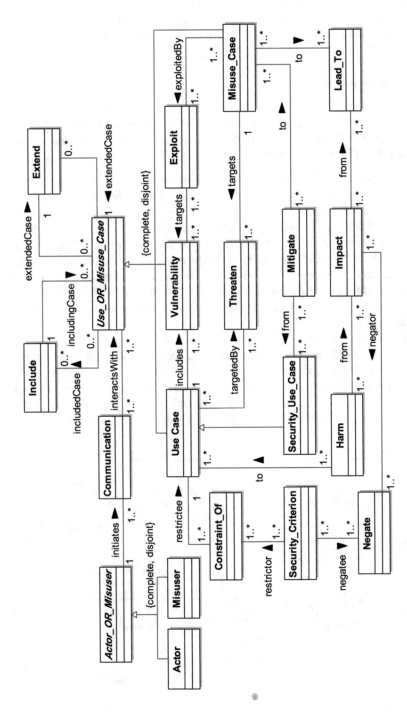

Fig. 7.5 Abstract syntax of security risk-oriented misuse cases, adapted from [130, 196]

To one or more *Impacts*. An *Impact Harms* one or more use cases by negating one or more *Security Criterions* that define a *Constraint Of* that *use case*. A *Security Use Case* is a specialised *Use Case* that *Mitigates* one or more *Misuse Cases*.

7.3   Examples

This section presents examples on how SROMUC could be applied to manage security risks. These examples are extracts taken from the Football Federation case, also considered in previous chapters.

Context, Asset and Security Objective Determination An asset diagram is presented in Fig. 7.6. This diagram could be seen as a standard use case diagram (with the addition of *security criteria* constructs). Here the emphasis is placed on two actors, Football Federation Employee and Umpire, who are using ERIS (*system asset*). The Football Federation Employe assigns umpire (see Assign umpire), whereas the Umpire has as his purpose to Submit game report. These use cases, basically, constitute the business assets of the system. Both security criteria (see Integrity of game report and Confidentiality of game report) are defined regarding the *game report*. However, it is not possible to model data objects using use cases.

Once the Umpire wants to submit the game report, he needs to provide his login name and password (to get access to ERIS). If they are correct, the game report is transferred (see Transfer game report), registered (see Register game report) and updated at the *Game storage*. These activities are characterised as system assets. However, the relationship *constraint of* is placed on them (e.g., Update game report and Transfer game report), since they support the *game report* through the process.

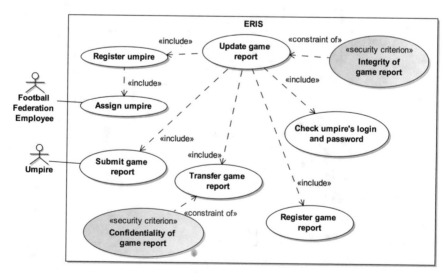

Fig. 7.6 Asset modelling

Risk Analysis A security risk scenario is presented in Fig. 7.7. Here, a *misuser* (i.e., Violator) intends to misuse the system by capturing and keeping the game report (see Read and keep game report for later use). This is included in the Intercept transfer of game report by exploiting the *vulnerability* (i.e., Transmission can be intercepted). The *misuse case* Intercept transfer of game report *threatens* the use case Transfer game report. This situation *leads to* the *impact* (i.e., Game report is not updated), which *harms* the transfer of game report and negates the security criterion (i.e., Confidentiality of team composition).

If the Violator succeeds, he could arrange the second security risk as illustrated in Fig. 7.8. Here the Violator collects information about accessing the game report (see misuse cases Obtain umpire's login name and Check game storage access repeatedly). After obtaining the umpire's user name, the Violator could brute force the password because of the *vulnerability* Number of checks is not limited. After getting the access to ERIS, the Violator is able to change the existing game report (e.g., Change game report). This threat leads to the *impact*, which harms the update of the game report and also means that an incorrect game report is stored in the game storage (see *impact* Incorrect game report stored in game storage).

Risk Treatment and Security Requirements Definition In this example we apply the security *risk reduction* decision. Figure 7.9 shows security requirements which refine this decision. The *security use case* Use secure communication defines a security requirement to mitigate the misuse of Intercept transfer of game report. Implementation of this requirement would lead to a shift of the communication

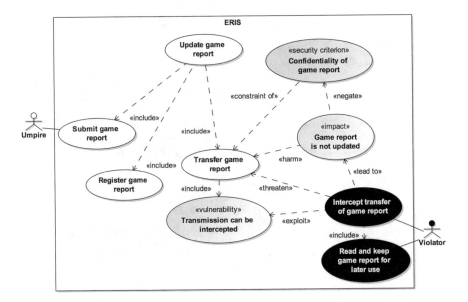

Fig. 7.7 Security risk: intercept transfer of game report

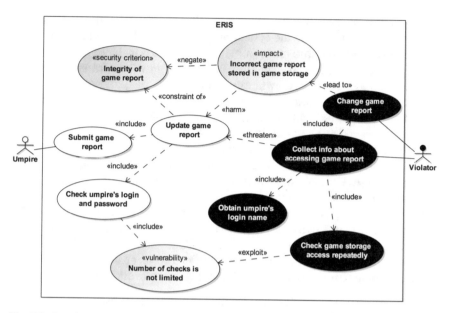

Fig. 7.8 Security risk: collect information about access and change of game report

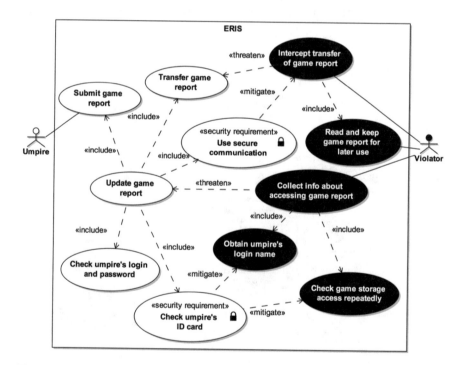

Fig. 7.9 Security risk treatment and security requirements

channel. The second risk is mitigated by introducing an umpire's authorisation using the ID card (see security use case Check umpire's ID card).

To finalise the example, it should be noted that misuse cases (like security risk-oriented BPMN and security risk-aware Secure Tropos) do not provide means for security *control* visualisation; thus these needs to be analysed using other means.

7.4 Textual Misuse Cases

Graphical use and misuse cases are typically used to define high-level scenarios and to indicate how different functional aspects are linked together. The scenario details are typically explained in the textual use/misuse case templates.

Templates encourage developers to write simple action sequences. Like ordinary use cases, misuse cases may be described textually using *misuse case templates*. There are two possible ways of expressing misuse cases textually [192]: lightweight descriptions and extensive descriptions. A *lightweight description* is embedded in an ordinary template (e.g., see [23, 45, 110]), which is extended with additional entries for threat specification. An *extensive description* supports a detailed analysis of security threats in a dedicated template [192, 196].

Table 7.1 shows an example of the extensive description. The misuse case Intercept transfer of game report (see Sect. 7.3) is detailed.

Alignment of Textual Template Entries In Table 7.2 it is shown how entries of the *extensive description* could be understood in terms of the ISSRM domain model [130]. For instance, the only *asset-related* entry is Related business rules, where some aspects of the *business asset* can be defined. But the majority of the *extensive description* concentrates on *risk-related* concepts.

Here, *risk* is addressed by the entry Stakeholders and risks; *vulnerability* by the entries Trigger, Assumption, and Precondition; *impact* by worst case threat; and *attack method* by the Basic path, Alternative path, and Extension points. In the entry Misuser profile, it is possible to give details of the misuser; it not only corresponds to the *threat agent*, but also allows the modeller to provide a detailed description (e.g., motivation and expertise) of the *threat agent*.

If a misuse case is specified at a higher level (e.g., Intercept transfer of game report; see Fig. 7.7), the Precondition would correspond to the *vulnerability*. But if a lower level of detail is specified (e.g., Change team composition), then the Precondition entry would define a system state where the misuse begins. Similar issues arise with other template entries, too.

A Mitigation points entry links a misuse case with security use cases. This indicates correspondence between mitigation points and *security requirements*. Further details of the risk treatment could be specified in the templates of other use cases (e.g., of Use secure communication from Fig. 7.9).

Table 7.1 Example of the misuse case (extensive) template (adapted from [192])

Name	Intercept transfer of game report
Summary	A violator establishes himself as man in the middle and captures the game report. He reads and keeps game report for later use.
Basic path	**bp1**: Violator establishes himself as man in the middle. **bp2**: Umpire submits game report to ERIS; **bp3**: Game report is transferred; **bp4**: Attacker intercepts transfer of game report; **bp5**: Attacker reads and keeps game report for later use (extension point ext1)
Mitigation points	**mp1**: Use secure communication
Extension points	**ext1**: Includes misuse case *Read and keep game report for later use.*
Trigger	Game report is submitted.
Assumption	**as1**: Transmission can be intercepted.
Precondition	**pr1**: Game report is not hidden (e.g., is not encrypted).
Worst case threat	Confidentiality of game report is negated; game report is not updated; transfer of game report is not reliable.
Mitigation guarantee	Use secure communication.
Related business rules	Game report is required to finalise the results of the game.
Misuser profile	Skilled. Knowledge of how to simulate man-in-the-middle attack, knowledge of how to intercept transferred messages. Motivated by some reward.
Stakeholder and risks	**Umpire**: Change of the confidentiality of the game report. Not able to received the game in time. Respectability of the Football Federation is lost.
Scope	Business environment.
Abstraction level	Confidentiality of game report.
Precision level	Focussed.

Table 7.2 ISSRM and entries of the misuse case template, adapted from [130]

ISSRM concepts	Misuse case template entries
Assets	–
IS assets	–
Business assets	Related business rules
Security criterion	–
Risk	Stakeholders and risks
Impact	Worst case threat
Event	–
Vulnerability	Assumption, Precondition
Threat	–
Attack method	Basic path, Alternative path, Extension points
Threat agent	Misuser profile
Risk treatment	–
Security requirements	Mitigation point
Control	–

7.5 Further Reading

A related approach to misuse cases is abuse cases [136]. It is an extension of use cases towards security; however, like misuse cases, it represents the behaviour that potential threats agent wish to perform using the software system.

Related literature reports a few interesting applications of misuse cases. For instance, in [9] misuse cases are applied in the trade-off analysis of conflicting requirements for railway train seats. Elsewhere, in [86], misuse cases are used in the train control scenario analysis. As highlighted in [9], trade-off analysis with misuse cases helps stakeholders to understand design as options rather than as fixed decisions. In [165, 211], the authors apply misuse cases for trade-off analysis of secure software architectures. Based on the identified misuse cases, i.e., security threats, and the security use cases, i.e, threat mitigation, the authors propose an approach to design architectural components and connect them to the candidate architectures. Trade-off analysis is performed by testing designed architectures against the identified security threats. This approach keeps the traceability between the security requirements and the architecture and gives rationale for the selected design decision.

In this chapter we discuss the misuse case extensions regarding security risk management. Our extensions are motivated by the application of the ISSRM domain model. In [39], an enhanced misuse case model is presented to define security requirements and a specification model following the Common Criteria paradigm [36]. Elsewhere, in [81], misuse cases are considered with respect to multi-channel information systems. The authors propose the concrete syntax extensions to indicate usage or misusage of various pieces of equipment in the system.

In [99], an experiment to test reusability of a threat model created using misuse cases is reported. The results show that the reuse option is the "preferred alternative" [99]; however, it is perceived as rather important since it could contribute to productivity and quality of modelling.

Although use and misuse case are rather easily understood by various stakeholders, they do not provide means for automating their testing or analysing. In [208], a language to model executable misuse case is presented. Use and misuse cases are defined using extended interaction overview diagrams. This way misuse case scenarios are defined in an executable form and their mitigation is expressed using aspect-oriented principles.

It should be noted that both use and misuse cases could be adapted for various purposes. In [9, 10] it is discussed that misuse cases could support elicitation of various non-functional requirements (like safety and usability) and definition of their test cases. Modelling principles for safety-related concerns are presented in [190]. Further, in [198] an experiment which compares safety hazard identification using graphical and textual misuse cases is reported. The authors observe that both techniques are rather easy to use. But since textual misuse cases include means for more detailed scenario definitions, they help capture more safety failure modes than graphical misuse cases.

In [104, 162], misuse cases are compared to attack trees. In [103], misuse cases and mal-activity diagrams (see Chap. 8) are compared for their capability of dealing with social engineering threats. And in [102] a combination of misuse case and system architecture diagrams are compared against misuse case maps. These language comparisons help us understand the advantages and disadvantages of modelling languages and identify system development stages where one or another language could be most efficiently applied.

7.6 Exercises

Exercise 7.1 How does the misuse use case process correspond to the security management process (see Fig. 2.2)?

Exercise 7.2 Create use and misuse case diagrams to express the system assets, their risks, and their risk treatment regarding asset integrity, availability and confidentiality in the Football Federation case.

Exercise 7.3 What content, asset-related, risk-related and risk treatment-related concepts are depicted in diagrams presented in Sect. 7.3. To structure your answer, fill in Table 7.3.

Exercise 7.4 Define an extensive misuse case template (see example in Table 7.4) for misuse case **Collect info about assessing game report** (Fig. 7.8).

Table 7.3 Template to support answer of Exercise 7.3

ISSRM concepts	Football Federation case
Business assets	
System assets	
Security criteria	
Risk	
Impact	
Event	
Vulnerability	
Threat	
Threat agent	
Attack method	
Risk treatment decision	
Security requirements	
Controls	

Table 7.4 Template to support answer of Exercise 7.4

Name	
Summary	
Basic path	
Mitigation points	
Extension points	
Trigger	
Assumption	
Precondition	
Worst case threat	
Mitigation guarantee	
Related business rules	
Misuser profile	
Stakeholder and risks	
Scope	
Abstraction level	
Precision level	

Chapter 8
Mal-activities for Security Risk Management

As discussed in Chap. 7, textual misuse case templates could be used to detail security risks and show how they threaten system functionality. Another possible technique could be malicious activity, or mal-activity, diagrams [191], UML activity diagrams extended to model negative system behaviour.

In this chapter, the alignment of mal-activity diagrams to security risk management concepts is presented [40]. We will discuss what language extensions are needed to express asset-, risk- and risk treatment-related concepts and how mal-activity diagrams can be applied to define malicious behaviour of the analysed system.

8.1 Activity and Mal-activity Diagrams

Activity diagrams are used to represent dynamic behaviour of the considered system. They include stepwise activities and actions with support for choice, iteration and concurrency and are intended to model both computational and organisational processes. For instance, activity diagrams could be used to model scenarios captured by a single use case or scenario, or express the details of a business rule [26, 158].

The major activity constructs are illustrated in Fig. 8.1. The modelled process typically begins with a *start* node that symbolises the default starting place. *Activity* represents an atomic action of the process flow. *Activity* nodes compose a *flow* in association with other activities and states.

Mal-activity diagrams are derived by extending the concepts of activity diagrams [191]. They deal with behavioural aspects of security problems. A basic way to build a mal-activity diagram is to build a normal process first and then add the *mal-activity* (unwanted behaviour) against this process. Thus some extra concepts such as *Mal-Activity*, *Mal-swimlane* and *Mal-decision*, are added and illustrated in Fig. 8.1. These concepts are just the opposite of normal activity diagram

© Springer International Publishing AG 2017
R. Matulevičius, *Fundamentals of Secure System Modelling*,
DOI 10.1007/978-3-319-61717-6_8

constructs. Additionally *Mitigation activity* and *Mitigation link* are defined to show the mitigation process.

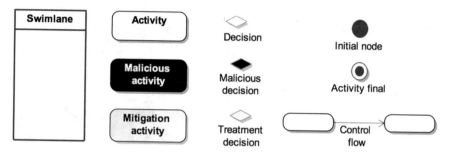

Fig. 8.1 Mal-activity constructs for asset concepts

8.2   Security Risk Management Using Mal-activities

How mal-activity diagrams could be used to manage security risks is presented in [40]. In this section we will discuss the major semantic alignment of mal-activity diagrams to the ISSRM domain model. We will also consider concrete and abstract syntax, showing suggested visual constructs and rules for combining them.

8.2.1   Semantics and Concrete Syntax

Asset-Related Concepts As discussed in Chap. 2, *asset* represents something of value for the organisation. A *business asset* is defined as information, process, or skill that is essential for the business. Activity diagrams are used to show the (*business*) workflow by combining together constructs like *activity* and *decision* using a *control flow* relationship, as illustrated in Fig. 8.2. These constructs are mapped to the ISSRM *business asset*. In addition, implicitly, *data* that are exchanged using control flows could be important to the business stakeholders, and are thus also recognised as *business assets*.

The ISSRM *system asset* is a component that supports a business asset. The activity *Swimlane* construct holds the other constructs (i.e., *activity* and *decision*) that are needed to support execution of workflows. Thus, all these constructs (i.e., *swimlane*, *activity*, *decision* and *control flow*) could be treated as ISSRM *system assets*. The *security criterion* construct (see Fig. 8.2) is introduced as an extension to the activity diagrams to model the ISSRM *security criterion*. This construct should be linked to the *activity* constructs which present the considered business asset.

Risk-Related Concepts An ISSRM *threat agent* is characterised by expertise, available means and motivation to harm the system, and the ISSRM *attack method* describes the means by which a *threat agent* carries out a *threat*. As shown in

Fig. 8.3, in mal-activity diagrams, a *mal-swimlane* (represented in the same way an ordinary *swimlane*) is used to define a *threat agent*, i.e., a malicious actor that could harm the system by performing malicious activities.

ISSRM	Mal-activity constructs	Concrete syntax
Asset	Process described using *Activity, Decision,* and *ControlFlow* constructs	
Business asset	(implicit) Objects used to perform activities	—
System asset	*Swimlane*	
supports	*ControlFlow;* (Implicit) *Swimlane* contains *FlowObjects* (representing Business assets)	
Security criterion	As informal comment linked to business asset	
constraint of		

Fig. 8.2 Mal-activity constructs for asset concepts, adapted from [40]

Mal-activity is the inverse of normal activity. These activities are done by malicious actors (i.e., *threat agents*) to harm the normal workflow. *Mal-decision* is a decision which is made with a malicious purpose. The *mal-activity* constructs combined using *mal-decision* and *control flow* constructs and placed in the *mal-swimlane* (representing the *threat agent*) correspond to the ISSRM *attack method*. As given in the definition, *threat agent* could use some means for which another *mal-swimlane* should be used. Thus, to conclude, the *attack method* is expressed using both the mal-process to capture the workflow of the *threat agent* and the *mal-swimlane* to capture the means used by the *threat agent*.

Mal-activity diagrams does not include constructs to model *vulnerability*. This construct is introduced as a greyed comment, as illustrated in Fig. 8.3. The ISSRM *impact* is the negative consequence of a risk that harms two or more assets. Using mal-activity diagrams it becomes possible to express *impact* with the *mal-activity* constructs situated in the *mal-swimlane* that represents the *attack method* (i.e., means).

Finally, other risk-related constructs, such as *threat*, *event* and *risk*, are defined using the combination of constructs used to model *threat agent*, *attack method*, *vulnerability* and *impact* following the principles suggested in the ISSRM domain model.

Risk Treatment-Related Concepts Risk treatment-related constructs are listed in Fig. 8.4. A *mitigation activity* shows the improvement of the process to mitigate the malicious behaviour, i.e., the *malicious activities*. Here, the *mitigation activity* construct is understood as the ISSRM *security requirement*. Since *swimlane* is used to aggregate all the mitigating activities, it is understood as the ISSRM *control*; in this way, the *control* is implemented by the *security requirements*.

ISSRM	Mal-activity constructs	Concrete syntax
Risk	Combination of constructs representing *Event* and *Impact*	
Impact	*Mal-activity*	
Event	Combination of constructs representing *Threat* and *Vulnerability*	
Vulnerability characteristic of	As informal comment linked to vulnerable system assets	
Threat	Combination of constructs representing Threat agent and Attack method	
Threat agent	*Mal-swimlane*	
Attack method	a) Process described using *Mal-activity, Mal-decision*, and *ControlFlows* b) *Swimlane* (as means to perform the attack)	a) b)
uses	(implicit) *Swimlane* contains *FlowObjects* (representing *Attack method*)	
targets, harms, leads to		
exploits, negates	–	–

Fig. 8.3 Mal-activity constructs for risk concepts, adapted from [40]

ISSRM	Mal-activity constructs	Concrete syntax
Risk treatment	–	–
Security requirement	*MitigationActivity*	
Control	*Swimlane*	
refines	–	–
mitigate	*MitigationLink*	– – – – →
implements	(implicit) *FlowObjects* (representing *security requirements*) are contained in the *Swimlane*	

Fig. 8.4 Mal-activity constructs for risk treatment concepts, adapted from [40]

8.2.2   Abstract Syntax

The abstract syntax of major mal-activity diagram constructs is shown in Fig. 8.5. Activity or mal-activity workflow starts with an *InitialState* (starting point) and finishes with a *FinalState* (end point). Mal-activity diagrams consist of three kinds of activity constructs: *Activity*, *Mal-activity* and *MitigationActivity*. *AnySwimlane* holds all the constructs of the mal-activity diagram. *AnySwimlane* could be classified as *Swimlane* or *Mal-swimlane*. Hence *Swimlane* contains *SwimlaneElements*, which could be *Activity*, *MitigationActivity* and *Decision*. *Mal-swimlane* includes *Mal-swimlaneElements*, which are *Mal-activity* and *Mal-decision*.

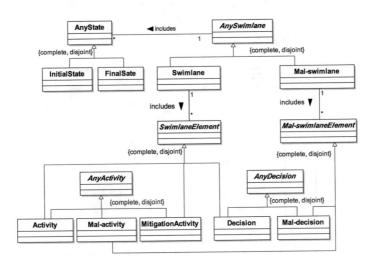

Fig. 8.5 Meta-model of mal-activity diagrams, adapted from [40]

Figure 8.6 shows how mal-activity constructs are related to each other using the *ControlFlow* construct. The *MitigationLink* construct indicates the place in the control flow where the identified risk should be mitigated. Finally, two new constructs—*SecurityCriterion* and *Vulnerability*—are introduced and linked according to *ControlFlow* (to identify system *vulnerability*) and *Activity* (to show *security criterion*).

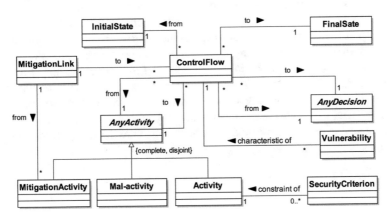

Fig. 8.6 Meta-model of mal-activity diagrams, adapted from [40]

8.3 Example

In this section we will continue with the previous example of the Football Federation case, where Umpire submits a game report, and the game report is registered in ERIS and then stored in the game storage. The context diagram using (mal-)activities is provided in Fig. 8.7. In this illustration we will consider Integrity of game report defined as the *security criterion* on the game report.

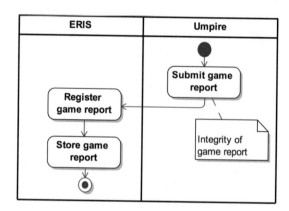

Fig. 8.7 Asset modelling using activity diagrams

Figure 8.8 presents Violator, who is using Intercepted channel to modify the intercepted game report (see Modify game report) and to pass it (see Pass game report) to ERIS. The security risk is possible because of the existing vulnerability, i.e., Transmission can be intercepted. By intercepting the channel (i.e., Intercept transfer of game report, understood as the attack method), Violator harms the transmission channel (i.e., implicit system asset). By modifying game (i.e., Modify game report, potentially treated as part of the impact), Violator harms the game report. Finally, by passing game report (i.e., Pass game report, potentially seen as another part of the impact), Violator negates the security criterion (i.e., Integrity of game report), because the changed game report is stored in the game storage.

In the next step one needs to decide what *risk treatment decision* should be taken. In Fig. 8.9, *risk reduction* is illustrated. Here, two *security requirements*, namely Use secure communication and Make game report not readable, are introduced to reduce the aforementioned risk. These security requirements are implemented in the Security module, which constitutes the security control in this example.

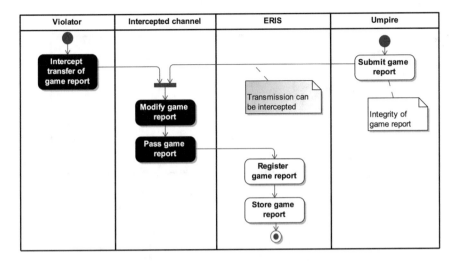

Fig. 8.8 Risk modelling using mal-activity diagrams

8.4   Further Reading

The literature suggests a few attempts to address security concerns using UML activity diagrams or other dynamic notations. For instance, in [101] misuse case maps (MUCM) are presented to capture and combine an attacker's behavioural view in the considered system with the system's architecture view. The goal of this method is to illustrate how security attacks could be performed in the architectural context.

Braz et al. propose a method to elicit security requirements through misuse activities [28]. The approach is to consider each activity in each use case and determine how it could be harmed by the internal and external attacker. Elsewhere, in [173], an extension of the activity diagrams is developed to specify security requirements in the business processes. These extensions are based on the business process security method. The authors also propose graphical notations for security requirements, audit registration, access control attack harm detection, integrity, non-repudiation and privacy. In this chapter we have considered how the mal-activities could support security risk management. In comparison to [28] and [173], our discussion follows the model which addresses the targeted security domain and suggests the rationale for why security requirements should be introduced.

8.5   Exercises

Exercise 8.1 What are the extensions of mal-activity diagrams to model security risk management? Discuss the conceptual language extensions and the process of language application.

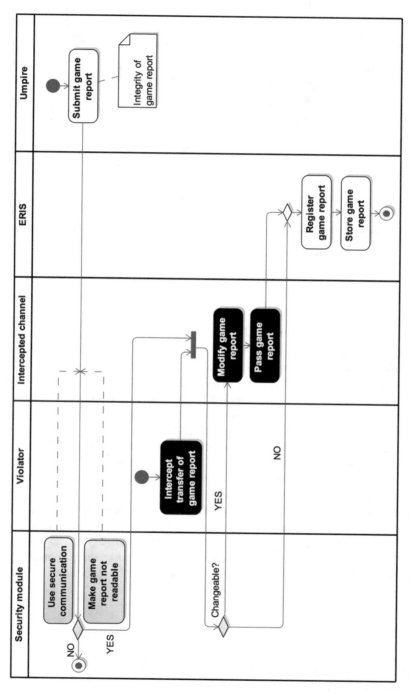

Fig. 8.9 Risk treatment modelling using mal-activity diagrams

Exercise 8.2 Discuss how *security risk* could be modelled using mal-activity diagrams. Describe modelling constructs used for each security risk constituency.

Exercise 8.3 Create mal-activity diagrams to manage security risks to the *Football Federation* system (i.e., ERIS).

Exercise 8.4 What content, asset-related, risk-related and risk treatment-related concepts are depicted in diagrams presented in Sect. 8.3? To structure your answer, fill in Table 8.1.

Table 8.1 Template to support answer of Exercise 8.4

ISSRM concepts	Football Federation case
Business assets	
System assets	
Security criteria	
Risk	
Impact	
Event	
Vulnerability	
Threat	
Threat agent	
Attack method	
Risk treatment decision	
Security requirements	
Controls	

Part III
Model-Driven Security Development and Application

Chapter 9
Transformations Between Security Risk-Oriented Modelling Languages

As discussed in the first and second parts of the book, security risk management is an important instrument to derive and reason about requirements and countermeasures. The systematic guidance on this process could be supported by different modelling languages. However, secure system development is a complex activity involving numerous stakeholders, including multiple perspectives, and considering various system and software aspects at different levels of abstraction. One way to deal with this complexity of secure system development is by supporting developers with systematic model transformation, thus allowing them to capture various stakeholder perspectives. In addition, this helps advancing systems with additional details that are not possible to capture in a single language model.

For example, as discussed in the second part of the book, the primary purpose of *BPMN* is business process modelling. *Secure Tropos* suggests a means to capture security constraint and reason about the achievement of security goals. *Misuse cases* define a list or sequence of steps taken by a misuser to cause harm to the stakeholders or the system itself. Finally, *mal-activities* are used to represent harmful behaviour of security attackers. In this chapter systematic guidelines for transformation between (some of) these modelling languages will be presented, thus illustrating how different secure system perspectives could be linked together.

9.1 Transformation Basis

9.1.1 Transformation Method

Figure 9.1 present the concepts of language transformation. The modelling languages (i.e., BPMN, Secure Tropos, Misuse cases, and mal-activity diagrams) considered in the second part of this book are aligned to the ISSRM domain model. This gives the base to derive semantic-based transformation rules which could be

© Springer International Publishing AG 2017
R. Matulevičius, *Fundamentals of Secure System Modelling*,
DOI 10.1007/978-3-319-61717-6_9

used to translate from *language A* to *language B*. This means that the *original model* created in *language A* could be transformed to the *target model* in *language B*.

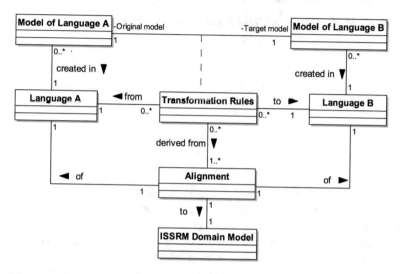

Fig. 9.1 Language transformation concepts

However, before illustrating the sets of the transformation rules, it is important to explain the principle of *semiotic clarity* [161, 207] and to show how the modelling languages fulfil these principles. According to this principle, there should be a one-to-one correspondence between a visual language construct and its referent concept in the semantic domain. If not, then there exist redundancy, overload, incompleteness and under-definition (excess) limitations of this language. *Redundancy* means that two language constructs have the same or overlapping semantics. *Overload* exists if the same language construct has several meanings. *Incompleteness* appears when a language does not convey information on a certain phenomenon. *Under-definition* (or *excess*) arises when a language construct has no semantics.

In the next section we will view over how the languages considered in Part II meet the semiotic clarity principle with respect to the domain model of security risk management.

9.1.2 Comparison of Modelling Languages

All four languages are aligned to the ISSRM domain model as discussed in Part II. Figure 9.2 shows a comparison of construct alignment of the *asset-related concepts*. Figure 9.3 presents how modelling languages express the *risk-related concepts*. Finally, Fig. 9.4 illustrates language correspondences to the *risk treatment-related concepts.* Below, we will compare each construct correspondence following the ISSRM concept. This discussion is based on the analysis given in [126].

Assets Only few language constructs have a clear semantics to present *assets*. For example, BPMN *data object* is used to express the *business assets*; BPMN *pool* and *data store*, misuse case *system*, and mal-activity *swimlane* are presenting the *system assets*. Further, the assets (both business and system) are described using a combination of several modelling constructs. This means that modelling languages have

- *overload* limitation, since the same construct combination could represent different ISSRM concepts;
- *underdefinition* limitation because, individually a language construct does not convey the asset semantics; and
- *redundancy* limitation (except the Secure Tropos), because more than one presentation of assets is possible using different constructs or their combinations.

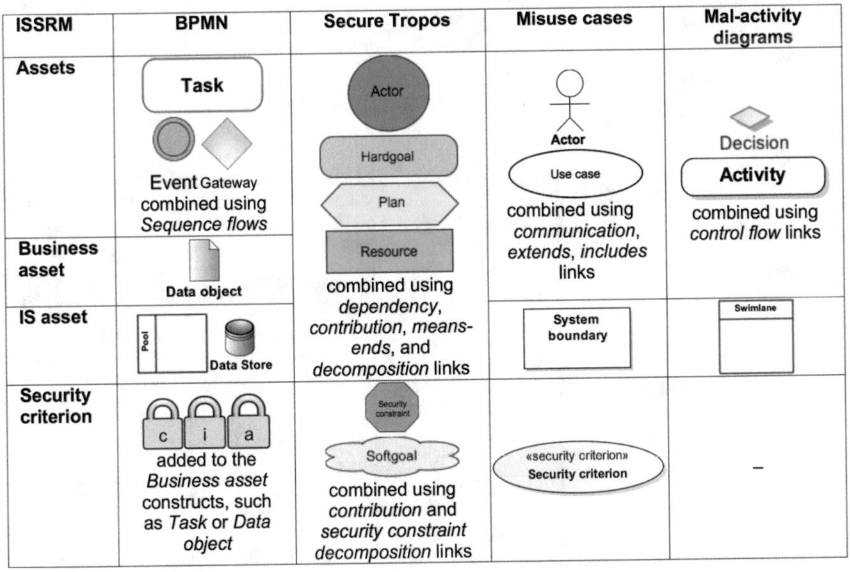

Fig. 9.2 Comparison of language alignments of asset-related concepts, adapted from [126]

Security Criterion Misuse cases have one-to-one correspondence between its *security criterion* construct and the ISSRM *security criterion*. BPMN contains the *incompleteness* limitation since the *lock* construct defines only the place where security criterion emerges. Secure Tropos allows expressing a security criterion using a security constraint and softgoal composition (i.e., *under-definition* limitation), and mal-activities do not give any construct for a security criterion (i.e., *incompleteness* limitation).

Risk None of the analysed languages allow modelling risk using one construct. Here, the *incompleteness* limitation is observed, because constructs, which are combined to express risk, correspond to the event and/or impact (i.e., have their meaning in the ISSRM domain).

ISSRM	BPMN	Secure Tropos	Misuse cases	Mal-activity diagrams
Risk	Combination of *Event* and *Impact*	Combination of *Event* and *Impact*	Combination of *Event* and *Impact*	Combination of *Event* and *Impact*
Impact		impacts →	«impact» Impact	Mal-activity contained in the *mal-swimlane* that expresses *attack method*
Event		Threat *or* combination of *Vulnerability*, and *Threat*	Combination of *Vulnerability* and *Threat*	Combination of *Threat* and *Vulnerability*, if it is implicitly defined
	Combination of *Vulnerability*, and *Threat*			
Vulnerability	**V** added to the *IS asset* constructs, such as *Task* or *Data store*	● added to the *IS asset* construct such as *Goal, Task, or Resource*	«vulnerability» Vulnerability	–
Threat	Combination of *Attack method* and *Threat agent*	Goal / Plan	Combination of *Attack method* and *Threat agent*	Combination of *Attack method* and *Threat agent*
Attack method	Task / Event Gateway combined using *Sequence flows*	Plan potentially combined with other *Tasks* using *decomposition* links	Misuse case potentially combined with other *misuse cases* using *includes* and *extends* links	As method: Mal-activity combined using *control flow* links As means Mal-Swimlane
Threat agent	Pool	Attacker	Misuser	Mal-Swimlane

Fig. 9.3 Comparison of language alignments of risk-related concepts, adapted from [126]

Impact Both BPMN and Secure Tropos have the *incompleteness* limitation. The *unlock* symbol, although indicating the harmed business asset and its security negation, gives no details about the harm to the IS asset. The Secure Tropos *impacts* link indicates the negated security criterion, but it does not present any harm to the assets. Using misuse cases and mal-activities one could provide the complete impact definition. In misuse cases it is done through the *impacts* construct (and related links of *harms* and *negates*). In mal-activities, the impact is specified using the *mal-activity* constructs placed in the *swimlane* that expresses the attack method.

Event Using all modelling languages, the *event* is expressed through a combination of constructs used to model *threat* and *vulnerability*. As in the *risk* example, this results in the *incompleteness* limitation for all languages, except Secure Tropos. In addition to the possibility of construct combination, Secure Tropos allows developers to model *event* using the *threat* construct, resulting in the *redundancy* limitation.

Vulnerability Similarly to *security criterion*, *vulnerability* could be completely defined using misuse cases. Using BPMN and Secure Tropos one could identify only a *vulnerability point*. And there is no construct to model *vulnerability* in mal-activities. In both cases this is an *incompleteness* problem.

Threat Using BPMN, misuse cases, and mal-activities, the *threat* is expressed by combining *threat agent* and *attack method* constructs (leading to *incompleteness*, as discussed for the *risk* concept).

In Secure Tropos, the *threat agent* (presented as actor; see below) uses *attack method* (a combination of plans; see below) and holds a *threat* as follows from the Secure Tropos definition [29, 148]. This means that the *threat* concept is not complete when combining a Secure Tropos goal and plan constructs.

Attack Method In BPMN, Secure Tropos and misuse cases, the *attack method* is defined by combining several modelling constructs. The languages have the *under-definition* limitation because individually these constructs do not have meaning regarding the ISSRM domain. Using mal-activities one could express the attack method either through a combination of the *mal-activity* and *mal-decision* constructs, or by the *mal-swimlane* construct. This results in the *redundancy* limitation.

Threat Agent All four modelling languages contain a clearly semantically defined construct for the threat agent: in BPMN—*pool*, in Secure Tropos—*actor*; in misuse cases—*misuser*; and in mal-activities—*mal-swimlane*.

Risk Treatment is a mental decision made by the modellers. So it is not a surprise that modelling languages are incomplete and do not provide any visual constructs.

Security Requirement Similarly to assets, the *security requirements* are defined by combining different constructs. This means the *under-definition* problem, since individually these constructs do not carry meaning regarding the ISSRM domain.

Control BPMN, Secure Tropos and misuse cases do not contain constructs for the control presentation. Using mal-activities, one could use a *swimlane* (which typically will contain mitigation activities and decisions) to express security controls.

Although syntactically it appears that languages nearly cover the whole ISSRM domain model, as discussed above, semantically the languages' similarities differ to rather large degree. Table 9.1 summarises the above comparison following the semiotic clarity criteria. *One-to-one* correspondence shows the ISSRM concepts, which have no limitations of semiotic clarity when using the analysed languages. The rest of the table shows the ISSRM concepts for which modelling languages have *redundancy*, *overload*, *incompleteness* and *under-definition* limitations.

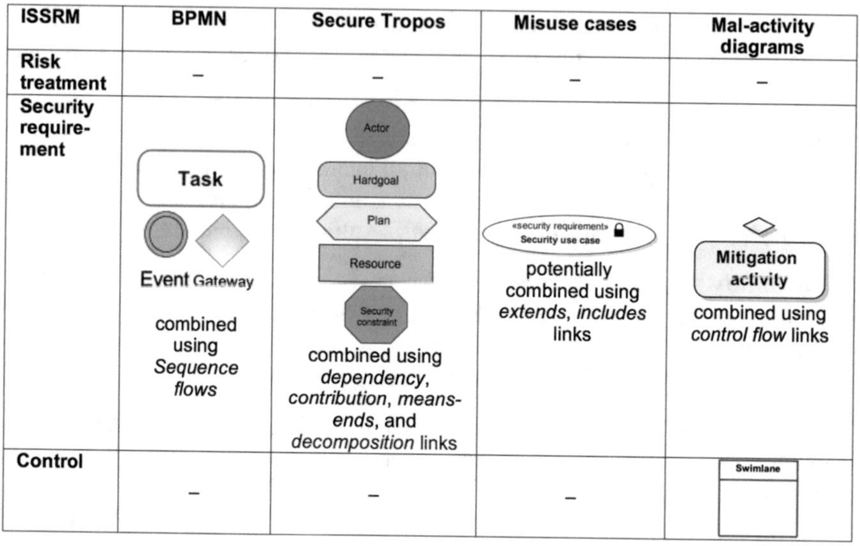

ISSRM	BPMN	Secure Tropos	Misuse cases	Mal-activity diagrams
Risk treatment	–	–	–	–
Security require-ment	**Task** Event Gateway combined using *Sequence flows*	Actor Hardgoal Plan Resource Security constraint combined using *dependency, contribution, means-ends,* and *decomposition* links	«security requirement» Security use case potentially combined using *extends, includes* links	Mitigation activity combined using *control flow* links
Control	–	–	–	Swimlane

Fig. 9.4 Comparison of language alignments of risk treatment-related concepts, adapted from [126]

Table 9.1 Comparing security risk-oriented/aware modelling languages, adapted from [126]

Semiotic clarity	BPMN	Secure Tropos	Misuse cases	Mal-activity diagrams
One-to-one correspondence	*Threat agent*	*Threat agent*	*Security criterion, Impact, Vulnerability, Threat agent*	*Impact, Threat agent, Control*
Redundancy	*Assets*	*Event*	*Assets*	*Assets, Attack method*
Overload	*Assets*	*Assets*	*Assets*	*Assets*
Incompleteness	*Security criterion, Risk, Impact, Event, Vulnerability, Threat, Risk treatment and Control*	*Risk, Impact Vulnerability, Threat, Risk treatment, and Control*	*Risk, Event, Threat, Risk treatment, and Control*	*Security criterion, Risk, Event, Vulnerability, Threat, and Risk treatment*
Under-definition (excess)	*Assets, Attack method, and Security requirements*	*Assets, Security criterion, Attack method, and Security requirements*	*Assets, Attack method, and Security requirements*	*Assets, and Security requirements*

It is not a surprise that the considered languages contain these limitations regarding *semiotic clarity*, because they were not designed to deal with security risk management in the first place. While applying them for their primary purpose (i.e., BPMN for business process description; Secure Tropos for secure goal definition; misuse cases for relation of functional and security requirements; mal-activities for identification of malicious processes), the *semiotic clarity* analysis could contribute with completely different results.

However, this analysis opens the way to define (security risk-based) model transformations between these languages. Our results show which language constructs could be transformed to the constructs of another language. Additionally, it gives an indication (*i*) what semantics is lost from the models when such a translation is performed; (*ii*) what semantics needs to be additionally defined in the resulting models; and (*iii*) what semantics is preserved during the model transformation. In the next section we illustrate a few sets of the transformations:

- From security risk-oriented BPMN to security risk-aware Secure Tropos (see Sect. 9.2)
- From security risk-aware Secure Tropos to security risk-oriented misuse cases (see Sect. 9.3)
- From security risk-oriented misuse cases to mal-activities for security risk management (see Sect. 9.4)

9.2 Transforming from Security Risk-Oriented BPMN to Security Risk-Aware Secure Tropos

A comprehensive introduction of the transformation guidelines from security risk-oriented BPMN to security risk-aware Secure Tropos is described in [13]. Here we will recapture the major transformation principles and provide an illustrative example.

Transformation Rules Transformation of the *BPMN* model to the *Secure Tropos* model could be done using these transformation guidelines:

- **TR.BPMN-ST.1**: BPMN *pool* is translated to the Secure Tropos *actor*.
- **TR.BPMN-ST.2**: In Secure Tropos, *dependencies* between actors are defined following the BPMN *messages flows*.
- **TR.BPMN-ST.3**: BPMN *task* is defined as *plan* in the Secure Tropos model.
- **TR.BPMN-ST.4**: BPMN *event* is defined as *hardgoal* in the Secure Tropos model.
- **TR.BPMN-ST.5**: BPMN *data object* and *data store* are translated to *resource* in the Secure Tropos model.

  Note: BPMN is used to represent dynamic aspects of organisation's business; thus, the model defines the workflow of the organisation. The Secure Tropos model captures the static concerns. This means that once the *tasks* and *goals* are represented as *plans* and *hardgoals* in Secure Tropos, one needs to introduce *means-ends* and *decomposition* relationships accordingly to illustrate how different *plans* are executed and *hardgoals* are achieved.

- **TR.BPMN-ST.6**: BPMN *lock* construct and its associated comment are translated to the Secure Tropos *security constraint*. The *restrict* relationship is defined from the *security constraint* to the appropriate construct.
  <u>Note</u>: The *security constraint* could also be defined on the *dependency* relationships.
- **TR.BPMN-ST.7**: The BPMN *pool* that presents the *threat agent* is translated to the Secure Tropos (malicious) *actor*.
- **TR.BPMN-ST.8**: BPMN *plans* and *message flows*, used to describe the *attack method*, are transformed to *plans* and situated within the malicious *actor* boundary in the Secure Tropos model.
  <u>Note</u>: Similarly to TR.BPMN-ST.5, the *decomposition* relationships need to be introduced to define how different *plans* depend on one another.
- **TR.BPMN-ST.9**: The BPMN *vulnerability* construct is translated to the *vulnerability point* and placed with the exploited constructs in the Secure Tropos model.
  <u>Note</u>: The actual vulnerability is not captured in the Secure Tropos model; thus, other means should be used to record it.
- **TR.BPMN-ST.10**: The BPMN *task* that presents the *security requirement* is transformed to the Secure Tropos *secure plan*.
  <u>Note</u>: Similarly to TR.BPMN-ST.5 and TR.BPMN-ST.8, the *decomposition* relationships needs to be introduced to define how different *secure plans* contribute to system security.

Transformation Example In Fig. 9.5, an extract of the Football Federation case as defined in Chap. 1 is presented. Here the Football Federation Employee submits initial Game info for the creation of the *Game* entry in the *Game storage*. Once the game entry is created (see Create game), the notifications are sent to Football Federation Employee and Umpire. Umpire next submits the Game report, which is then updated (see Update game report) in the game storage. In the final step, the Football Federation Employee needs to confirm the submitted game report (see Update confirmation).

Let's assume that there exists a Violator who observes that the access control mechanism is not defined in ERIS, as illustrated in Fig. 9.6. Therefore the Violater is able to submit and register Faulty game info, Faulty game report and Faulty confirmation. In other words, this security risk creates a *faulty game entry* in the game storage, thus negating its integrity.

To mitigate the security risk, one needs to introduce access control mechanisms as illustrated in Fig. 9.7. The mechanism includes access checking tasks such as Check permission to create game, Check permission to update game report, and Check permission to update confirmation. These tasks then becomes part of the game entry creation process.

Next we illustrate, how this model represented using security risk-oriented BPMN, could be translated to security risk-aware Secure Tropos. After applying the transformation rules listed above, the resulting security risk-aware Secure Tropos representation is displayed in Fig. 9.8.

Following TR.BPMN-ST.1 the Football Federation Employee, Umpire and ERIS *pools* are translated to Secure Tropos *actors*. In the security risk-oriented

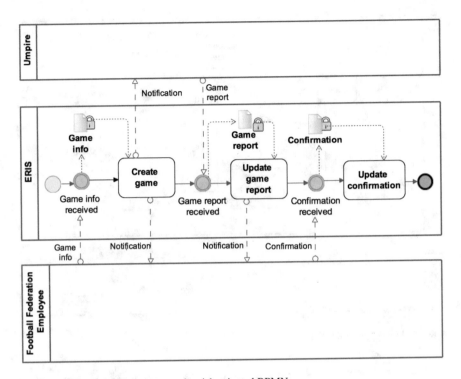

Fig. 9.5 Asset modelling using security risk-oriented BPMN

BPMN model there exist six *message flows* which are recaptured in Fig. 9.8 according to TR.BPMN-ST.2. All BPMN tasks (e.g., Create game, Update game report, and Update confirmation) are translated to Secure Tropos *plans* TR.BPMN-ST.3. Similar transformations are performed regarding the BPMN *events* as defined in TR.BPMN-ST.4 (see Game info received, Game report received, and Confirmation received). *Data object* (e.g., Game info, Game report and Confirmation) are translated according to TR.BPMN-ST.5. Following the TR.BPMN-ST.6 rule, in the given example *security constraints* (i.e., Integrity of game info, Integrity of game report, and Integrity of confirmation) restrict their appropriate business assets as illustrated in Fig. 9.8.

Figure 9.6 shows how Violator could harm the business and system assets. Following TR.BPMN-ST.7, the *Violator pool* is translated to the Secure Tropos *actor*. All the BPMN constructs, i.e., *tasks* and *message flows* (e.g., Register faulty game info, Register faulty game report, and Register faulty confirmation) used to present the *attack method* are translated to the Secure Tropos *plans*. As noted in TR.BPMN-ST.8, the *decomposition* and relationships must be introduced by the developer. Additionally, in Secure Tropos model one needs to define the *threat agent goal*, in the current example given as Faulty game created. This is needed to complete the definition of security *threat*.

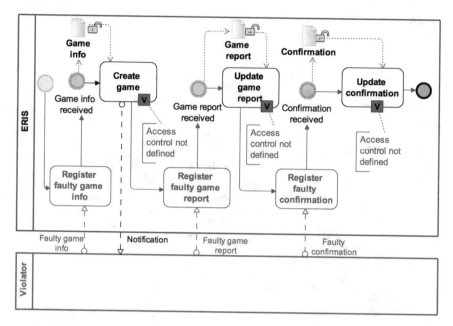

Fig. 9.6 Risk modelling using security risk-oriented BPMN

Following the TR.BPMN-ST.9 rule, *vulnerability points* are introduced to *plans* Create game, Update game report and Update confirmation. The BPMN model does not include explicit definitions of the *exploits* and *target* relationships. However, following the model logics, one could capture them implicitly and introduce them to the Secure Tropos model as illustrated in Fig. 9.8.

In Fig. 9.7, security countermeasures (i.e., Check permission to create game, Check permission to update game report, Check permission to update confirmation) are introduced to mitigate the identified risk. Following the TR.BPMN-ST.10 rule, these tasks are translated to *secure plans* in the Secure Tropos model as shown in Fig. 9.8.

Model Completion The guidelines defined in this section are rather informal and based on the logic of the modelling of both the BPMN and the Secure Tropos languages. Additional model elements need to be introduced to complete the Secure Tropos model. As discussed above, for example, one needs to define:

- *decomposition* and *means-ends* relationships to illustrate how *plans* are decomposed and *goals* are achieved;
- *security criteria* to restrict dependencies among the actors;
- malicious *goal(s)* to complete the definition of security threats;
- *exploits* and *targets* relationships to show how vulnerabilities (i.e., vulnerable points) are exploited and system assets are attacked;
- aggregated attack view to illustrate how the security events could be mitigated.

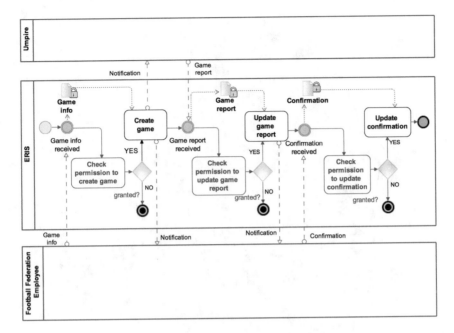

Fig. 9.7 Risk treatment modelling using security risk-oriented BPMN

9.3   Transforming from Security Risk-Aware Secure Tropos to Security Risk-Oriented Misuse Cases

The major principles of transforming the security risk-aware Secure Tropos models to the security risk-oriented misuse cases[1][2] are defined in [2]. In this section we recall the major transformation rules and illustrate them using the Football Federation example. Firstly, we present the set of transformation rules; then we illustrate how they can be applied to the *Football Federation* case

Transformation Rules To transform the *Secure Tropos* model to the *misuse case* diagram, the following transformation rules are applied:

- **TR.ST-MUC.1**: An *actor* that presents the (software) system in Secure Tropos is translated to a misuse case software *system boundary*.
- **TR.ST-MUC.2**: Secure Tropos *goal* and *plan*, which belong to the (software) system Tropos actor, are translated to *use case* in the misuse case diagram.
- **TR.ST-MUC.3**: Secure Tropos *means-ends* and *decomposition* links are translated to the misuse case *includes* relationship.

---

[1]To simplify the discussion in this section we will call security risk-aware Secure Tropos simply Secure Tropos, and security risk-oriented misuse cases simply misuse cases. Similar short names will be used for the security risk-oriented BPMN and mal-activities for security risk management.

[2]The transformation rules for the misuse case diagrams to the Secure Tropos models are defined in [5].

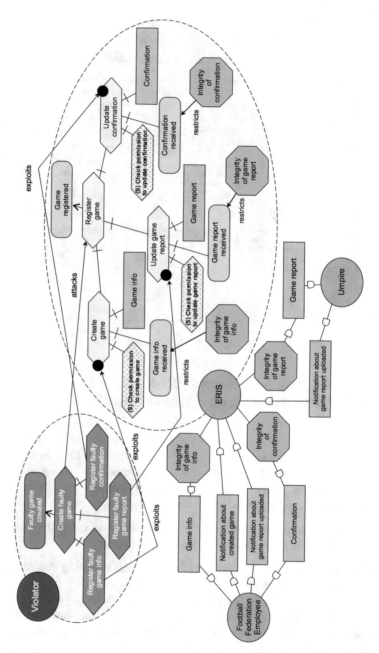

Fig. 9.8 Security risk management using security risk-aware Secure Tropos

- **TR.ST-MUC.4**: A Secure Tropos *actor* that presents the organisational actor (or the actor from the system environment) is translated to a misuse case *actor*.
- **TR.ST-MUC.5**: Secure *Dependency* links from Secure Tropos are translated to communication *association* in the misuse case diagram.
- **TR.ST-MUC.6**: Secure Tropos *Security constraint* is translated to misuse case *Security criterion*.
- **TR.ST-MUC.7**: A Secure Tropos *restricts* link is translated to a misuse case *constraint of* relationship.
- **TR.ST-MUC.8**: A Secure Tropos *actor* that *exploits* and/or *targets* elements of other actors is translated to *misuser* in the misuse case diagram.
- **TR.ST-MUC.9**: The Secure Tropos *goal* and *plan* that belong to the *actor* who exploits and/or targets constructs of other actors are translated to *misuse case* in the misuse case diagram.
  Following TR.ST-MUC.3, one should translate the *means-ends* and *decomposition relations* to misuse use case *includes*. A *communication* link is defined between the *misuser* and the top level misuse case in the misuse case hierarchy.
- **TR.ST-MUC.10**: A Secure Tropos *vulnerability point* is translated to a *vulnerability* in the misuse cases diagram. The newly translated *vulnerability* will not carry any name (it needs to be defined by the modeller), but the *includes* relationships should be defined between the asset use case and this *vulnerability*.
- **TR.ST-MUC.11**: A Secure Tropos *exploits* link should be represented by two relationships in the misuse case diagram: (*i*) as a *threatens* relationship from the misuse case to the asset *use case*, and (*ii*) as an *exploit* relationship from the misuse case to the asset *vulnerability*.
- **TR.ST-MUC.12**: Secure Tropos *goal* and *plan*, which express security requirements (and controls), are translated to (security) *use case* in the misuse case diagram.
- **TR.ST-MUC.13**: A Secure Tropos *mitigates* link is translated to a *mitigates* relationship in the misuse case diagram. However, since the misuse case *mitigates* is defined between *security use case* and *misuse case*, one needs to identify the 'from' and 'to' ends of the relationship.

Transformation Example Since security risk management is an iterative process as described in Chap. 2 (see Fig. 2.2), we will continue the example of *game creation* from Fig. 9.8. Hence we assume that previously introduced security requirements (such as Check permission to create game, Check permission to update game report, Check permission to update confirmation) become part of the ERIS system. The new context model is presented in Fig. 9.9.

In the updated diagram a few additional plans are introduced—Check FFE's login name and password and Check umpire's login name and password. These plans clarify how the permissions to perform targeted actions are ensured. In addition, this also means that the Game info and Confirmation can be submitted only if access to the Football Federation Employee is granted (i.e., *security constraint* Only if access to FFE is granted contributes to the integrity of the game info and confirmation in particular and to Integrity of Game in general. A

corresponding security constraint (i.e., Only if access to umpire is granted) is
defined regarding the Game report.

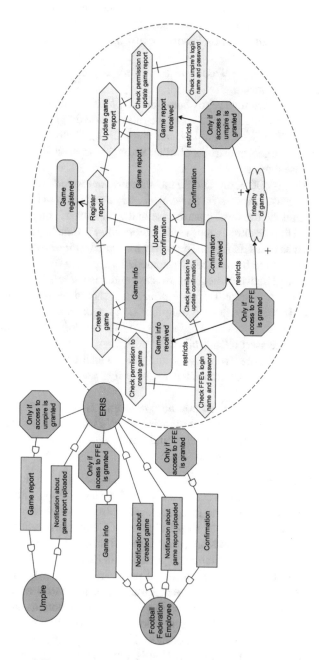

Fig. 9.9 Asset modelling using security risk-aware Secure Tropos

The problem arises, as illustrated in Fig. 9.10, if Violator observes that it is possible to check access to ERIS repeatedly (see Check game storage access repeatedly). This way he could receive access and change the game entry in the game storage (see violator's *goal* Access received and game changed). To mitigate this security risk, the countermeasure of using users' (e.g., Football Federation Employee's and/or Umpire's) ID cards for authorisation is suggested (see plans Check FFE's ID card and Check umpire's ID card) in Fig. 9.11.

Following the transformation rules defined above, we will illustrate how to translate this security risk-aware Secure Tropos analysis to the security risk-oriented misuse cases. The resulting misuse case diagram is displayed in Fig. 9.12.

Following TR.ST-MUC.1, the ERIS actor is expressed as the *system boundary*. All the goals and tasks (e.g., Register game, Create game, Game info received, Check permission to create game, Check FFE's login name and password, and others) are used to define the use case hierarchy as defined in rules TR.ST-MUC.2 and TR.ST-MUC.3.

Following TR.ST-MUC.4, both actors—Football Federation Employee and Umpire—are translated to misuse case actors. The Secure Tropos *dependency* relationships are translated to misuse case communications, thus linking actor Football Federation Employee with use cases Create game, Update confirmation, Game info received and Confirmation received, and actor Umpire with use cases Update game report and Game report received, as defined in TR.ST-MUC.5. Note that the information carried by the Secure Tropos *dependum* is not represented in the misuse case diagram.

Next, security constraints Only if access to FFE is granted and Only if access to umpire is granted are translated to the misuse case *security criterion* following TR.ST-MUC.6. They are linked to the asset use cases using the *constraint of* relationships as defined in TR.ST-MUC.7.

In general, it is easy to notice that by applying transformation rules TR.ST-MUC.1 to 7, one transforms the Secure Tropos *asset model* to a misuse case *asset model*.

Following TR.ST-MUC.8, Violator, who presents the threat agent (see Fig. 9.11), is expressed as *misuser* in misuse cases, as illustrated in Fig. 9.12. According to TR.ST-MUC.9, the violator's goals (i.e., FFE's login and password received and Umpire's login and password received) and plans (i.e., Get access and change game, Get access and change game info or confirmation, Get access and change game report, Change game info or confirmation, Change game report, and Check game storage access repeatedly) form the misuse case hierarchy, as illustrated in Fig. 9.12. Violator is linked to the Get access and change game via a *communication* relationship.

In Secure Tropos model, *plans* Check FFE's login name and password and Check umpire's login name and password have a *vulnerability point*. Therefore, as defined in TR.ST-MUC.10, a *vulnerability* is included in the misuse case diagram. This vulnerability is exploited by misuse case Check game storage access repeatedly. Also as defined in TR.ST-MUC.11, a threaten link is introduced from Get access and change game to Register game.

The last two transformation rules are defined to define security countermeasures. To translate the security requirements (i.e., CheckFFE's ID card and Check

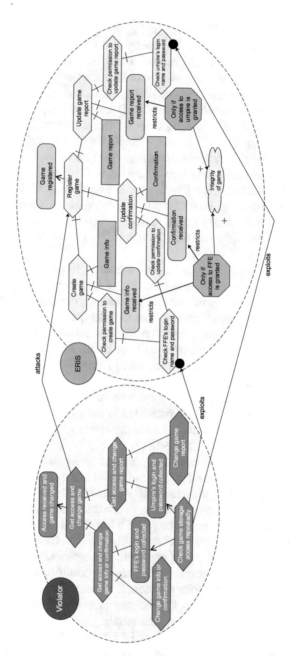

Fig. 9.10 Risk modelling using security risk-aware Secure Tropos

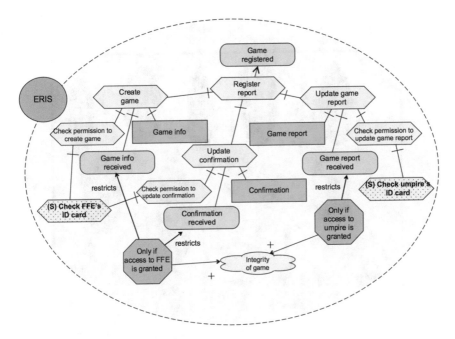

Fig. 9.11 Risk treatment modelling using security risk-aware Secure Tropos

umpire's ID card) to security use cases (see Fig. 9.12), one needs to follow rule TR.ST-MUC.12. According to TR.ST-MUC.13, the mitigate relationship is introduced. The 'from' and 'to' ends of this relationship need to be defined by the modeller. In the given example, the *mitigates* is defined between the *security use cases* and *misuse case* Get access and change game.

Model Completion The transformed misuse case model is not complete. The following details should be added by the system modeller:

- The name of *vulnerability*. In our example, it is defined as Not limited number of tries.
- *Impact* and its relationships (e.g., leads to, negates, and harms) should be defined by the modeller.
- Following TR.ST-MUC.14, the modeller needs to identify the 'from' and 'to' ends of the *mitigates* relationship.

9.4 Transforming from Security Risk-Oriented Misuse Cases to Mal-activities for Security Risk Management

This section presents the transformation rules to translate the security risk-oriented misuse case model to mal-activities for security risk management. The idea of such

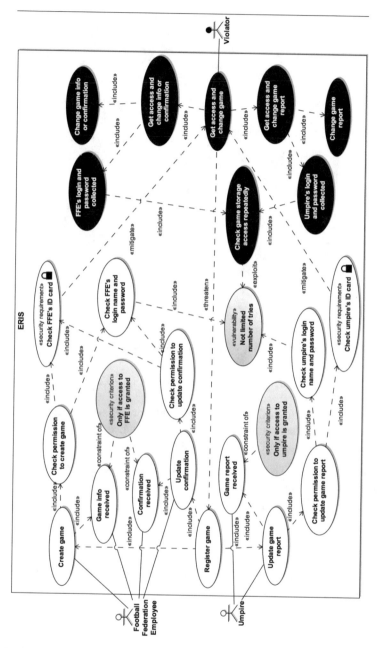

Fig. 9.12 Security risk management using security risk-oriented misuse cases

a transformation is presented in [160]. Here will summarise the major guidelines and will illustrate with an example taken from the *Football Federation* case.

Transformation Rules To transform such *misuse case* model to the **mal-activities**, the following transformation rules are applied:

- **TR.MUC-MAL.1**: A *system boundary* that presents a software system in the misuse case diagram is translated to *swimlane* in mal-activities.
- **TR.MUC-MAL.2**: A (mis)use *actor* is translated to a *swimlane* in mal-activities.
- **TR.MUC-MAL.3**: A *use case* construct is translated to an *activity* construct.
  Note: The developer needs to decide in which swimlane the activity will be situated. Modelling includes definition of the "dialog" between the system and its actors. All the activities performed by the system actors need to be placed in the actor swimlane and all activities performed by the system under the system swimlane.
  Note: The rule also does not define how the sequence flow needs to be introduced between the activities—this also depends on the developer's decision. To complete the (mal-)activity model, additional activities need to be introduced to define the complete sequences of the activities.
- **TR.MUC-MAL.4**: The (mis-)use case *security constraint* is translated to the (mal-)activity *security constraint*.
- **TR.MUC-MAL.5**: The *misuser* is translated to the *mal-swimlane*.
  Note: Both misuse case *misuser* and mal-activity *mal-swimlane* present the *threat agent*, which is characterised by motivation, expertise and means to perform the attack. These means (used to carry on the *attack method*) in mal-activities could be represented using another *mal-swimlane*, which needs to be introduced by the developer.
- **TR.MUC-MAL.6**: The *misuse case* construct is translated to the *mal-activity*.
  Note: As in TR.MUC-MAL.3, the developer needs to specify where the mal-activities will be situated: (*i*) in the *mal-swimlane* of *threat agent*, thus presenting the *attack method*, or (*ii*) in the *mal-swimlane* of the threat agent's means, thus presenting the *impact*.
- **TR.MUC-MAL.7**: The misuse case *vulnerability* is translated to the mal-activity *vulnerability*.
- **TR.MUC-MAL.8**: A *security use case* is translated to *mitigation activity* in mal-activities.
  Note: To highlight and group the risk countermeasures, a *swimlane* presenting a *security control* needs to be introduced. Appropriate sequence flows and extra mitigation means (e.g., checks) should be introduced to the mal-activity diagram by the developer.

Transformation Example To illustrate these transformation rules, we will continue the previous example (see Fig. 9.12) and will iterate the security risk management process (see Fig. 2.2) one more time. Hence, again (see Fig. 9.13) the integrity of the game (decomposed to **Integrity of game info**, **Integrity of game report** and **Integrity of confirmation**) will by considered. This time the emphasis is placed on the transfer of the data from the users (i.e., Football Federation Employee and Umpire) to the ERIS system. The transfer use cases are characterised in Transfer game info, Transfer game report and Transfer confirmation. Integrity should be checked once the data is received (see use cases Game info received, Game report received and Confirmation received).

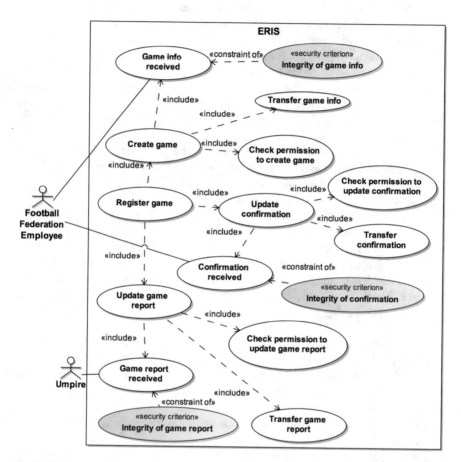

Fig. 9.13 Asset modelling using security risk-oriented misuse cases

The potential security risk is described in Fig. 9.14. It arises when Violator has the means to intercept transferred data (see Intercept transfer), and modify and pass (see Modify and pass intercepted game info, Modify and pass intercepted game report and Modify and pass intercepted confirmation) it to ERIS. This becomes possible because there exists the vulnerability that the Transmission can be intercepted. The risk even could harm the transfer of the data, modifying the game info, game report and confirmation (see impact Game info modified, Game report modified and Confirmation modified), thus negating their integrity.

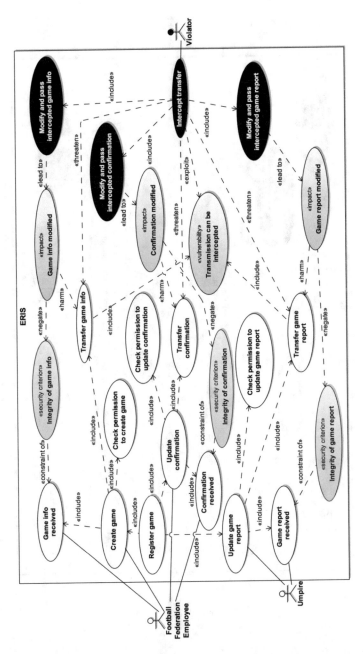

Fig. 9.14 Risk modelling using security risk-oriented misuse cases

To mitigate the identified a risk (see Fig. 9.15), one needs to introduce the security use case **Use secure communication**. This use case mitigates misuse case **Intercept transfer**.

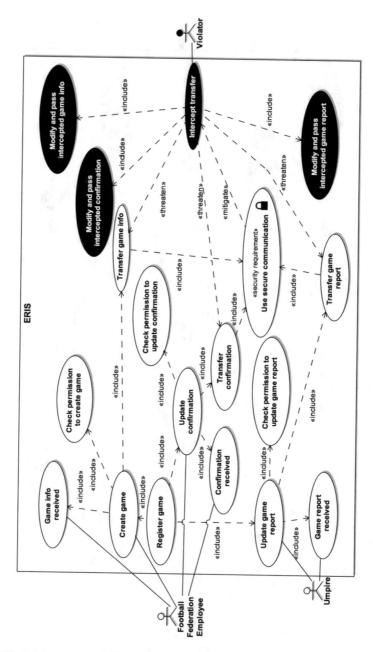

Fig. 9.15 Risk treatment modelling using security risk-oriented misuse cases

The translated model of mal-activities for security risk management is displayed in Fig. 9.16. Hence, the *system boundary* ERIS and actors Football Federation

Employee and Umpire are translated to *swimlanes* (see TR.MUC-MAL.1 and TR.MUC-MAL.2). Following the TR.MUC-MAL.3 rule, all the use cases (e.g., Check permission to create game, Transfer game info, Game info received and others) are expressed as activities. The use case security criteria (i.e., Integrity of game info, Integrity of game report and Integrity of confirmation) are defined as security criteria in the mal-activity model following the rule TR.MUC-MAL.4.

The Violator is defined as a *swimlane* following TR.MUC-MAL.4. To complement the model with the threat agent's means (i.e., Intercepted Channel), which could be posed by the Violator, one needs to introduce another *swimlane*. As defined by TR.MUC-MAL.6, the *misuse cases* (i.e., Intercept transfer, Modify and pass intercepted game info, Modify and pass intercepted game report, and Modify and pass intercepted confirmation) are translated to *mal-activities*. Vulnerability constructs are introduced in Fig. 9.16 following TR.MUC-MAL.7.

To capture the security requirements, one needs to apply the TR.MUC-MAL.8 rule. The *use case* Use secure communication is translated to mal-activities, as shown in Fig. 9.16.

Model Completion While translating the misuse case model to the mal-activity diagram, there are a number of steps that need to be introduced by the developer manually. For instance, developer needs to define:

- *swimlanes* to present *attack method* and *control*;
- in which *swimlanes* the transformed *activities* and *mal-activities* need to be situated;
- relationships (i.e., flows) with regard to the sequences among *activities*, *mal-activities*, and *security activities*;
- *security constraint* and *vulnerability* places in the model.

Finally, the mal-activity model could be always strengthened by investigating additional misuse case definitions, e.g., provided using the textual misuse case templates (see Table 9.2).

9.5   Further Reading

In this section we will highlight a few studies which consider transformations between security models and specifically concern the aforementioned modelling languages—BPMN, Secure Tropos, misuse cases and mal-activities. For example, in [17] the transformation from the BPMN *business process models* is performed to the *Secure Tropos* models to capture security constraints, mechanisms, and threats and to incorporate them back into the business process model. Transformations from the *Secure Tropos* to *business processes* help also in deriving secure business process designs from the organisationals actors, their goals thus capturing the systematic reasoning for the security means [17].

In [172], the transformation from the *secure business processes* (expressed in security-extended BPMN) to the UML *class diagrams* and *use case diagrams* is

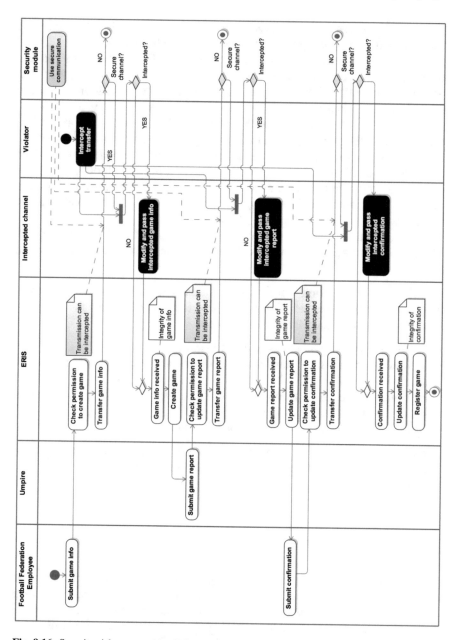

Fig. 9.16 Security risk management using mal-activities

presented. This transformation should show security requirements defined in the business processes could be further refined to security controls and systematically introduced in the secure system design solution. Similarly, an integration of the

Table 9.2 Textual misuse case Intercept transfer of team composition

Name	Intercept transfer
Summary	An attacker establishes himself as man in the middle and captures the messages (i.e, Game info, Game report, and Confirmation). He modifies the messages and passes them to ERIS.
Basic path	**bp1**: Attacker intercepts transfer of data: • **bp2.1**: Attacker modifies and passes intercepted data (extension points ext2.1); • **bp2.2**: Attacker modifies and passes intercepted data (extension points ext2.2); • **bp2.2**: Attacker modifies and passes intercepted data (extension points ext2.3).
Mitigation points	**mp1**: Make team composition not readable; **mp2**: Use secure communication;
Extension points	**ext2.1**: Includes misuse case *Modify and pass intercepted game info*. **ext2.2**: Includes misuse case *Modify and pass intercepted game report*. **ext2.3**: Includes misuse case *Modify and pass intercepted confirmation*.
Trigger	Game data are submitted to ERIS.
Assumption	**as1**: Unsecure transfer channel.
Precondition	**pr1**: Data is not encrypted.
Worst case threat	Integrity of game is negated; intended game data are not received; ERIS transfer channel is not reliable.
Mitigation guarantee	Attacker is not able to intercept communication channel. Even if the team composition is intercepted, attacker is not able to read and change it.
Related business rules	Team composition is required, because only the officially registered team composition is possible to use during the games.
Misuser profile	Skilled. Knowledge of how to perform man-in-the-middle attack, knowledge of how to change transferred messages. Motivated by some reward received or fame.
Stakeholder and risks	**Team Representative**: Change of the integrity of the game. Respectability of the Football Federation is lost.
Scope	Business environment.
Abstraction level	Integrity of game.
Precision level	Focussed.

goal-driven security requirements engineering using Secure Tropos and *secure system design* using UMLsec is considered in [149]. The integration is performed through translation of the aligned concepts of Secure Tropos and UMLsec. The approach allows checking and tracing how security requirements are fulfilled. It also helps incorporate the configuration data, e.g, user permissions.

El-Attar proposes a formal misuse case description to support transformation of misuse cases to mal-activity diagrams [60]. This description facilitates the collaboration between the business analysts (expected authors of the misuse cases) and the software developers (expected authors of the mal-activity diagrams). The model transformation could help evolve the system and software models and support development of consistent system representations using different notations.

9.6 Exercises

Exercise 9.1 Following the alignment of modelling languages to the ISSRM domain model, discuss similarities and differences between:

- Security risk-oriented BPMN *and* security risk-aware Secure Tropos;
- Security risk-oriented BPMN *and* security risk-oriented misuse cases;
- Security risk-oriented BPMN *and* mal-activities for security risk management;
- Security risk-aware Secure Tropos *and* security risk-oriented misuse cases;
- Security risk-aware Secure Tropos *and* mal-activities for security risk management;
- Security risk-oriented misuse cases *and* mal-activities for security risk management.

Exercise 9.2 Following the transformation guidelines given in Sect. 9.2, transform the *security risk-oriented BPMN* model (see Figs. 9.5, 9.6 and 9.7) to the *security risk-aware Secure Tropos* model.

Exercise 9.3 Following the transformation guidelines given in Sect. 9.3, transform the *security risk-aware Secure Tropos* model (see Figs. 9.9, 9.10, and 9.11) to the *security risk-oriented misuse case* model.

Exercise 9.4 Following transformation guidelines given in Sect. 9.4, transform the *security risk-oriented misuse case* model (see Figs. 9.13, 9.14 and 9.15) to the model of *mal-activities for security risk management*.

Exercise 9.5 Discuss what are the semantic similarities and differences in the textual misuse case template (see Table 9.2) and the mal-activity diagram model (see Fig. 9.16).

Exercise 9.6 Using the transformation method defined in Sect. 9.1, define the model transformation guidelines from

1. *Security risk-oriented BPMN* to:

   - *Security risk-oriented misuse cases*;
   - *Mal-activities for security risk management.*

2. *Security risk-aware Secure Tropos* to:

   - *Security risk-oriented BPMN*;
   - *Mal-activities for security risk management.*

3. *Security risk-oriented misuse case* to:

   - *Security risk-aware Secure Tropos*;
   - *Security risk-oriented BPMN*.

4. *Mal-activities for security risk management* to:

   - *Security risk-oriented BPMN*;
   - *Security risk-aware Secure Tropos*;
   - *Security risk-oriented misuse cases*.

Illustrate your guidelines with an example.

Chapter 10
Role-Based Access Control

Access is a specific type of interaction between a subject and an object that results in the flow of information from one to the other [177]. Following this definition, *access control* is the process of limiting access to the resources of a system only to authorised programs, processes, or other systems [177].

Role-based access control (RBAC) is a method to define and assess security access to different system artefacts, including data, functions and services. In this chapter we will introduce the major RBAC terms, and present the requirements for RBAC solution development and administration. Implementation of the RBAC solutions could be performed using model-driven security technologies. In the chapter we will discuss how SecureUML and UMLsec modelling languages could be applied when developing RBAC models and their applications.

10.1 Family of RBAC Models

The family of the role-based access control (RBAC) modelling consists of four models [65]: core RBAC, hierarchical RBAC, constrained RBAC and symmetric RBAC. In this section, firstly we will present the major RBAC concepts and principles (i.e., discuss the core RBAC model); then the extensions of the core RBAC are surveyed.

Core RBAC [65, 177] is illustrated in Fig. 10.1. A *User* is defined as a human being, but this concept could also be extended to machines, networks, or intelligent autonomous agents. A *Role* is a job function within the context of an organisation. Some associated semantics include authority and responsibility conferred on the user assigned to the role. *Session* is a mapping between a user and an activated subset of roles the user is assigned to. *Permission* is an approval to perform an operation on one or more protected objects. An *Operation* is an executable image of a program, which upon invocation executes some function for the user. Hence, the

© Springer International Publishing AG 2017
R. Matulevičius, *Fundamentals of Secure System Modelling*,
DOI 10.1007/978-3-319-61717-6_10

operation types and secured objects depend on the type of the system where they are implemented. *User assignment* and *permission assignment* are many-to-many relationships. The first describes how users are assigned to their roles. The second characterises the set of privileges assigned to a role.

The core RBAC defines how users acquire permissions through roles, how user assignments and permission assignments are defined, monitored, and controlled. In this chapter will focus our discussion on the core RBAC model.

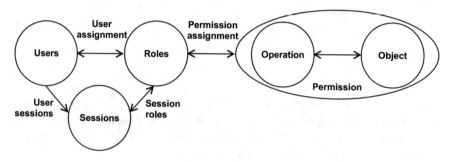

Fig. 10.1   Core RBAC, adapted from [65, 177].

Extensions of core RBAC are: (*i*) hierarchical RBAC, (*ii*) constrained RBAC, and (*iii*) symmetric RBAC [65, 177]. In addition to the core RBAC, the *hierarchical RBAC* includes role hierarchies. A *hierarchy* is a partial order defining a seniority relation between roles, whereby senior roles acquire the permissions of the juniors. For example, role r_1 inherits role r_2 only if all permissions of r_2 are also permissions of r_1 and all users of r_1 are also users of r_2. There are two types of hierarchy definition [65]: in *general hierarchical RBAC*, an arbitrary partial order is defined to support role hierarchy; in *restricted hierarchical RBAC*, some restrictions (e.g., tree or inverted tree structure) are imposed on the role hierarchy.

The *constrained RBAC*, in addition to the hierarchical RBAC, introduces constraints such as static separation of duty, dynamic separation of duty, prerequisite roles, and cardinality constraints [65]. *Separation of duties* spreads responsibility and authority for an action or task over multiple users, thereby raising the risk involved in committing a fraudulent act by requiring the involvement of more than one individual. The RBAC respects the static and dynamic separation of duties through user-role assignment and through role activation during the same session. The *prerequisite roles* are based on competency and the appropriateness needed. *Prerequisite constraints* require that a user be assigned to a role only if the user is already assigned to the role's prerequisites. Finally, *cardinality constraints* are used to restrict the number of users assigned to a role, the number of roles a user can play, the number of roles a permission can be assigned to, or the number of sessions a user is allowed to activate at the same time.

Finally the *symmetric RBAC* extends the constrained RBAC by adding support for permission-role review with performance comparable to that of user-role review [65]. This means that the roles to which a particular permission is assigned can be determined, as well as the permissions assigned to a specific role. For example, by identifying the permissions of a single user, the manager of policy should have way to revoke all permissions of this user and then to reassign all revoked rights to another user with the same or a different set of permissions [65].

10.2 RBAC Administration

System (security) administrator is the individual who establishes the system security policies, performs the administrative roles and reviews the system audit trails [65]. Three major functional requirements groups of the RBAC administration are (*i*) *administrative functions*, (*ii*) *supporting system functions*, and (*iii*) *review functions*.

Administrative functions include *creation* and *maintenance* of element sets and relations for building the various component RBAC models [65]. The basic element sets are *Users, Roles, Operations*, and *Objects*, as illustrated in Fig. 10.1. Operations and objects are predefined by the underlying system for which RBAC is deployed. Administrators manage users and roles.

They also define relationships between roles and operations and relationships between roles and objects. The two main RBAC relations are *user-to-role assignment* and *permission-to-role assignment*. Therefore administrative functions also include tasks to create and delete instances of user-to-role assignments, to assign and to de-assign users. Functions to manage permission-to-role assignments, to grant permissions and to revoke permissions need to be defined.

Supporting system functions are required to support the RBAC model constructs (e.g., RBAC session attributes and access decision logic) during user interaction with a system [65]. For example, management of an active role is necessary for regulating access control for a user in a session. Functions relating to the adding and dropping of active roles and other auxiliary functions include:

- Creation of user session and assignment of default set of active roles to the user.
- Addition of the active role to the current session.
- Deletion of the active role from the current session.
- Determination of whether the session subject has permission to perform the requested operation on an object.

Review functions helps us to review the results of the actions created by administrative functions. For instance, after creation of the user-to-role assignment and permission-to-role relations, it should be possible to view the contents of those relations from both the user and the role perspectives. The review functions include:

- *View assigned users* (mandatory)—viewing the set of users assigned to a given role;
- *View assigned roles* (mandatory)—viewing the set of roles assigned to a given user;

- *View role permissions*—viewing the set of permissions granted to a given role;
- *View user permissions*—viewing the set of permissions a given user gets through his or her assigned roles;
- *View session roles*—viewing the set of active roles associated with a session;
- *View session permissions*—viewing the set of permissions available in the session;
- *View role operations on object*—viewing the set of operations a given role may perform on a given object;
- *View user operations on object*—viewing the set of operations a given user may perform on a given object.

10.3   RBAC Modelling Languages

To reason about the RBAC rules, one could apply security modelling languages to prepare the RBAC model. In this section, SecureUML [21, 119] and UMLsec [100] are presented for this purpose. We will illustrate the major language principles and define how they could complement each other [127, 128].

10.3.1   SecureUML

Principles SecureUML [21, 119] is an extension of the standard UML language for the role-based access control modelling. The abstract syntax of SecureUML is illustrated in Fig. 10.2. This meta model introduces concepts like *User*, *Role* and *Permission* as well as relationships between them. Protected resources are expressed using the standard UML elements (i.e., *ModelElement*). In addition, *ResourseSet* represents a user-defined set of model elements used to define permissions and authorisation constraints.

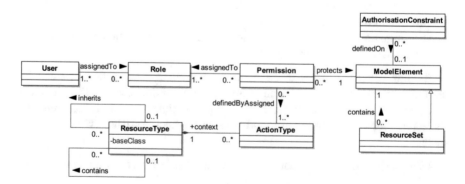

Fig. 10.2 Abstract syntax of SecureUML, adapted from [21, 119]

Permission is defined by assigned *ActionType* elements used to classify permissions. Here every *ActionType* represents a class of security-relevant operations (e.g., insert, update, select, and delete) on a particular type of protected resource. On the other hand a *ResourceType* defines all action types available for a particular meta-model type. An *AuthorisationConstraint* is a part of the access control policy. It expresses a precondition imposed on every call to an operation of a particular resource. This precondition usually depends on the dynamic state of the resource, the current call, or the environment. The authorisation constraint is attached either directly or indirectly, via permissions, to a particular model element representing a protected resource.

Example In Fig. 10.3 we present a SecureUML model to illustrate the RBAC policy of ERIS. Let's say there are three *users*, Bob, John and Karl, who play different *roles* in the system. Bob is a FootballFederationEmployee. And John and Karl both play the role of Empire. There also exists the protected resource Game characterised by three attributes gameInfo, gameReport and confirmation. The Game could be accessed both by the FootballFederationEmployee and by Umpire; however, they have different permissions. This means that a certain restriction on changing the state (changing the value of the attributes) of this resource needs to be defined for FootballFederationEmployee and Umpire.

Association class FFEmployeePermission characterises two actions allowed for the FootballFederationEmployee: (*i*) action submitGameInfo (of type Insert) defines that FootballFederationEmployee can submit game info and in this way initialise the creation of new Game (game's attributes gameReport and confirmation are assigned *null* values); the action is executed by performing operation createGame() (see class Game); and (*ii*) action submitConfirmation (of type Update) allows changing the confirmation of the Game by executing operation updateConfirmation(). To strengthen these permissions we define authorisation constraints AC#1 and AC#2.

AC#1:

```
context  Game :: createGame (): void
     pre:  self . responsibleFFE . assignedUser  −>
     exists ( i  |  i . assignedUser  =  'Bob')
```

AC#2:

```
context  Game :: updateConfirmation (): void
     pre:  self . responsibleFFE . assignedUser  −>
     exists ( i  |  i . assignedUser  =  'Bob')
```

Authorisation constraint AC#1 means that operation createGame() can be executed, by one *user* Bob assigned to the role FootballFederationEmployee.[1]

---

[1] As illustrated in [119], SecureUML model might contain both *objects* (i.e., Bob, John, and Karl) and *classes* (i.e., FootballFederationEmployee, Umpire). This results in restrictive authorisation

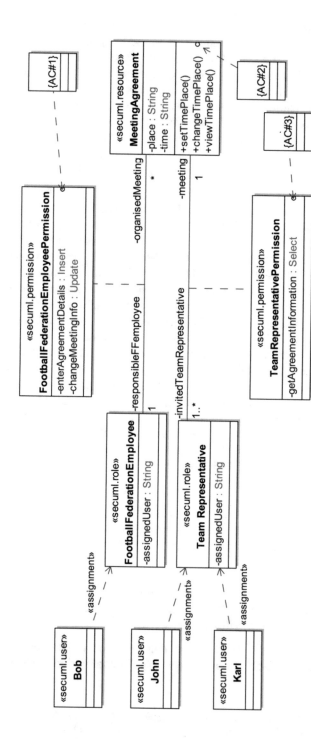

Fig. 10.3 Example of SecureUML model

Similarly, the authorisation constraint AC#2 defines a restriction for operation updateConfirmation().

Association class UmpirePermission defines a restriction for the Umpire *role*. It defines an action submitGameReport (of type Update) that says that only Umpire can update the value of attribute gameReport in the Game. To enforce this permission, an authorisation constraint AC#3 is defined.

AC#3:

```
context  Game :: updateConfirmation ( ): void
    pre:  self . assignedUmpire ->
          exists (p1|p1. assignedUser='John ')  and
    self . assignedUmpire ->
          exists (p2|p2. assignedUser='Karl ')  and
    self . assignedUmpire ->size  = 2
```

Authorisation constraint AC#3 says that only users John and Karl who have an assigned role Umpire can execute operation updateConfirmation().

Figure 10.4 presents the security action used to define the permission. In the current example, security actions Update (to *update* data), Insert (to *insert* new data), and Select (to *select* data) are used. Security action Delete (to *delete* data) is not used in the current example.

10.3.2 UMLsec

Principles UMLsec is an extension of the standard UML profile extension using stereotypes, tagged values and constraints; see Table 10.1. Constraints specify security requirements. Threat specifications correspond to actions taken by the adversary. Thus, different threat scenarios can be specified based on different adversary strengths.

Here we focus on the «rbac» stereotype, its tagged values and constraints [100]. This stereotype enforces RBAC in the business process specified in the UML *activity diagram*. It has three associated tags, {protected}, {role}, and {right}. The tag {protected} describes the states in the activity diagram, access to whose activities should be protected. The {role} tag may have as its value a list of pairs (*actor, role*), where *actor* is an actor in the activity diagram and *role* is a role. The tag {right} has as its value a list of pairs (*role, right*), where *role* is a role and *right* represents the right to access a protected resource. The associated constraint requires that the actors in the activity diagram only perform actions for which they have the appropriate rights.

---

constraints AC#1, AC#2 and AC#3. In case the user assignment relationship was not specified, the precondition might be expressed as self.responsibleFFE.assignedUser=caller, where *caller* is a set of *users* (assigned to a *role*) on behalf of whom the operation is executed.

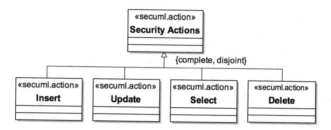

Fig. 10.4 Security actions used in SecureUML model

Table 10.1 Extract of UMLsec stereotypes, adapted from [100]

Stereotype	Base class	Tags	Constraints	Description
rbac	*subsystem*	*protected, role, right*	*only permitted activities executed*	*enforces RBAC*
fair exchange	subsystem	start, stop, adversary	after start eventually reach stop	enforce fair exchange
guarded access	subsystem		guarded object accessed through guards	access control using guarded object
guarded	object	guard		guarded object
data security	subsystem	adversary, integrity, authenticity	provides secrecy, integrity, authenticity, freshness	basic data security constraints

Example Figure 10.5 illustrates an application of UMLsec to model game creation. FootballFederationEmployee will *submit game info*. Next, Umpire will *submit game report*. In the final step, FootballFederationEmlpoyee submits *game confirmation*.

This diagram carries an «rbac» stereotype, meaning that the security policy needs to be applied to the protected actions. For instance, the FootballFederation's action Submit game info leads to the action Create game in the Game swimlane.

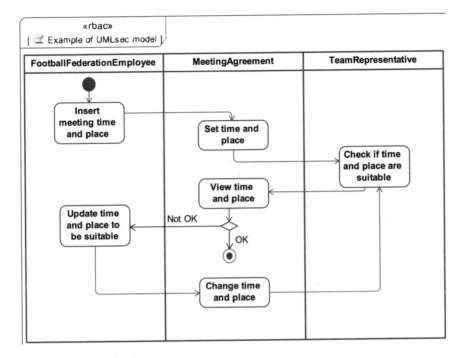

Fig. 10.5 Example of UMLsec model

Create game is executed if and only if there exists an associated tag, that defines
the following: (*i*) Create game is a protected action, (*ii*) *Bob* plays the role of
FootballFederationEmployee, and (*iii*) FootballFederationEmployee enforces
the action Create game. This associated tag (AT#1) is defined as follows:

AT#1:

```
{protected = Create game}
{role = (Bob, FootballFederationEmployee)}
{right = (FootballFederationEmployee,
                            Create game)}
```

Similarly, the sets of associated tags are defined for other two protected actions,
Update game report (see AT#2) and Update confirmation (see AT#3). Note that
both John and Karl can initiate execution of action Update game report (AT#2),
since they both play the role of Umpire.

AT#2:

```
{protected = Update game report}
{role = ([John, Karl], Umpire)}
{right = (Umpire, Update game report)}
```
AT#3:

```
{protected = Update confirmation}
{role = (Bob, FootballFederationEmployee)}
{right = (FootballFederationEmployee,
                              Update confirmation)}
```

10.3.3   Comparison

Extension Mechanisms A comparison of extension mechanisms of SecureUML and UMLsec is summarised in Table 10.2 [127]. Both approaches originate from UML. SecureUML is developed through the explicit meta-model presented in Fig. 10.2. UMLsec does not have an explicit meta-model, but the general UML meta-model is implicitly extended with security modelling concerns.

Table 10.2 Comparison extension mechanisms of SecureUML and UMLsec, adapted from [127]

Criteria	SecureUML	UMLsec
Meta-model	Explicit, based on the RBAC model	Not explicit, as the UML profile extension
UML profile	Mainly *class* diagram	The whole UML profile (i.e., *use cases, class, activity, state, component,* and other diagrams)
Extensions mechanism	Stereotypes, tagged values and authentication constraints	Stereotypes, tagged values and constraints
Constraints	Written in OCL	Constraint language is not identified

   Both SecureUML and UMLsec are proposed as "lightweight extensions", namely new stereotypes, tagged values and constraints are introduced. The difference is in the stereotype meaning. SecureUML is specifically oriented to the terminology of the RBAC model, and defines stereotypes, such as «secuml.user», «secuml.role», «secuml.permission», «secuml.action», and «secuml.resource». This means that SecureUML extends mainly the profile of UML class diagrams. UMLsec has a broader scope. It extends the whole UML profile by extending base classes such as model *subsystem, link, node, dependency,* and *object.* The extension stereotypes are applied to different UML diagrams. Hence, here the *rbac* stereotype is only one extension of the subsystem base class, applied to the activity diagram. Authorisation constraints in SecureUML are written in the object constraint language (OCL). In UMLsec no specific constraint language is mandated.

Modelling Targets and Application Methods A comparison of modelling targets and application methods of SecureUML and UMLsec is summarised in Table 10.3 [127]. In the security risk management literature, a security criterion expresses a problem domain by "characterising the security needs" [133]. Security requirements describe a solution domain by defining a condition "we wish to make true by installing the system in order to mitigate risks" [133] (see, Chap. 4). We did not observe how SecureUML could model security criteria; however, it is basically meant for modelling of solutions, especially through RBAC models. This results in SecureUML application guidelines, basically oriented towards RBAC development.

Table 10.3 Comparing modelling targets and application methods of SecureUML and UMLsec, adapted from [127]

Criteria	SecureUML	UMLsec
Security criteria	Not identified	Confidentiality, integrity (and derived ones, like authenticity and others)
Security requirements/ controls	RBAC	RBAC, but also non-repudiations, secure communication links, secrecy and integrity, authenticity, freshness, secure information flows, guard access
Method	Development of the RBAC models	Not explicit, but implicitly supports standard security management methods

UMLsec is meant to perform a formal analysis of system security. The language could be applied to both problem and solution domains. In a UMLsec model, one can define confidentiality, integrity, and a number of derived criteria (e.g., authenticity, etc.). To satisfy the identified security criteria, UMLsec proposes solution stereotypes, such as security policies for «fair exchange», «rbac», «non-repudiation», and others (see Table 10.3). The application of UMLsec implicitly supports standard security risk management approaches (see, Sect. 2) to identify secure assets, to define security criteria, to analyse risks, to determine security requirements, and to define controls.

Construct Semantics In Table 10.4 we compare SecureUML and UMLsec constructs regarding the RBAC concepts and relationships (see Fig. 10.1). Firstly, we observe that both modelling languages cover RBAC concepts and relationships. This means that they are able express security policies through RBAC. Secondly, SecureUML addresses RBAC through the defined stereotypes, while UMLsec expresses RBAC concepts and relationships through the associated tags and their values. At the example level, both languages use the same (e.g., for *Users*, *Roles*, and *Objects*) or very similar (e.g., for *Operations*) labels for RBAC concepts.

Some modelling and labelling differences are observed when it comes to relationship definition. In SecureUML, the *User assignment* relationship is modelled through a UML-stereotyped dependency without defining any label. In UMLsec, the specific associated tag {role} is defined for a user-to-role assignment. Different labelling is also used to specify *Permission assignment*. In SecureUML, this is done through stereotyped association classes, which might carry a name depending on the modelled context. In UMLsec, the associated tag {right} is used for this purpose.

Table 10.4 Comparing SecureUML and UMLsec constructs regarding the RBAC concepts and relationships, adapted from [128]

	RBAC concepts	SecureUML construct	UMLsec construct
1	**User** (concept)	Class stereotype «secuml.user»	*Actor* value of the association tag {role}
2	**User assignment** (relationship)	Dependency stereotype «assignment»	Associated tag {role}
3	**Roles** (concept)	Class stereotype «secuml.role»	Expressed in two places: • *Activity partition* • *Role* value of the associated tag {role}
4	**Permission assignment** (relationship)	Association class stereotype «secuml.permission»	Expressed in two places: • *Action* • Associated tag {right}
5	**Object** (concept)	Class stereotype «secuml.resource»	*Activity partition*
6	**Operation** (concept)	Operation of «secuml.resource» class	Expressed in two places: • *Action* • Associated tag {protected}
7	**Permission** (concept)	Authorisation constraints	Not defined

Finally, we note that UMLsec does not provide explicit means to define *Permission* itself. This is rather left implicit at the diagram level when defining the values for all the associated tags ({protected}, {role}, and {right}). In SecureUML, *Permission* is explicitly defined through authorisation constraints expressed in OCL (see, for instance, the preconditions AC#1, AC#2, and AC#3).

10.3.4   Transformation

Following the semantic similarities of both modelling languages in this section, we list a number of guidelines leading to semi-automated transformation between RBAC models expressed in these languages. Some of these rules could be directly implemented in the modelling tools, resulting in semi-automated support for RBAC model transformations (proof of concept is reported in [97]). To discuss and to illustrate the transformation guidelines we apply them to the SecureUML models presented in Fig. 10.3 (resulting model provided in Fig. 10.6) and 10.5 (resulting model shown in Fig. 10.7).

Transforming SecureUML Model to UMLsec The following transformation guidelines are applied to transform the SecureUML model (see Fig. 10.3) to the UMLsec model (see Fig. 10.6):

- **SU1.** A class with a stereotype «secuml.resource» is transformed to an *activity partition* in the UMLsec model (Table 10.4, line 5), and the *operations* of this class become *actions* belonging to this partition (Table 10.4, line 6). In addition, each operation becomes a value the UMLsec associated tag {protected}.

  Example The class Game (see Fig. 10.3) is represented as an activity partition in Fig. 10.6. The operations createGame(), updateGameReport(), and updateConfiramtion() are shown as actions in this partition. Three associated tags (see Table 10.5 {protected} are defined: {protected=(createGame)}, {protected=(createGameReport)}, and {protected=(updateConfirmation)}.

- **SU2.** A relationship with a stereotype «assignment» used to connect users and their roles is transformed to an associated tag {role}.

  Example In Fig. 10.3 we specify associated tags {role=(Bob, FootballFederationEmployee)}, {role=(John, Umpire)}, and {role=(Karl, Umpire)}, as provided in Table 10.5.

- **SU3.** A SecureUML class with the stereotype «secuml.roles» is transformed to the UMLsec *activity partition* (Table 10.4, line 3). The attributes of an association class that connects the «secuml.role» class with the«secuml.resource» class become *actions* in the corresponding activity partition (Table 10.4, line 4).

  Example In Fig. 10.6 we define *activity partitions* FootballFederationEmployee (with the *actions* submitGameInfo and submitConfirmation grabbed from the class FFEpermission) and TeamRepresentative (with the *action* submitGameReport defined from the class UmpirePermission);

- **SU4.** The SecureUML association class with the stereotype «secuml.permission» defines the role value for the UMLsec associated tag {right} (Table 10.4, line 4). The value of *right* can be determined from the *authorisation constraint* defined for the attribute of the SecureUML association class.

  Example This rules leads to the association tags {right =(FootballFederationEmployee, submitGameInfo)} and {right =(Umpire, submitGameReport)} captured in Table 10.5.

  Note The *authorisation constraint* might help us identify the relationship between two actions, as shown in Fig. 10.6 between *actions* submitGameInfo and createGame and between *actions* submitConfirmation and updateConfirmation.

  Note A complete definition of the association tag {right} is not always possible because (*i*) it might be that no association constraint is defined at all (no additional security enforcement is needed), or (*ii*) an authorisation constraint might be defined at a different place (e.g., to strengthen the *operations* of the «secuml.resource» classes) in the SecureUML model, as shown for the authorisation constraint AC#2 in Fig. 10.3.

- **SU5**. The received activity diagram is annotated with the «rbac» stereotype (see Fig. 10.6).

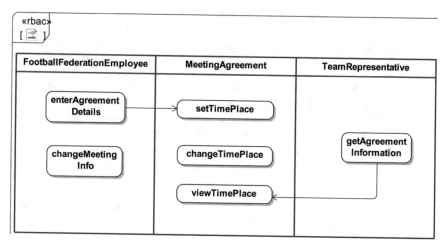

Fig. 10.6 Transformed UMLsec model

Table 10.5 summarises the resulting association tags. However, as mentioned above, we are not able to determine all the association tags required in the model. For example, the {right} association tag is captured from the association class «secuml.permission» and its link to the authorisation constraint. However, not all association constraints are links to the association classes «secuml.permission»: For example, in Fig. 10.3 the authorisation constraint AC#2 is linked to class MeetingAgreement. This means that the association tag {right= (MeetingInitiator, changeTimePlace)} needs to be written manually by the developer. This means also that SecureUML is not concerned with behavioural aspects.

Table 10.5 Automatically translated association tags

Transformation rule	Association tags
SU1.	{protected=(createGame)} {protected=(updateGameReport)} {protected=(updateConfirmation)}
SU2.	{role=(Bob, FootballFederationEmployee)} {role=(John, Umpire)} {role=(Karl, Umpire)}
SU4.	{right =(FootballFederationEmployee, createGame)} {right =(Umpire, updateGameReport)}

To complete the UMLsec activity diagram (e.g., Fig. 10.6), a developer needs to specify information that was not possible to capture from the SecureUML diagram. For instance, the developer needs to define initial and final nodes. Other control flows (including the conditionals ones) need also to be specified. For instance, in Fig. 10.6 control flows between setTimePlace, getAgreementInformation, viewTimePlace and changeMeetingInfo and others might be defined as a logical sequence of activities.

Transforming UMLsec Model to SecureUML The transformation from UMLsec to SecureUML is defined by means of five guidelines. To illustrate these rules, we will analyse the extract of ERIS presented in Fig. 10.5. The resulting SecureUML model is illustrated in Fig. 10.7. The guidelines are:

- **US1.** *Association tags* {protected} allow identifying the *operations* that belong to a secured resource (Table 10.4, line 6). The *activity partitions* which hold these *operations* are transformed to the SecureUML *class* with a stereotype «secuml.resource» (Table 10.4, line 5).

  Example In Fig. 10.7 a *class* Game is defined. It has three *operations*, Create game(), Update game report(), and Update confirmation().
- **US2.** The UMLsec *activity partitions* which do not hold secured protected actions can be transformed to «secuml.role» stereotyped classes (Table 10.4, line 3).

  Example In Fig. 10.7 two «secuml.role» classes—FootballFederation Employee and Umpire—are defined.
- **US3.** *Association tag* {role} allows identifying the «assignment» *dependency* relationship (Table 10.4, line 2) between *classed* with a stereotype «secuml.user» and their «secuml.role» stereotypes.

  Example In Fig. 10.7 three «assignment» dependency links are defined: (*i*) between Bob and FootballFederationEmployee, (*ii*) between John and Umpire, and (*iii*) between Karl and Umpire.
- **US4.** From UMLsec *association tag* {right} we are able to identify on which *operations* the role can perform *security actions* (Table 10.4, line 4). Thus, from each occurrence of this *association tag* in the SecureUML model, a corresponding *association class* between a «umlsec.role» and a «umlsec.resource» is introduced.

  Example In Fig. 10.7 two *association* classes: (*i*) between FootballFederationEmployee and Game, and (*ii*) between Umpire and Game—are defined.
- **US5.** In the UMLsec activity diagram it is possible to identify the *security actions* that are carried towards the secured *operations* (see Table 10.4, line 4): these are unprotected actions performed before the protected ones.

  Example In Fig. 10.5 the action Submit game info is performed before protected action Create game: Submit game info is transformed to the *attribute* of the *association class* (see Fig. 10.7). Similar transformations are performed for the *attributes* Submit confirmation and Submit game report.

Note It is not possible to identify the type of security action.

The SecureUML model needs to be completed manually with the information, not captured from the UMLsec model:

- the *attributes* of the «umlsec.resource» class that define the state of the secured resource(s). For instance, in Fig. 10.7 attributes place:String and time:String could be introduced in class Game.
- necessary *authorisation constraints* for the SecureUML model. For instance, in Fig. 10.7 no authorisation constraints (such as AC#1, AC#2, and AC#3) are captured.
- *multiplicities* for all the association relationships.

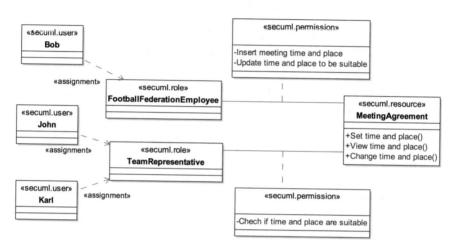

Fig. 10.7 Transformed SecureUML model

- *association class names*. For instance, in Fig. 10.7 names—FootballFederation EmployeePermission and Umpire—should be given for association classes.
- *action types* for the identified actions. For instance, action Submit game info type is Insert, Submit confirmation type is Update, and Submit game report type is Update.

Finally, the developer could include additional model attributes if/as required. For instance, in order for the translated model (Fig. 10.7) to correspond to Fig. 10.5, one needs to define attributes assignedUser:String. These attributes would carry the information about the *users* assigned to the *roles*.

10.4   Model-Driven Security

This subsection discusses the principles of model-driven security. It is illustrated through the role-based access control example in relational databases.

Model-driven development refers to the systematic use of models and model transformations to support the software development lifecycle. In Chap. 9 it was illustrated how models could be translated for the system and software analysis purposes. However, model-driven development typically means that the software code is generated from models and thus models need to be used efficiently and effectively [111, 176, 197]. The major vision of model-driven development is to decrease the effort of code writing and to move this effort to system modelling and design. The simplified principle is illustrated in Fig. 10.8 (upper part). Model-driven software development includes three major stages: (*i*) definition of the system/software model, (*ii*) systematic development of the set of the transformation rules, and (*iii*) application of these rules to generate executable software code from the model.

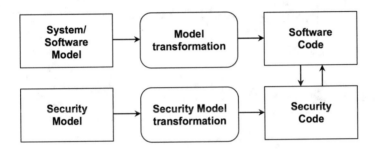

Fig. 10.8 Simplified principle of model-driven development

Model-driven security integrates security models with system/software design models, thus producing security design models [43, 111]. The simplified principle is illustrated in Fig. 10.8 (lower part). The security model is defined separately from the system model. Then, using the transformation rules, the security model is translated to security code. Finally, using tools, the software code and security code are automatically generated into system architectures, including the complete (e.g., access control) infrastructure.

Security Model Transformation   Following the previous example (see Sect. 10.3), we will illustrate how the RBAC policy defined in the SecureUML security model is transformed into *database views* and *instead-of triggers*, which implement the security constraints. In Fig. 10.9 secured *resources* (i.e., *objects* of class Game) are equipped with a stereotype, «secuml.resource ». The two roles (i.e., FootballFederationEmployee and Umpire carrying stereotype «secuml.role») have different sets of permissions (i.e., FFEpermission and UmpirePermission). Two authorisation constraints—FFEauthConstraint and UmpireAuthConstraint: restrict the permissions of the defined roles. These constraints are expressed in PL/SQL to simplify the model transformation to security constraints.

To transform the defined security model to *security code* (see Fig. 10.8), one needs to introduce transformation rules that correspond to security actions: (*i*) *Insert*, for entering new data; (*ii*) *Update*, for changing the existing data; (*iii*) *Select*, for viewing existing data; and (*iv*) *Delete*, for deleting data. By applying these transformation rules[2] the SecureUML security model (i.e., Fig. 10.9) is translated to the *database views* and *instead-of triggers*, which implement security authorisation constrains on the secured data. The PL/SQL security authorisation constraint is illustrated in Fig. 10.10 for the *Insert* security action.

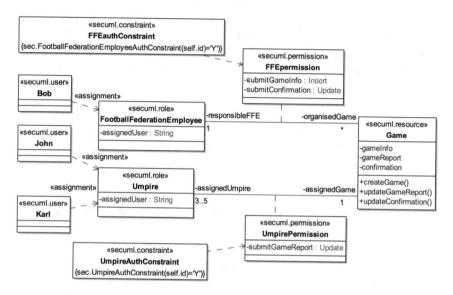

Fig. 10.9 Updated SecureUML model

The **Insert** authorisation constraint (Fig. 10.10) specifies what new data assigned to a valid **Role** a **User** can *insert* into a table. It is implemented through an *instead of insert trigger* (i.e., Game_sec_insert_trg) on the *secured resource* (i.e., Game). Execution of the trigger results in success or failure. If there is no security violation and if new inserted values are valid, the trigger will give a positive result. Otherwise the update action will result in an exception.

The *Insert* authorisation constraint is row-based because it is not possible[3] to insert only parts of a row into a table. This means that before the actual *insert* is performed, a Boolean security constraint is checked. The Boolean constraint consists of the *implicit role constraint* (i.e., sec.is_role(FootballFederationEmployee), captured from the class FootballFederationEmployee and association class FFEpermission), and *explicit constraints* (i.e., sec.FootballFederationEmployeeAuth Constraint(self.id) = 'Y', captured from the class FFEAuthConstraint).

Other authorisation constraints—*update*, *select*, and *delete*—are defined similarly [129].

---

[2]In the current example, these security rules are defined using the Velocity template language, URL: http://velocity.apache.org/engine/devel/user-guide.html.

[3]Table columns could be complemented with default values, which will be used when the value of the column is not specified in the *insert* statement; however, this is not supported in the developed transformation templates.

```
-- Imported common-sql.vtl
CREATE OR REPLACE TRIGGER Game_sec_insert_trg
  INSTEAD OF INSERT ON Game
  REFERENCING NEW AS NEW
  FOR EACH ROW
DECLARE
  ex_denied EXCEPTION;
BEGIN
  IF sec.is_role('FootballFederationEmployee') = 'Y' AND
     sec.FootballFederationEmployeeAuthConstraint(self.id)='Y'
  THEN
    INSERT INTO Game (
          gameInfo, gameReport, confirmation)
    VALUES (
          :NEW.gameInfo, :NEW.gameReport, :NEW.confirmation);
  ELSE
    RAISE ex_denied;
  END IF;
EXCEPTION
  WHEN ex_denied THEN
    raise_application_error (-20000, 'Access denied!');
END;
/
```

Fig. 10.10   Transformed *Insert* authorisation constraint

Applying Authorisation Constraints   As the final step, the generated SQL code
and *security authorisation constraints* code could be intertwined together, for
execution on a database management system such as SQL*Plus,[4] developed by
Oracle.

10.5   Further Reading

Access Control Approaches   A summary of recent access control models, policies
and mechanisms is reported in [108]. The authors tend to propose a unified
metamodel including *discretionary access control* (DAC), *mandatory access control*
(MAC) and *any policy* (e.g., role-based access control [65, 177], attribute-based
access control [89, 90], usage control model [164], risk-adaptive access control
[138, 185] and token-based access control [169]) access control mechanisms and
models. A major similarity between the access control models is that they all
concern the definition of subjects (entities which requests the access), objects
(entities on which requests are given) and permissions (which specify the type and

---

[4]https://docs.oracle.com/cd/B19306_01/server.102/b14357/qstart.htm.

level of the access). The major differences are the ways of specifying permissions rules and the ways of estimating access control levels.

Attribute-based access control (ABAC) [89, 90] grants access to objects after assessing permission rules against the *attributes* of subjects and objects, operations, and the environment relevant to the received access request. This helps specify rules without taking into account individual relationships between the subjects and objects. And, thus, the access decision depends on the attribute values, and not the subject-object relationships which specify the permission rules.

The *usage control model (UCON)* [164] definition is based on the monitoring of the use of the resource; this may enforce change of the access permissions and reassessment of the subject's rights on the targeted resource. The final access decision is made by estimating *authorisation, obligation* and *condition* constraints, through which access rights are specified.

Risk-adaptive access control (RAdAC) [138, 185] has the property of adapting the access permissions based on the continuous changes in the environment. The permission is granted after estimating the situational factors, such as people, information technology components, objects, environment properties and heuristics. The access request is granted after assessing the both the security risk level and the operation need; thus, after estimating the dynamism of the environment, the access permission much depends on the changes in the environment.

In this chapter we have analysed the RBAC model, which in principle presents the underlying bases for a access control. This model could be seen as coarse-grained access control definition. However, the dynamic environments and various domains require fine-grained access models. Thus the underlying RBAC principles could be taken into account and extended with the fine-grained properties as illustrated with the presentation of the ABAC, UCON, and RaDAC models and a number of other RBAC model extensions (e.g., for Web services [83], mobile systems [85], location support services [47], database management systems [24], collaborative environments [184] and others).

Model-driven security is used for the development of access control constraints [183]. A framework to support the modelling of RBAC system using XACML architecture is proposed in [210]. It uses the UML Profile mechanism and integrates security with the system development cycle. Elsewhere, in [6], the authors apply UML to represent access control features of the security model and to support policy validation using OCL. This improves understanding and articulates the security model and its associated policies. In [41], a UML Profile for RBAC is proposed to integrate access control specifications with the development process. The RBAC constraints are embedded into the UML Profile; they also include separation of duties and cardinality constraints. In [200], the authors consider how to dynamically define document structure and security policies over this structure without losing context-based information. SecureUML is applied to define RBAC policy on XML documents. This combination allows one to create and update document structure and its security concerns when designing the document itself.

In [7], a method to recover the RBAC security model from automatically recovered structural and behavioural models of Web applications is introduced. Elsewhere, in [183], the Spring Framework applications are analysed to derive access permissions. They are visualised in the RBAC models and contribute to developers understanding of the existing system, thus facilitating the needed access changes.

10.6 Exercises

Exercise 10.1 Define RBAC administration functions for the *Football Federation* system ERIS.

Exercise 10.2 Analyse the *Football Federation* case and define the SecureUML model representing the role-based access control policy regarding the data gathered and registered about Team. When analysing, consider the following questions:

- What is the object and what are its attributes?
- What operations change the values of the attributes?
- What are the roles?
- What are the security actions?
- What are the permissions of the roles towards the object?
- Who are the users?

Exercise 10.3 Analyse the *Football Federation case* and define the UMLsec model representing the role-based access control policy regarding the data gathered and registered about Team. When analysing, consider the following questions:

- What is the object and what are its operations?
- What are the roles?
- What are the role's rights?
- What are the associated tags?
- Who are the users?

Exercise 10.4 Football league match report.
  Figure 10.11 illustrates the match report filled by different people. Their "fillings" are provided in blue.
  Define role-based access control models using

- SecureUML;
- UMLsec.

  Consider the following scenario: the football game report is started before the match, continued during the match, and finalised once the match is over. The new report is created by the league secretary, who is employed by the Football Federation. The league secretary fills in initial information such as league name, his own contact data, region, division, and game numbers as well as the names of the competing teams. Once done, the league secretary informs the team representatives, so that they could provide the team composition for the game, including player names and their registration numbers. The team composition should be provided no later than 2 h before the game.

WOLFS FOOTBALL LEAGUE MATCH REPORT FORM

League Secretary
CALEX KARUUNA
20 STREET ALLEA
CITY

Each team representative is to sign this form and ensure that all details are correct and that all players are registered with the ERIS system.

LEAGUE NAME	WOLFS			DIVISION		A	
REGION	AA			GAME		45	

HOME TEAM NAME			Final score:	AWAY TEAM NAME			Final score:
Green Rabbits			3	Orange Carrots			2

FULL NAME	REG, NO	CARDS	GOALS	FULL NAME	REG, NO	CARDS	GOALS
[1] John	1			Joeph	11		
[2] Peter	2	YY->R	1	Boris	1		
[3] Arnold	3	Y		Pran	2		
[4] Davy	5			Ferdinand	10	Y	
[5] Kayle	6	Y	1	Vassilyi	3	Y	
[6] King	7			Svetoslav	4		1
[7] Shark	9	Y		Jevgenyi	5		
[8] Anupras	10			Matheus	6		1
[9] George	11		1	Annis	55	YY->R	
[10] Gerome	12	Y		JP	7		
[11] Sergey	15				69		

	Full time score	Extra time score	Penal-ties		Full time score	Extra time score	Penal-ties
	2	1	-		2	0	-

Signature of Home Team Representative			YES	Signature of Away Team Representative			YES
HomeSignedIt			~~NO~~	*AwaySignedIt*			~~NO~~

I am satisfied with my opponents registration/performance (Please indicate YES or NO above)

Home Team Caution		Away Team Caution	
No problem, everything is OK		No problem, everything is OK	

Umpire Name	Referee signature	Umpire Comment	
Billy-Goat the Beard	*BilGoalB*	No comments	

Confirmation by league secretary	Confirmed	~~Not confirmed~~	Confirmation date 2020.02.20

Fig. 10.11 Match report form

During the match the game report needs to be maintained by the umpire, who needs to register the scored goals and "given" cards. The umpire is also responsible for filling in the match results, including the scores (including final, full time, extra time and penalties). After the match, the umpire needs to invite the team representatives to sign the report and (optionally) provide comments. Once signatures from the team representatives are received, the umpire himself comments and signs the report. After the game the report is sent to the league secretary for confirmation.

Exercise 10.5 What are the similarities and differences between SecureUML and UMLsec?

Exercise 10.6 Transform:

- the model presented in Fig. 10.3 to the UMLsec model;
- the SecureUML model received during Exercise 10.2 to the UMLsec model.

What association tags should be presented with the new UMLsec model? Complete the translated UMLsec model with missing details of the UMLsec representation.

Exercise 10.7 Transform:

- the model presented in Fig. 10.5 to the SecureUML model.
- the SecureUML model received during Exercise 10.3 to the SecureUML model.

What authorisation constraints should be presented with the new SecureUML model? Complete the translated SecureUML model with missing details of the SecureUML representation.

Exercise 10.8 Explain the principles of the model-driven security.

Chapter 11
Secure System Development Using Patterns

Security engineering requires security-related knowledge and is a time-consuming activity. However, typically, although business analysts are experts in their analysed domain, they have limited knowledge and expertise in developing secure business processes, and thus secure systems. They need to rely on best security practices, information security standards, or security experts. In this chapter we will discuss the use of *security patterns* to secure business processes and systems. The idea is that the majority of systems does not require new solutions; thus it is possible to reuse existing knowledge. In this way, analysts are able to introduce relevant and proper security requirements based on their rationale and later reason about security countermeasures.

This chapter, firstly, gives an overview of security pattern classifications and introduces some security risk-oriented patterns to secure business processes. Secondly, it presents a method for security requirements elicitation from business processes (SREBP).

11.1 Security Patterns

The attention to software patterns was drawn after the Gamma et al. book on design patterns [74]. Nowadays, patterns are developed for different stages and domains of software development and maintenance (e.g., software architecture, programming levels, business process management and workflow, server components, and many others). Patterns describe both the process and the phenomenon that creates this process. For instance, patterns could be used to characterise the configuration element both for software design and software architecture. Pattern presents a high-level, proven solution that resolves the given problem optimally. At the same time, patterns are generic, in some cases independent of and in other dependent on a particular implementation technology. Patterns support understanding of a problem

© Springer International Publishing AG 2017   171
R. Matulevičius, *Fundamentals of Secure System Modelling*,
DOI 10.1007/978-3-319-61717-6_11

and its solution. They could also tell a story and initiate a dialog to explain the considered problem and to influence the problem solution.

Security pattern "describes a particular recurring *security problem* that arises in a specific *context*, and presents a well-proven generic *solution* for it. The solution consists of a set of interacting roles that can be arranged into multiple concrete design structures, as well as a process to create one particular such structure" [64, 182]. The *context* describes the situation, its general environment and conditions, under which the problem occurs. In the context of security, a *problem* occurs whenever an asset is protected in an insufficient way against abuse, or a situation arises that can allow security violations. Appropriate *solutions* are determined by the context, the problem and the forces of the pattern. A discussion of the benefits and drawbacks of a solution (i.e., the trade-off analysis) helps our understanding of how the forces have been resolved.

The above definition is supported by the terms of the ISSRM domain model. For instance, both *system assets* and *business assets* could be jointly used to describe the specific security context, where the security problem, expressed using the *risk-related* concepts, could be identified. The security solution is then defined using the *risk treatment* concepts.

The application of security patterns has a number of benefits [182]. Firstly, security patterns codify basic security knowledge in a structured and understandable way. Their representation is familiar to business analysts, systems engineers, security analysts and software developers, who constitute the key audience in systems development. Since patterns are already used to capture organisation and system engineering knowledge, using patterns to capture security knowledge helps us improve the integration of security into systems, where it clearly needed. Finally, using the patterns at nearly all system levels allows one to focus in a single common structure and terminology, which helps us integrate system components at different levels.

11.2 Security Pattern Taxonomy

In [182], Schumacher et al. classify security patterns into (*i*) enterprise security and risk management patterns, (*ii*) identification and authentication patterns, (*iii*) access control model patterns, (*iv*) system access control architecture patterns, (*v*) operating system access control patterns, (*vi*) accounting patterns, (*vii*) firewall architecture patterns, (*viii*) secure Internet application patterns, and (*ix*) cryptographic key management patterns. This taxonomy is illustrated in Fig. 11.1 and discussed below.

The scope of *enterprise security and risk management patterns* include a policies, directives, or constraints that apply across the enterprise. These patterns are applied for enterprise asset valuation, threat and vulnerability assessment, risk determination, enterprise security approaches and services, and enterprise partner communication.

The purpose of *identification and authentication patterns* is to identify an individual and confirm the individual's identity. These patterns introduce require-

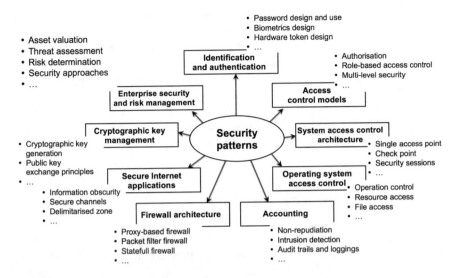

Fig. 11.1 Security pattern taxonomy, adapted from [182]

ments and produce design options for the identification and authentication services. Examples are patterns on procedural identification and authentication, physical identification and authentication, automated identification and authentication design alternatives, which also include password design and use, biometrics design alternatives, hardware token design alternatives and others.

Patterns on *access control models* describe security policies and security restrictions at the architectural level and the application level. The examples of these patterns are models for authorisation, role-based access control, role-right definition, reference monitoring, and multi-level security.

System access control architecture patterns handle the architecture of software systems to be secured, based on a generic set of access control requirements. They tend to introduce security solutions for separate system components or individuals. The examples include patterns on access control requirements, single access points, check points, security sessions, limited access and others.

Operating system access control patterns concern access of files. Also, they provide solutions on how operating systems should control and authorise processes when creating, monitoring, and executing system processes.

Accounting patterns deal with monitoring, registering and presenting harmful security issues that happen through operational activities. They support this with information so that appropriate solutions should be found. Examples of accounting patterns are about security accounting (and auditing) requirements and design, non-repudiation requirements and design, intrusion detection requirements and design, audit trails and logging requirements and design and others.

Firewall architecture patterns represent trade-offs between complexity, speed, and security solutions. Some may also introduce design solutions to prevent attacks on particular network layers. Examples are patterns on proxy-based firewalls, packet filter firewalls, stateful firewalls and others.

Secure Internet applications patterns concentrate on secure Internet applications and provide guidelines for their implementation. Examples are patterns of information obscurity, protection reverse proxies, secure channels, demilitarised zones, integration reverse proxies, known partners, front doors and others.

Cryptographic key management patterns describe how to secure communication, e.g., using Internet and other distributed public services. The patterns describe cryptographic key generation, sessions and public key exchange principles.

11.3   Security Risk-Oriented Patterns

Security risk-oriented patterns [4] could be seen as the class of the enterprise security and risk management patterns. Since they are developed following the principles of the ISSRM domain model (see, Sect. 2), they support identification and valuation of system assets, determination of their security criteria, assessment of security threats, vulnerabilities, and overall risk. These patterns also support definition of security requirements and introduction of security countermeasures. Patterns are represented using the security risk-oriented BPMN (see, Sect. 5). Five security risk-oriented patterns are introduced in this section:

- **SRP1** Securing data from unauthorised access;
- **SRP2** Securing data that flow between business entities;
- **SRP3** Securing business activity after data is submitted;
- **SRP4** Securing business service against DoS attacks;
- **SRP5** Securing data stored/retrieved from the data store.

SRP1: Securing Data from Unauthorised Access   The SRP1 pattern describes how to secure (confidential) data from access by unauthorised people or device [4]. In Fig. 11.2, a user requests **data** (i.e., a confidential business asset). In response to this request the **data** are retrieved (using the **retrieval interface** characterised as the IS asset) and provided to the user.

The problem arises (see Fig. 11.3) if retrieval of the confidential data is allowed to any user (independently of whether she or he is malicious or not) without checking his or her access permissions to the data. Such a risk event would lead to the disclosure of the confidential data: these data might be sent to business competitors, compromising the business itself. On the technical level it would bring into compromise the reliability of the data retrieval (and potentially storage) device.

To reduce this risk, the *check for the access right(s)* should be implemented, as illustrated in Fig. 11.4. This means that one needs to define clearance or trust levels (for accessing people or devices) and data sensitivity levels. Additionally, the verification procedure of clearance levels against sensitivity levels should be established. The implementation of these requirements would lead to application of access control (see, Sect. 10) models.

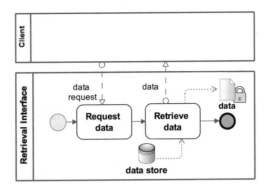

Fig. 11.2   SRP1: asset modelling

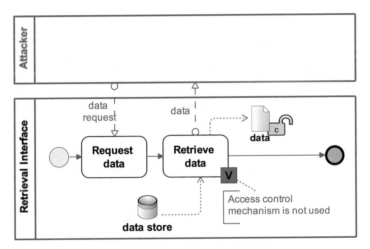

Fig. 11.3   SRP1: risk modelling

SRP2: Securing Data that Flows Between Business Entities A pattern addresses the electronic transmission of *data* between two entities [4], as illustrated in Fig. 11.5. Its scenario indicates that the client fills in the form and submits data through the Input interface to the Server for data employment. Here the *confidentiality* and *integrity* of data are two important security criteria; data correspond to business assets; and system assets are defined as Input interface and Server.

The assumption is made that the data are transmitted using Transmission medium (i.e., another system asset), as illustrated in Fig. 11.6. However, this situation faces (at least) two vulnerabilities. Firstly, such a transmission medium could be intercepted by an Attacker (i.e., threat agent) who has the means to intercept it by acting as a proxy. Secondly, since data are not encrypted, they could be misused, for example, modified and passed to the Server. This event would harm data, would lead to the loss of transmission medium reliability, and would negate data integrity (and confidentiality).

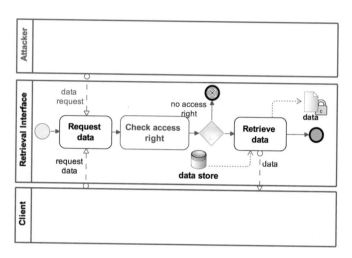

Fig. 11.4 SRP1: risk treatment modelling

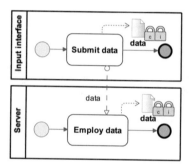

Fig. 11.5 SRP2: asset modelling

A potential risk treatment decision includes risk reduction by making data unreadable and verifying the received data. In Fig. 11.7, these security requirements are introduced to reduce the identified risks. The implementation includes introduction and application of the cryptographic algorithms and the checksum algorithms.

Another risk treatment decision, risk avoidance, could be applied, resulting in the change of the transmission medium. This could result in, for example, physical data delivery.

SRP3: Securing Business Activity After Data is Submitted This ensures valid data entry into business processes by rejecting the unwanted malicious data [4]. As illustrated in Fig. 11.8, it secures the business activity (i.e., any activity after data is submitted) of which *integrity* and *availability* have to be ensured. Hence, the data could be submitted by any entity to the input interface. The activity Submit data is vulnerable, as shown in Fig. 11.9, because it does not check the incoming data, which could be submitted by an Attacker (i.e., threat agent) who is

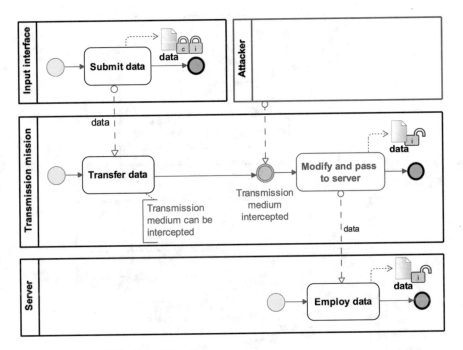

Fig. 11.6 SRP2: risk modelling (threat to integrity)

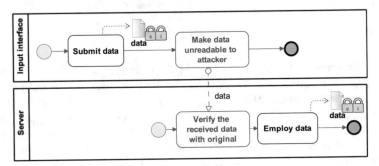

Fig. 11.7 SRP2: risk treatment modelling

capable of writing malicious scripts (e.g., cross-site scripting, like SQL queries or xPath injections [75]). Executing these scripts enable an attacker to read/write the confidential business data or change the business rules. If this happens, it risks the confidentiality and integrity of the data itself, and any activity after data is submitted may be harmed, become unavailable or lose its integrity; additionally the input interface would be compromised.

To mitigate the risk(s), the pattern introduces a security requirement of filtering the incoming data, as illustrated in Fig. 11.10. This security requirement could be implemented in input validation [75], input sanitisation [72], input filtration [75], or/and input canonicalization [42] security controls.

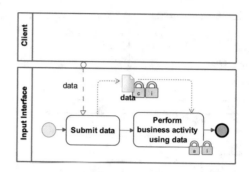

Fig. 11.8 SRP3: asset modelling

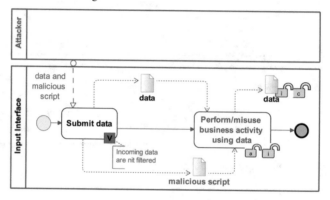

Fig. 11.9 SRP3: risk (malicious script) modelling

SRP4: Securing a Business Service Against DoS Attacks The patterns [4] ensures the availability of a business service by protecting the IS from a denial of service (DoS) attack [121]. The major idea is to protect the business services (i.e., business assets), which are provided by a server, in order to guarantee the availability of this business service, as illustrated in Fig. 11.11. The pattern assumes that there exists an attacker capable of hacking a large number of computers that simultaneously request this business service (see Fig. 11.12). The attacker is able to target the server because the used protocol (e.g., TCP, ICMP, or DNS) allows handling unlimited number of requests for a service [37]. Hence, the impact of the risk event is that the server becomes incapable of operating resulting in the business service becoming unavailable to ordinary users.

To reduce the DoS attack, one needs to implement a security requirement for checking for abnormal requests, as shown in Fig. 11.13. This requirement would include filtering and classifying of incoming requests, detecting abnormal requests, and discarding the attacking ones. Implementation of the requirements would result in detection [105, 156], filtering [201], and response to attack [123] techniques.

SRP5: Securing Data Stored In/Retrieved from the Data Store The pattern ensures the data privacy at the data store from *insiders* (i.e., administrators or malware that could infect the data store) [4]. The main goal of this pattern is to prevent

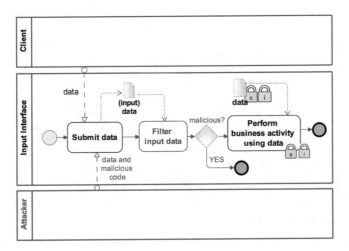

Fig. 11.10   SRP3: risk treatment modelling

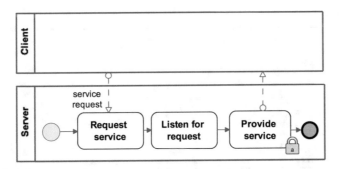

Fig. 11.11   SRP4: asset modelling

the flow control of information from leaking horizontally across the departments (i.e., at the same level). Let's assume (see Fig. 11.14) that there exists a storing/retrieval interface (i.e., system asset) which helps clients (*i*) to store the client's data (i.e., business asset) in the data store and (*ii*) to retrieve them when needed.

Let's assume that there exists an attacker, i.e., a malicious insider who has privileges to access the data store and also retrieve data directly from it (see Fig. 11.15). If the storing/retrieval interface (including the queries to the database) are designed in a way that data are stored/retrieved in a plain format, the insider could view the client's data, thus negating the data confidentiality.

To reduce this security risk, one needs to introduce security requirements (see Fig. 11.16) that help in making data *invisible* before they are stored in the data store and making them *visible* after they are retrieved from the database. A security requirement for monitoring for malicious changes at the data store should also be introduced. Implementation of these security requirements would result in application of auditing, cryptographic, and/or data protection techniques [87].

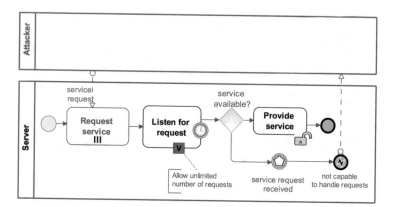

Fig. 11.12 SRP4: risk modelling

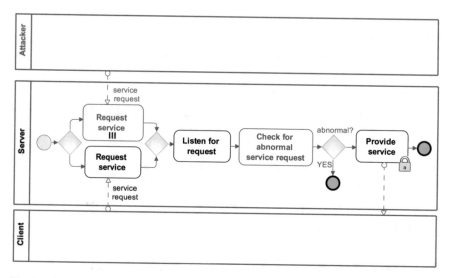

Fig. 11.13 SRP4: risk treatment modelling

11.4   Security Requirements Elicitation from Business Processes

A method for security requirements elicitation from business processes SREBP suggests means to derive security requirements from the business processes by applying security risk-oriented patterns [1]. In this section we will present the major principles of the SREBP method and will illustrate it through the Football Federation case.

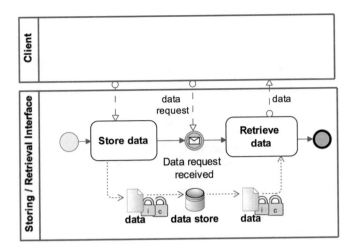

Fig. 11.14 SRP5: asset modelling

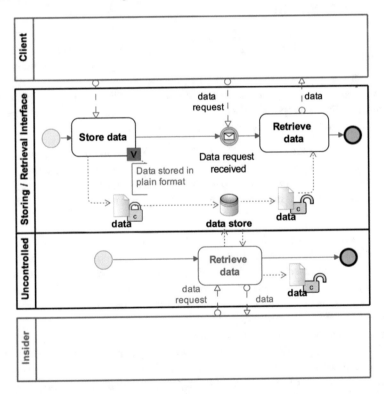

Fig. 11.15 SRP5: risk (data retrieval) modelling

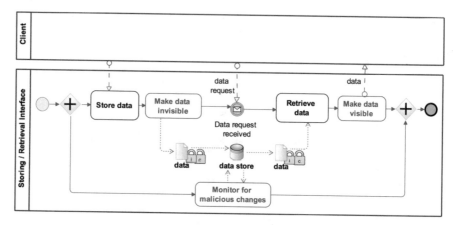

Fig. 11.16 SRP5: risk treatment modelling

11.4.1 SREBP Method

To present the SREBP method [1, 178] we will apply the component-based method view [79], which requires the description of method perspective (procedure for the modelling process from a particular perspective), framework (relationships between the individual method components), cooperation principles (a range of specialist skills for cooperation between different roles) and all method components (consisting of concepts, procedures, and notations).

Perspective The major goal of the SREBP method is to identify the organisation's assets, determine its security objectives, and elicit its security requirements. Using the method, the business/security analysis can derive security requirements from the business processes and introduce them as security restrictions back to the business processes.

Cooperation Among Stakeholders Typically, security engineering requires a close collaboration between the *business analyst* (i.e., the specialist of the business domain) and the *security analyst* (i.e., the specialist of the security domain) [4, 178]. Being experts in the business domain, business analysts have limited or no expertise in security engineering. They have to rely on best security practices, information security standards, or security experts.

The business analyst introduces to the security analyst the business context and describes the enterprise's workflow. In this way the security analyst (in collaboration with the business analyst) identifies what the business assets are, what security objectives (in terms of confidentiality, integrity, and availability) should be taken into account, and what the system assets to support the identified business assets are.

Once the security requirements are derived from the business process models, they can be used to annotate the original business process models. The annotated business model is returned back to the business analyst. But the feedback could also include security risk models. Another collaboration might be on security requirements trade-off analysis. However, this activity is not emphasised in the SREBP method.

SREBP Components The SREBP method components are listed in Table 11.1. The majority of these concepts, i.e., *business asset, security criterion, system asset, security risk*, and *security requirements*, are taken from domain model for the information systems security risk management (see, Sect. 2). But the SREBP method also includes a few concepts, i.e., *security risk-oriented patterns, pattern occurrence, security model*, which result from the application and performance of the base ISSRM concepts.

Table 11.1   SREBP method components, adapted from [178]

Concepts	Procedures	Notations
Value chain	Created by the business analyst, expresses how the enterprise business functions are related in order achieve enterprise's goals	BPMN
Business process diagram	Created by the business analyst, expresses the use of the computerised information system. These diagrams should express the use of data objects, data flows and data stores	BPMN
Business asset	Identified from the value chain	Textually and/or graphically
Security criterion	Identified by understanding importance of the business assets	Textually and/or graphically
System asset	Identified when analysing the business process diagrams	Textually and/or graphically
Security risk (and its major components)	Identified from the business process diagrams by instantiating the security risk-oriented patterns	Security risk-oriented BPMN
Security requirements	Identified from business process diagram by applying the security risk-oriented patterns and by instantiating pattern security parts	Documented textually as security requirements statements, and graphically using UML notations depending on the analysed contextual area
Security risk-oriented patterns	Artefact used to guide security risk requirements derivation from the business process diagrams. The patterns describe recurring security risks that arise within business processes. To mitigate the risks, the patterns recommend security requirements	Documented textually in the structured template [4] and graphically using security risk-oriented BPMN (see Section 11.3)
Pattern occurrence	Identified in the business process diagram using security risk-oriented patterns	Highlighted in the analysed business process diagram
Security model	Derived from the business process model and the result of security risk-oriented pattern application	Represented graphically using UML notations depending on the analysed contextual area and applied pattern

In the second column of Table 11.1, the procedures used to identify the relevant concepts are presented. Hence the business analyst creates *value chain* and *business process diagrams* as the part of the organisation's business process management. The *asset-related concepts* are identified from the *value chain* and *business process diagrams*, and *security risk-related* and *risk treatment-related concepts* are defined using the *security risk-oriented patterns*.

The third column presents the notations used to represent concepts. A notable set of concepts is expressed using textual language, which is supported with targeted graphical notations. Since SREBP is meant to consider business processes, the majority of the notations are BPMN or security risk-oriented BPMN. The security requirements models are represented using UML.

SREBP Conceptual Framework In Fig. 11.17, the relationships between the SREBP method components are described. Hence, the *Business process diagram* expands the *Value chain diagram*. The *Business assets* are elicited from the *Value chain*. The security analyst in cooperation with the business analyst determines the *Security objective* for each identified *Business asset*. *System asset* supports *Business asset*, which are also refined when considering the *Business process diagram*. When applying *Security risk-oriented patterns*, *Pattern occurrences* are found in the *Business process diagram*. *Pattern occurrences* result in a *Security model*, which is extracted from the *Business process diagram* based on the used *Security risk-oriented pattern*. *Security requirements* are derived from the *Security model* and they define the security constraints on *Assets*.

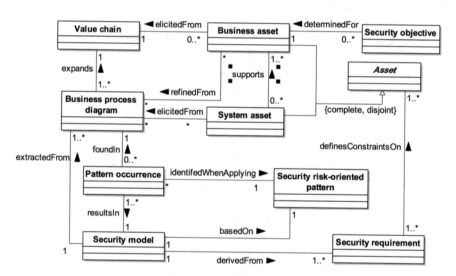

Fig. 11.17 The SREBP framework, adapted from [178]

Figure 11.18 presents an SREBP process. It consists of two stages: (*i*) business asset identification and security objective determination, and (*ii*) security requirements elicitation. The second stage includes three activities: identify patterns, extract security model and derive security requirements.

During pattern identification one need to find pattern occurrences in the business process diagram. One could apply methods of hierarchical0level matching, business perspective matching, structural similarity and semantic similarity matching [3]. Once the pattern occurrences are determined, one could extract the security model.

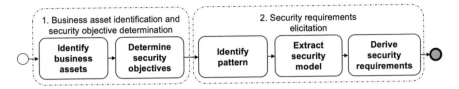

Fig. 11.18 The SREBP process, adapted from [178]

Depending on the chosen security risk-oriented pattern, different activities for security model extraction could be performed (see, Fig. 11.19). After extracting the security model, it becomes possible to derive and document security requirements.

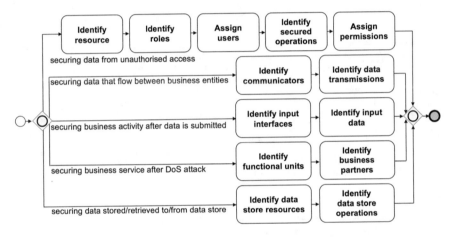

Fig. 11.19 SREBP activity Extract security model, adapted from [178]

11.4.2 Pattern Application

In this section, we will analyse the running example—the extract of the Football Federation case presented in Chap. 1. We will apply the SREBP method and illustrate how security risk-oriented patterns could help in determining security requirements.

To start performing the security requirements elicitation one needs to collect knowledge of an organisation's *values* from the *value chain* and the *business functions*. The value chain is presented in Fig. 1.6. In Fig. 11.20 a detailed workflow of **Register game report** process is given. The process has two business partners (Umpire and FootballFederationEmployee) expressed as swimlanes, while ERIS is identified as a system.

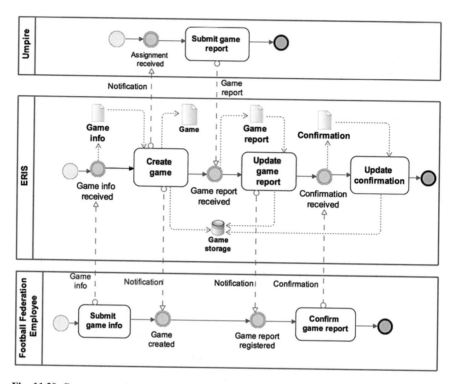

Fig. 11.20 Process to register game report (re-captured Fig. 1.7)

11.4.2.1 Business Asset Identification and Security Objective Determination

The first stage starts with the analysis of the *value chain* (see Fig. 1.6) from which the assets that must be protected against security risks are determined. The stage requires collaboration between security analysts and the stakeholders from the analysed enterprise. It consists of two activities:

(*i*) *Identify business assets*: During this activity the central artefacts considered in the value chain are identified. Typically, further details of these artefacts are considered in the business process model. The value chain can either have a single artefact used in all the processes or be comprised of multiple artefacts in each operational business process. In the Football Federation case, it is possible to identify important artefacts from each business activity. The protected assets include **Team, Player, Umpire, League and region, Timetable,** and **Game.** In this discussion we will focus on **Game** (and its registration process).

(*ii*) *Determine security objectives*: The activity addresses the determining of key security objectives—confidentiality, integrity and availability—for identified business assets. The following security objectives for business asset Game are defined:

- (*i*) Game should be confidential (at least some its attributes or at least at some stage in its existence), i.e., no unauthorised individual should read it and its relevant data;
- (*ii*) Game should be integral, i.e., the Game and its relevant data should not be tampered; and
- (*iii*) Game and its relevant data should be available to the business partners at any time.

11.4.2.2   Security Requirements Elicitation

At the second stage, the security requirements elicitation is performed using security risk-oriented patterns. It is important to note that each artefact—*data* or *process*—separately considered and protected by the patterns, contributes to the security of the business asset (i.e., Game) identified at the first stage.

Securing Data from Unauthorised Access   The major concern of this pattern is to protect the confidentiality of the identified business asset, in our example the Game, when it is being manipulated by the system asset (i.e., the ERIS). The security threat arises if the Game and its attributes (like (Game info, Gamereport, and Confirmation) are accessed by users who does not have access permissions. The risk event would: (*i*) negate confidentiality of Game, (*ii*) lead to unintended use of the Game data , and (*iii*) harm the ERIS's reliability.

A way to mitigate the security risk is through the introduction of an access control mechanism, for example, the Role-Based Access Control (RBAC) model (see, Chap. 10). The RBAC model (see, Fig. 11.21) is elicited by performing the following activities:

- (*i*) *Identify resource*: Hence, the business asset (i.e., Game) is defined as a resource that needs to be protected from unauthorised access. The protected resource is characterised by its attributes—gameInfo, gameReport and confirmation—that add value to the asset.
- (*ii*) *Identify role*: The swimlanes are considered as an outside role while the lanes of an information system corresponds to an internal role. We consider both out-side and internal roles, since they both could access the secured business asset i.e., Game. These roles (e.g., Umpire and FootballFederationEmployee) are modelled using the ≪role≫ stereotype in RBAC security model (see Fig. 11.21).
- (*iii*) *Assign users*: This activity assigns roles to users, which are instances of some role. Usually it is not possible to elicit concrete users from the operational business process. This requires expertise of and collaboration with domain experts.

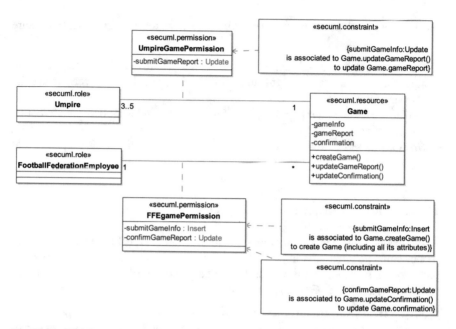

Fig. 11.21 RBAC security model - register game report business process

(*iv*) *Identify secured operation*: An operation is an executable set of actions that can change the state of the protected resource. For instance, createGame, updateGameReport and updateConfirmation are secured operations.

(*v*) *Assign permissions*: Permissions specify the security actions—namely, *Insert* and *Update*—over secured operations that the role can perform to change the state of the protected resource. For example, the Umpire role has permission to update Game's attribute gameReport.

The developed security model (see Fig. 11.21) suggests the refinement of the security requirement *check for the access rights* to the following context-specific security requirements:

- **SecReq.1:** Umpire should be able to *update* the gameReport.
- **SecReq.2:** FootballFederationEmployee should be able to *insert* the Game (i.e., create a new instance of Game, including gameInfo, gameReport, and confirmation).
- **SecReq.3:** FootballFederationEmployee should be able to *update* the confirmation.

The security model (i.e., Fig. 11.21) defines how authorised parties should access the protected resources. However, it does not support capturing scenarios like *entailment constraints* [91], *delegation constraints* [19] and *usage control* [164]. These requirements could be determined in the collaboration between business and security analysts.

Securing data that flows between business entities is used to exchange data between business partners (e.g., Umpire and Football Federation Employee) and the system (e.g., ERIS). Here, data, like game info, different notifications, game report, confirmation, etc., need to be protected when they are transmitted over the (untrusted) communication channel, i.e., Internet. To define security requirements, one needs to performs two activities:

(i) *Identify communicators*: Communicators are the entities that transmit or receive data. Operational business processes are considered to identify the system and their business partners who exist outside of an organisation but transmit/receive data to/from the organisation. In Fig. 11.22, we illustrate a security model for communication channel between ERIS and Umpire using a UML interaction diagram. ERIS is modelled as the system that communicates with the Umpire identified as the business partner.

(ii) *Identify data transmission*: One needs to determine the business asset and/or its relevant data transmitted or received between the identified communicators over the untrusted communication channels, i.e., Internet. For example, game report is communicated between Umpire and ERIS; thus, they require to be protected.

The above activities result in the following security requirements for the Umpire and ERIS and correspondingly for other entities (e.g., Football Federation Employee, Team Representative, etc.) that communicate with ERIS:

- **SecReq.4:** ERIS should have unique identity in the form of key pairs (public key, private key) certified by a certification authority.
- **SecReq.5:** Umpire should encrypt and sign game report (and other data communicated to ERIS) using keys before sending it to ERIS.

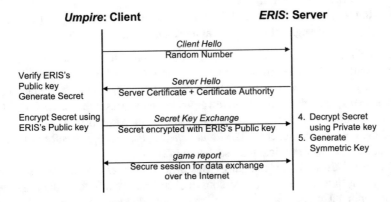

Fig. 11.22 TLS protocol implementation, adapted from [16]

A security requirements implementation could be fulfilled by the standard transport layer security (a.k.a., TLS) protocol [16] (see Fig. 11.22). As the first contact, the Umpire sends ERIS a *handshake* message, which includes a random number. Then the ERIS responds with its public key and information about the certification authority. After verification of the ERIS's public key, the Umpire generates the secret and sends it to the ERIS encrypted with the ERIS's public key. The ERIS then decrypts the secret using the private key and generates symmetric session keys. The keys enable Umpire and ERIS to establish a secure session for data exchange. The encryption keeps the transmitted data (e.g., game report, etc.) confidential, and signing it ensures that the received data is not tampered. The secure communication continues until it is not explicitly terminated by Umpire or ERIS.

Securing business activity after data is submitted ensures that the input data submitted by business partners are correct and complete. In this contextual area two activities are suggested:

(*i*) *Identify input interfaces*: The activity identifies the system input interfaces from the operational business processes that have incoming message flows. The input interfaces are those activities of the information system that receives input from the enterprise stakeholders.

(*ii*) *Identify input data*: The activity identifies the input data received by the input interfaces from the enterprise's business partners.

In the Football Federation case, Update game report could be treated as the input interface of ERIS that receives the game report from Umpire. The threat agent can exploit the vulnerability of the input interfaces by submitting the data with malicious scripts. If this happens the availability and integrity of any activity (e.g., Update confirmation) after the input interface (e.g., Update game report) may be misused or negated. To avoid this risk the following security requirements are suggested:

- **SecReq.7:** Update game report should filter the input (i.e., game report).
- **SecReq.8:** Update game report should sanitise the input (i.e., game report) to transform it to the required format.
- **SecReq.9:** Update game details should canonicalise the input (i.e., game report) to verify against its canonical representation.

Input filtration (i.e., SecReq.7) validates the input data against the secure and correct syntax [42]. The string input should be checked for length and character set validity (e.g., allowed and blacklisted characters). The numerical input should be validated against their upper and lower value boundaries. *Input sanitisation* (i.e., SecReq.8) should check for common encoding methods used (e.g., HTML entity encoding, URL encoding, etc.). The *input canonicalisation* (i.e., SecReq.9) verifies the input against its canonical representation [42].

Securing business service against Dos attacks secures the network infrastructure of the system. The system is composed of several small functional units, which can be deployed at either a single location or multiple locations connected through the Internet. The goal is to guarantee availability of these functional units. Two activities are performed:

(*i*) *Identify functional-unit*: A functional unit is an activity or sub-process implemented on an independent network infrastructure to provide certain functionality to an enterprise's information system. A system can be comprised of one or more functional units. For instance, the ERIS system (see Fig. 11.20) consists of three functional-units, Create game, Update game report, and Update confirmation, which could be deployed on an independent network infrastructure connected through the Internet to form a single system (i.e., ERIS). Here, the elicitation of security requirements for Update game report is illustrated (see Fig. 11.23).

(*ii*) *Identify business partner*: Business partners are the external entities that can access the network infrastructure in order to communicate with the enterprise information system. The access involves any request type necessary to receive or send data. For instance, Umpire could be treated as an external entity that communicates with ERIS.

In Fig. 11.20, ERIS has a functional unit Update game report offered to Umpire. The threat agent may exploit the hosts in the channel and hack them because of the protocol (e.g., TCP, ICMP or DNS [37]) vulnerability, i.e., the ability to handle an unlimited number of requests for service. When receiving simultaneously multiple requests, ERIS will not be able to handle them; thus, the services become unavailable. The above activities helps us develop a security model (see Fig. 11.23) that defines three types of firewalls [182]—Packet Filter Firewall, Proxy Based Firewall and Stateful Firewall. The security model introduces the following requirements to mitigate the risks:

- **SecReq.10:** Update game report should establish a rule base (i.e., a collection of constraints used by different firewalls) to communicate with the Umpire.
- **SecReq.11:** Packet Filter Firewall should filter the Umpire's address to determine if that is not a host used by the threat agent.
- **SecReq.12:** Proxy Based Firewall should communicate to the proxy which represents Update game report to determine the validity of the request received from Umpire.
- **SecReq.13:** State Firewall should maintain the state table to check the Umpire's request for additional conditions on established communication.

It is important to notice that the communication between the Umpire (and also Football Federation Employee) and the ERIS is bidirectional. Similar requirements must be taken into account when ERIS sends messages back to the business party.

Securing data stored in/retrieved from the data store is used to define how data are stored in and retrieved from the associated databases (e.g., Game storage). If the threat agent is capable of accessing and retrieving the data, their confidentiality and integrity would be negated resulting in harm to the business asset (i.e., the Game report) and its supporting system assets (i.e., ERIS). To prevent unauthorised access to the datastore, the access control model could be defined:

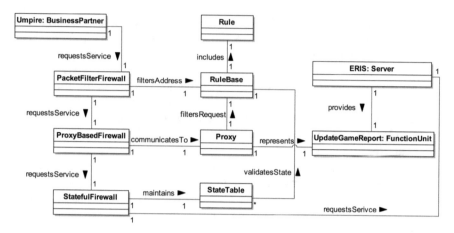

Fig. 11.23 Firewall architecture, adapted from [182]

(*i*) *Identify* **Datastore** *resource*: For example, **Game storage** is identified as a single collective resource. The identified business assets and their related data in the operational process models are modelled as resource attributes. This means that the attributes **Game info**, **Game report**, and **Confirmation** will represent the attributes of business asset **Game**.

(*ii*) *Identify* **Datastore***'s operations*: The activity identifies operations that save and retrieve the data identified in previous activity to and from **Game storage**. These operations are modelled as operations of **Game storage**'s resource.

Once the resource and operations are modelled, the activities *identify role* and *assign permissions* are performed as described earlier (see discussion on *securing data from authorised access*). This results in a security RBAC model for **Game storage**, given in Fig. 11.24.

Once we identify access control policies, it becomes possible to introduce security requirements for monitoring and auditing (i.e., *monitor for malicious changes*) and for hiding data/ and making it visible (i.e., *make data invisible* and *make data visible*), as illustrated in Fig. 11.16. The following security requirements should be taken into account:

- **SecReq.14:** The **ERIS** should audit the operations after the retrieval, storage or any other manipulation of data in the **Game storage**.
- **SecReq.15:** The **ERIS** should perform operations to hide/unhide data when they are stored/retrieved to/from the **Game storage**.

Auditing (supported by the access control policy) is the process of monitoring and recording selected events and activities [153]. It determines who performed what operations on what data and when. This is useful for detecting and tracing security violations performed on **gameInfo**, **gameReport** and **confirmation**.

A possible implementation of SecReq.15 is through cryptographic algorithms. The encryption offers twofold benefits: (*i*) the data would not be seen by the Game storage users (e.g., by the database administrator) where the circumstances do not allow one to revoke their permissions; (*ii*) due to any reason if someone gets physical access to the Game storage she or he would not be able to see the confidential data stored.

11.4.2.3   Once Security Requirements Are Elicited

Once security requirements are elicited, one needs to understand whether they all need to be implemented. This basically includes requirements prioritisation and security trade-off analysis. For instance, implementing all security requirements might be costly. In addition, although this can guarantee a certain level of security, it would influence the efficiency and performance of the system. Thus the optimal decision on security requirements needs to be found once requirements are derived by applying the security risk-oriented patterns.

11.5   Further Reading

A classical overview of software requirements patterns is presented in [209]. After introducing the notion of patterns for software requirements, the author describes the pattern taxonomy for information, user functions, data, performance, flexibility and access control. The security pattern taxonomy [182] viewed over in this chapter is one possible classification. Elsewhere, [25] differentiates between *available system patterns* and *protected systems patterns*. The first group is concerned with system availability and provides security approaches that give continuous access to the services and resources. The second group concerns protection of privileged resources by providing a set of methods that protect valuable assets against unauthorised use. In [52], secure design patterns are introduced and classified into (*i*) *architectural-level patterns* to describe the high-level distribution of the tasks and communication protocols between different modules; (*ii*) *design-level patterns* to design standards of high-level system modules; and (*iii*) *implementation-level patterns* to deal with low-level security concerns. These patterns are appropriate for adjusting the application of a particular functionality in the system. To support pattern classification, Slavin et al. suggest feature diagram hierarchies to support more confident and expert-like decisions in efficient time [194].

Nine modelling approaches are compared in terms of modelling constructs to represent security patterns [20]. Elsewhere, in [22], a framework to link security standards with a security engineering method is proposed. The author illustrates how goal-oriented Si*/Secure Tropos [18, 77, 77, 78, 125], CORAS [122], and problem frames [96] could be used to ensure compliance with security standards.

Security risk-oriented patterns, discussed in this chapter, could be considered within different model representations. For instance, besides pattern application in

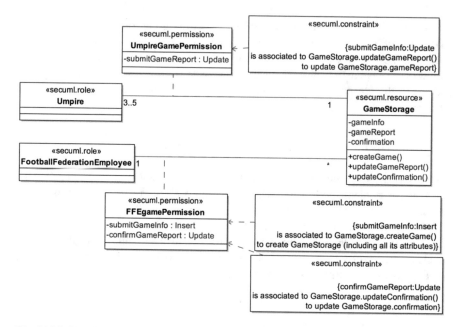

Fig. 11.24 RBAC security model (e.g., used for auditing)

business processes, application of SRPs is illustrated within the models of security risk-aware Secure Tropos [175]. The study illustrates how SRP could initiate security requirements derivation and security trade-off analysis.

11.6   Exercises

Exercise 11.1 What are the similarities and differences between the different security pattern taxonomies: STRIDE [188], CAPEC [145], security threat taxonomy for distributed systems [205], pattern taxonomy suggested by Schumacher et al. [182], etc.?

Exercise 11.2 Based on your experience, develop a new security risk-oriented pattern.

Exercise 11.3 For the *Football Federation* process model (see Fig. 1.5), apply the method of security requirements elicitation from business processes (SREBP) and derive the security requirements for the **Team** asset.

As illustrated in Fig. 1.5, **Team** asset is characterised by the attributes

- teamInfo—team info;
- teamRep—team representative;
- participationDecision—decision about participation; and
- regionAndLeague—region and league, where team decided to participate.

The solution should illustrate the application of security risk-oriented patterns and include:

- SRP1: Security model (i.e., RBAC model) and the derived list of security requirements
- SRP2: Security model (i.e., collaboration model) and the derived list of security requirements
- SRP3: Derived list of security requirements (describing the input filtering)
- SRP4: Security model (i.e., class diagram) and derived list of security requirements (describing the requirements for the firewall architecture)
- SRP5: Security model (i.e., RBAC model regarding the database) and derived list of security requirements (including auditing and information hiding requirements).

Exercise 11.4 Discuss how security risk-oriented patterns could be defined using:

- Security Risk-aware Secure Tropos;
- Security Risk-oriented Misuse Cases;
- Mal-activities for security risk management.

Part IV
Concluding Remarks

Chapter 12
Secure System Development

In this book we have analysed different methods, frameworks, techniques and processes for modelling of secure software systems. However, activities of system requirements engineering, modelling and design are a part of overall secure software system development. So it is important how the modelling and design approach is situated within various stages of secure software system development. To conclude this book, we will look now at three secure system development processes, namely Microsoft secure system development lifecycle [88], open Web application security project (OWASP) and its comprehensive lightweight application security process (CLASP) [82] and Cigital's seven security touchpoints (Seven Touchpoints) approach [137]. The chapter gives their comprehensive overview and comparison. To complete the discussion we will consider shortly how different secure system development approaches suit the various stages of secure system development.

12.1 Secure System Development Processes

During secure system development, stakeholders have to decide and select the development activities. Traditional system and software engineering lifecycles, such as Waterfall, V-model, Spiral, Prototype development, Agile, Incremental development, could be a good starting option. However, traditional development lifecycles do not take into account security concerns in particular. Therefore, there exist approaches which focus on *security development* techniques, methods, and tools. In this section we survey three secure system development lifecycles: Microsoft Secure System Development Lifecycle [88], Open Web Application Security Project (OWASP) and its Comprehensive Lightweight Application Security Process (CLASP) [82], and Seven Touchpoints for Software Security [137].

© Springer International Publishing AG 2017
R. Matulevičius, *Fundamentals of Secure System Modelling*,
DOI 10.1007/978-3-319-61717-6_12

12.1.1 Microsoft Secure System Development Lifecycle

The Microsoft secure system development lifecycle (SSDL) is a set of activities performed to develop and deliver a secure software solution [88].[1] These activities are
grouped in seven stages (see Fig. 12.1): training, requirements, design, implementation, verification, release and response. Although the SSDL stages are security-
specific, they are very alike to traditional software development (e.g., Waterfall,
V-model, etc.) stages. Below we will briefly characterise each stage separately.

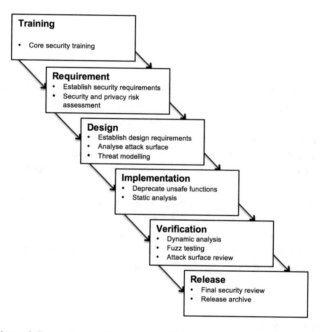

Fig. 12.1 Microsoft Secure System Development lifecycle, adapted from [88]

Training Using the SSDL approach, much attention is much put on the training of
the organisation's employees. This helps them to be aware of the analysed problem.
Also, it is emphasised that annual training should be maintained in light of recent
developments and security solutions. In addition, a measurement program should be
established and maintained to assess the employees' knowledge and skills.

Requirement This stage consists of activities to establish security requirements and
to assess security and privacy needs. Here, security risk assessment helps us define
the functional system characteristics that might require a thorough security review.
During this stage one also determines the necessity for threat modelling, security
design reviews and penetration testing. At the requirements stage one considers
privacy concerns as well as measures for data sensitivity.

---

[1]An up-to-date description of the SSDL could be found at https://www.microsoft.com/en-us/SDL.

Design Detailed system and architecture design are supported through security threat modelling with the goal to decrease the security attack surface. SSDL emphasises the *STRIDE* approach [188] and supports its application by suggesting supporting resources and documents. Both the design and architecture solutions should be continuously reviewed.

Implementation and Verification SSDL emphasises applying coding standards to avoid security flaws and testing standards to detect potential security risks. These activities include using automated tools and conducting manual code reviews to capture and correct code mistakes. The testing activities cover black box testing. SSDL describes procedures to ensure that the final software product meets security requirements.

Release During the release stage the software product should undergo a final security review. This is an independent software examination, typically conducted by the organisation's security team. If any problems are found during the final security review process, the previous SSDL stages need to be revised to understand the flaw rationale.

12.1.2   OWASP CLASP

Open Web Application Security Project (OWASP)[2] and its Comprehensive Lightweight Application Security Process (CLASP) tend to move security analysis into the early stages of software system development [82]. It includes security engineering-related activities and their supplementary resources (e.g., concepts, best practices, core security principles, check-listed coding guidelines, vulnerability checklists, and others). Generic CLASP perspectives are presented in Fig. 12.2. These five perspectives are divided into activities and process components. The choice of the activities and the order of their execution are left open and depend on the modeller's perspective and the software requirements. CLASP introduces the roles responsible for different security solutions. In addition, each activity is assigned the resources necessary for this activity execution.

The major CLASP activity groups (i.e., best practice guidelines) are:

- *Defining awareness program.* People should consider security to be an important project goal. This means that team members need to be trained and people should be aware of the security settings as well as of the consequences if these settings are misused. The project team officer needs to be assigned. Some schemas of reward to organisation's employees could be established for handling security-related issues.
- *Assessing application.* These activities include security requirements engineering and design. The typical tasks involve source-level reviews and the definition of security tests.

---

[2]See also: https://www.owasp.org/.

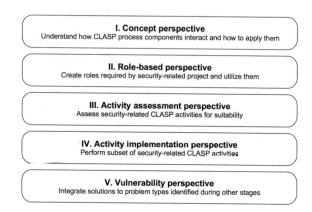

Fig. 12.2 CLASP perspectives and their relationships, adapted from [82]

- *Capturing security requirements.* Requirements are captured using both offensive and defensive means, including threat modelling and use and misuse case-driven analysis. CLASP also supports identifying the attacker's profile for the simpler specification of the threat origin.
- *Implementing secure development practices* includes annotating of software system components with security-related properties and applying the principles of secure software development. This also means managing the needed resource, respecting development contracts and organising component interfaces.
- *Building of vulnerability remediation procedures.* Handling system vulnerabilities requires continuous monitoring and reacting to new emerging flaws. The activities include addressing reported security issues and managing security flaw disclosure processes.
- *Definition and monitoring of metrics* includes selecting metrics, collecting metrics and evaluating the results. CLASP acknowledges the importance of testing, but focusses more on white box testing. It suggests automating security analysis and computing of metrics by using dynamic or static tools. In the later stages, CLASP suggests penetration testing, too.
- *Publishing operational security guidelines.* Security awareness is an important aspect of secure systems. CLASP emphasises specifying the database security configuration, and also building operational security guides and publishing them for interested system users.

12.1.3   Seven Touchpoints

The Cigital's Seven Security Touchpoints (Seven Touchpoints) approach provides a set of best practices that have been gathered over the years from extensive industrial experience [137]. The Touchpoint approach recognises the importance of security risk management and, thus, includes both "destructive" (i.e., attacks, exploits, software breaking, etc.) and "constructive" (i.e., design, defence, etc.) activities. As illustrated in Fig. 12.3, the seven touchpoints are (*i*) code review, (*ii*) risk analysis, (*iii*) penetration testing, (*iv*) risk-based security tests, (*v*) abuse cases, (*vi*) security requirements, and (*vii*) security operations.

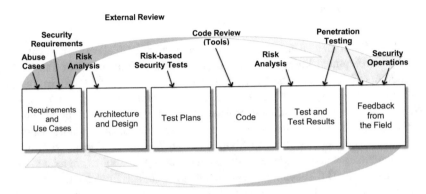

Fig. 12.3 Seven Security Touchpoints, adapted from [137]

The main goal of the Seven Touchpoints approach is to capture security bugs as early as possible. Therefore, the approach suggests using *automated tools* for *code review* as the "best way" to identify implementation defects.

The Seven Touchpoints approach advises that *abuse cases* be used in order to describe the system's behaviour under attack. Two critical activities of abuse cases are: creating anti-requirements and attack models. Anti-requirements are for describing what can go wrong. An attack model is for describing how the attack could be achieved.

Another important point of the approach is *risk analysis*. It emphasises security risk management methods to identify and keep track of risks over time as the software system develops. This includes application of attack resistance methods, including the use of the checklists of the known attacks (e.g., STRIDE [188], CAPEC [145]). An important activity is ambiguity analysis, which includes discovering new risks, finding unclear paths of system performance, and analysing trust, data sensitivity and threat models.

Penetration testing is a special type of system testing when an attack on the system is performed with the intention of finding security weaknesses, gaining access to it, its functionality and its data. Touchpoints also acknowledges unit testing as an important part of security testing (i.e., breaking system security down into a number of discrete parts).

Risk-based security testing is a mix of constructive and destructive activities that requires black-and-white box approaches. Testers must ground both the system's architectural reality and the attacker's mindset.

For release and deployment, the Seven Touchpoint approach suggests using event monitoring and event logging (i.e., *security operations*). Both techniques will gather data for risk event analysis and the determination of possible response actions.

12.1.4   Comparison

In [51] De Win et al. give an extensive theoretical and empirical comparison of three security development lifecycles. The observations are summarised in Table 12.1. The authors observe that the SSDL puts strong emphasis on the education and awareness, project inception and release, deployment and support activities. Like OWASP CLASP concentrates on project inception and release, deployment and support activities, but in addition strongly addresses analysis and requirements and architectural and detailed design activities. Seven Touchpoints much concentrates on implementation and testing (e.g., three out of seven touchpoints are related to the testing activities). But Touchpoints also includes a lot of activities related to analysis and requirements and architectural and detailed design. If one intends to select the secure system development process, she needs to estimate various stakeholder perspectives and the type of the developed software system.

12.2   Security Approaches in Secure Systems Development Processes

In Table 12.2 we provide tentative suggestions about the stages (and for which activities) of the secure system development processes the considered security approaches could be applied. We, however, do not limit this alignment, as the approach could be used for different purposes. Hence this table could suggest some hints when selecting security approaches.

Firstly, Table 12.2 illustrates a different focus of the secure system development processes. For example, Seven Touchpoints places a large emphasis on testing activities; however, security testing was not in the scope of this book. Secondly, it should be noted that while the stages of *Education and awareness* are not explicitly mentioned in Table 12.2, the security modelling approaches need to be learnt before applying them for secure system development. Similarly, at the stages of *Release, deployment and support*, the project could benefit if explicit requirements are defined using the models. This could help explain the decisions made while supporting and maintaining security solutions. In addition, it could help validate the security solutions through the reverse engineering of security models [183].

Finally, while analysing the secure system development processes, one could easily notice that the majority of activities centres around the *analysis and requirements* and *architectural and detailed design* (although one should not underestimate other

Table 12.1 Comparing security development approaches, adapted from [51]

Stages	SSDL	CLASP	Touchpoints
Education and awareness	1. Baseline education and advanced education 2. Focus on awareness, knowledge of security engineering knowledge	1. Base level and advanced education 2. Focus on all project roles 3. Emphasis on accountability 4. Tends to improve awareness by sharing all security artefacts	1. No separate touchpoint, but recognises that people should be sufficiently trained 2. A knowledge management framework established to share security knowledge
Project inception	1. Decision about the methodology, personnel, tools, and targeted security bugs	1. Assignment of the security officer and determining influence of security on other development roles 2. Motivation plan by institutional accountability and by means of reward 3. Metric definition, collection and management 4. Organisational policy management	1. Stress on the creation and continuous execution of an improvement program
Analysis and requirements	1. Use scenarios as the means in threat modelling	1. Identifies resources, trust boundaries, capabilities for resources and roles, and attacker profiles 2. Uses threat modelling and requirements specification means 3. Deals with business requirements, functional security requirements, conflict resolution, etc.	1. Touchpoint dedicated to threat modelling based on abuse cases 2. Extra security requirements identified based on laws and regulations, commercial considerations and contractual obligations
Architectural and detailed design	1. Supports threat modelling 2. Focusses on operational environment 3. Assesses user privacy 4. Tends to reduce attack surface (by reduction of privileges)	1. Supports threat modelling 2. Audits both security and non-security requirements 3. Focusses on reduction of access points 4. Annotates design models 5. Secures configuration of data bases	1. Main focus on threat modelling 2. Includes threat identification and risk assessment 3. Tends to remove ambiguity
Implementation and testing	1. Provides secure coding guidelines 2. Encourages both using automated tools for verification and manual code inspection 3. Focus on *black box* testing	1. Emphasises on *white box* security testing 2. Includes implementation of interface contracts 3. Reviews specification from developers perspective	1. Big emphasis on security testing – three (out of seven) touchpoints deals with testing 2. Stress on importance of risk-based testing 3. Emphasis on code review using automated tools
Release, deployment and support	1. Focus on response plan (i.e., where, when vulnerability is determined)	1. Requests stakeholder to sign the code, so to provide a way to validate the origin and integrity of the product	1. Limited support in this activity (fine tuning access controls, configuring the monitoring and logging)

stages as well). In this book we have considered a number of different approaches for security and security risk management, modelling, and engineering.

Table 12.2 Security approaches in the secure system development processes

Security approaches	SSDL	CLASP	Touchpoints
ISSRM	Requirements, Design	Assessing application, Capturing security requirements, Implementing secure development practices, Definition and monitoring of metrics	Risk analysis
STRIDE	Design	Capturing security requirements	Risk analysis
Threats for distributed systems	Design	Capturing security requirements	Risk analysis
Seven pernicious kingdoms	Design, Implementation	Building vulnerability remediation procedures	Code review, Security operations
Security Risk-oriented BPMN	Requirements	Capturing security requirements	Security requirements
Security Risk-aware Secure Tropos	Requirements, Design	Capturing security requirements	Abuse cases, Security requirements
Security Risk-oriented Misuse Cases	Design	Capturing security requirements	Abuse cases, Security requirements
Mal-activities for Security Management	Design	Capturing security requirements	Abuse cases, Security requirements
Secure model transformations	Requirements, Design	Implementing secure development procedures	Security requirements
RBAC	Design, Implementation	Implementing secure development procedures, Definition and monitoring of metrics	Security requirements, Security operations
SecureUML	Design, Implementation	Implementing secure development procedures	Security requirements, Security operations
UMLsec	Design, Implementation	Implementing secure development procedures	Security requirements, Security operations
Model-driven security	Design, Implementation	Implementing secure development procedures	Security requirements, Code review
Security patterns	Requirements, Design	Capturing security requirements, Implementing secure development practices	Security requirements, Abuse cases, Risk analysis, Security operations
SREBP	Requirements, Design	Capturing security requirements, Implementing secure development practices	Security requirements, Abuse cases, Risk analysis

12.3   Tools

The main emphasis of this book is placed on the modelling approaches of secure software systems. We focussed on the determination, modelling and engineering of security requirements using different modelling languages. We also illustrated how the created models could be used to represent different secure system perspectives. Models also provide rationale for security decisions and implementation of security controls. In the book we do *not* emphasise the use of any specific modelling or engineering tools because, when knowing the modelling approach, security engineers could select tools based on their preference, knowledge, usability and other factors.

However, in this book we have extensively used the generic UML modelling tool.[3] Modern modelling tools contain comprehensive means to introduce extensions for the traditional modelling languages, as illustrated in Chaps. 5, 7, and 8.

There exist a number of modelling tools to deal with goal-oriented approaches, such as *i**, Tropos and Secure Tropos.[4] More specifically, the Secure Tropos approach considered in Chap. 6 is supported by the tool SecTro [166] (recently, the second version, SecTro2, of the tools released).

These tools suggest comprehensive means to introduce security engineering methods and support application of these methods. For example, to prove the concept of model transformation (see Chap. 9), a tool is introduced to illustrate transformation of Security Risk-aware Secure Tropos models to/from Security Risk-oriented Misuse Cases diagrams [193]. This was done by combining the generic UML tool (i.e., MagicDraw) and the SecTro2 tool.

There exist also few extensions of generic UML modelling tools to support: (*i*) multiple perspective RBAC management using the SecureUML and UMLsec modelling languages [97], (*ii*) model-driven development [111, 129, 199, 200] (see Sect. 10); (*iii*) reverse engineering of the security constraints to the security models [183].

12.4 Exercises

Exercise 12.1 Following the discussion given in Sect. 12.1, compare activities and sub-activities of the SSDL, OWASP CLASP, and Seven Touchpoints approaches.

Exercise 12.2 How could traditional software development lifecycles, e.g., Waterfall, V-model, Spiral, prototyping development, etc. (choose one or few), be combined with

- SSDL;
- OWASP CLASP;
- Seven Touchpoints?

Exercise 12.3 Which secure system development process would you recommend to develop a secure software system in the *Football Federation* case?

Exercise 12.4 In this book a lot of different security engineering approaches—like methods, techniques, processes—and frameworks were considered. Let's assume that you need to apply some secure system development lifecycle (SSDL, OWASP CLASP or Seven Touchpoints) and select various security engineering approaches at different stages of the lifecycle. Which approach would you use at the different stages of the lifecycles?

---

[3]For example, MagicDraw; see https://www.nomagic.com/products/magicdraw.

[4]For example, see http://istarwiki.org/tiki-index.php.

References

1. Ahmed, N.: Deriving security requirements from business process models. Ph.D. thesis, University of Tartu, Tartu (2014)
2. Ahmed, N., Matulevičius, R.: Towards transformation guidelines from secure tropos to misuse cases (position paper). In: Proceedings of the SESS'11, pp. 36–42 (2011)
3. Ahmed, N., Matulevičius, R.: A taxonomy for assessing security in business process modelling. In: Proceedings of RCIS 2013, pp. 1–10. IEEE (2013)
4. Ahmed, N., Matulevičius, R.: Securing business process using security risk-oriented patterns. Comput. Stand. Interf. **36**, 723–733 (2014)
5. Ahmed, N., Matulevičius, R., Mouratidis, H.: A model transformation from misuse cases to secure tropos. In: Proceedings of the CAiSE'12 Forum at the 24th International Conference on Advanced Information Systems Engineering (CAiSE), pp. 7–12 (2012)
6. Ahn, G.J., Hu, H.: Towards realizing a formal RBAC model in real systems. In: Proceedings of the 12th ACM Symposium on Access Control Models and Technologies (SACMAT'07), pp. 215–224 (2007)
7. Alalfi, M.H., Cordy, J.R., Dean, T.R.: Recovering role-based access control security models from dynamic web applications. In: Proceedings of the 12th International Conference on Web Engineering (ICWE'12), pp. 121–136 (2012)
8. Alberts, C.J., Dorofee, A.J., Stevens, J., Wooky, C.: Introduction to the OCTAVE approach. Technical Report, Software Engineering Institute, Carnegie Mellon University (2003)
9. Alexander, I.: Initial industrial experience of misuse cases in trade-off analysis. In: Proceedings of the IEEE Joint International Conference on Requirements Engineering, pp. 61–68 (2002)
10. Alexander, I.: Misuse cases: use cases with hostile intent. IEEE Softw. **20**, 58–66 (2003)
11. Alexander, I., Stevens, R.: Writing Better Requirements. Pearson Education Ltd, Boston (2002)
12. Alter, S.: The Work System Method, Connecting People, Processes and IT for Business Results. Work System Press, Larkspur, CA (2006)
13. Altuhhova, O.: An extension of business process model and notation for security risk management. Master thesis, University of Tartu (2013)
14. Altuhhova, O., Matulevičius, R., Ahmed, N.: An extension of business process model and notification for security risk management. Int. J. Inform. Syst. Model. Design (IJISMD) **4**(4), 93–113 (2013)
15. Anderson, R.: Security Engineering: A Guide to Building Dependable Distributed Systems, 2nd edn. Wiley, New York (2008)

© Springer International Publishing AG 2017
R. Matulevičius, *Fundamentals of Secure System Modelling*,
DOI 10.1007/978-3-319-61717-6

16. Apostolopoulos, G., Peris, V., Saha, D.: Transport layer security: how much does it really cost? In: Proceedings IEEE INFOCOM'99 the Conference on Computer Communications, vol. 2, pp. 717–725 (1999)
17. Argyropoulos, N., Alcañiz L.M., Mouratidis, H., Fish, A., Rosado, D.G., de Guzmán, I.G.R., Fernandez-Medina, E.: Eliciting security requirements for business processes of legacy systems. In: Proceedings of PoEM 2015, pp. 91–107 (2015)
18. Asnar, Y., Giorgini, P., Mylopoulos, J.: Goal-driven risk assessment in requirements engineering. Requir. Eng. **16**, 101–116 (2011)
19. Atluri, V., Warner, J.: Security for workflow systems. In: Gertz, M., Jajodia, S. (eds.) Handbook of Database Security, pp. 213–230. Springer, New York (2008)
20. Bandara, A., Shinpei, H., Jurjens, J., Kaiya, H., Kubo, A., Laney, R., Mouratidis, H., Nhlabatsi, A., Nuseibeh, B., Tahara, Y., Tun, T., Washizaki, H., Yoshioka, N., Yu, Y.: Security patterns: comparing modeling approaches. In: Software Engineering for Secure Systems: Industrial and Research Perspectives, pp. 75–111. IGI Global, Hershey, PA (2010)
21. Basin, D., Doser, J., Lodderstedt, T.: Model driven security: From UML models to access control infrastructure. ACM Trans. Softw. Eng. Methodol. (TOSEM) **15**(1), 39–91 (2006)
22. Becker, K.: Pattern and Security Requirements: Engineering-Based Establishment of Security Standards. Springer, New York (2015)
23. Bernardez, B., Duran, A., Genero, M.: Metrics for Use Cases: A Survey of Current Proposals, pp. 59–98. Imperial College Press, London (2005)
24. Bertino, E., Bonatti, P.A., Ferrari, E.: TRBAC: A temporal role-based access control model. ACM Trans. Inf. Syst. Secur. (TISSEC) **4**(3), 191–233 (2001)
25. Blakley, B., Heath, C.: Security design patterns. Technical Report, The Open Group (2004)
26. Börger, E., Cavarra, A., Riccobene, E.: An ASM semantics for UML activity diagrams. In: Proceedings of the 8th AMAST 2000, pp. 293–308. Springer, Berlin (2000)
27. Braun, R., Esswein, W.: Classification of domain-specific BPMN extensions. In: The Practice of Enterprise Modeling. LNBIP, pp. 42–57. Springer, Heidelberg (2014)
28. Braz, F.A., Fernandez, E.B., VanHilst, M.: Eliciting security requirements through misuse cases. In: Proceedings of the 19th International Conference on Database and Expert System Application, pp. 328–333 (2008)
29. Bresciani, P., Perini, A., Giorgini, P., Fausto, G., Mylopoulos, J.: TROPOS: an agent-oriented software development methodology. J. Auton. Agent. Multi-Agent Syst. **25**, 203–236 (2004)
30. Brooke, P.J., Paige, R.F., Power, C.: Approaches to modelling security scenarios with domain-specific languages. In: Security Protocols 2012. LNCS, vol. 7622, pp. 41–54. Springer, Berlin (2012)
31. Brucker, A., Hang, I., Lückemeyer, G., Ruparel, R.: SecureBPMN: modeling and enforcing access control requirements in business processes. In: Proceedings of the 17th ACM Symposium on Access Control Models and Technologies, pp. 123–126. ACM, New York (2012)
32. BSI: BSI Standard 100-1 version 1.5. Information Security Management System (ISMS). Bundesamt für Sicherheit in der Informationstechnik (BSI), Bonn (2008)
33. BSI: BSI Standard 100-2 version 2.0. IT-Grundschutz Methodology. Bundesamt für Sicherheit in der Informationstechnik (BSI), Bonn (2008)
34. BSI: BSI Standard 100-3 version 2.5. Risk Analysis Based on IT-Grundschutz. Bundesamt für Sicherheit in der Informationstechnik (BSI), Bonn (2008)
35. BSI: BSI Standard 100-4 version 1.0. Business Continuity Management. Bundesamt für Sicherheit in der Informationstechnik (BSI), Bonn (2009)
36. CC: Common Criteria for Information Technology Security Evaluation, CC v3.1. Release 4. https://www.commoncriteriaportal.org/cc/ (2015). Last Checked 02 Feb 2016
37. Chang, R.: Defending Against flooding-based distributed denial-of-service attacks: A tutorial. IEEE Commun. Mag. **40**(10), 42–51 (2002)
38. Cherdantseva, Y., Hilton, J., Rana, O.: Towards SecureBPMN: aligning BPMN with the information assurance and security domain. In: Business Process Model and Notation. LNBIP, pp. 107–115. Springer, Heidelberg (2012)

39. Choi, S., Kim, S., Lee, G.: Enhanced misuse case model: a security requirement analysis and specification model. In: Computational Science and Its Applications - ICCSA 2006, pp. 618–625 (2006)
40. Chowdhury, M.J.M., Matulevičius, R., Sindre, G., Karpati, P.: Aligning mal-activity diagrams and security risk management for security requirements definitions. In: Requirements Engineering: Foundation for Software Quality, pp. 132–139. Springer, Heidelberg (2012)
41. Cirit, C., Buzluca, F.: A UML profile for role-based access control. In: Proceedings of the 2nd International Conference on Security of Information and Networks (SIN'09), pp. 83–92 (2009)
42. Clarke, J.: SQL Injection Attacks and Defense. Syngress Publishing, Boston (2011)
43. Clavel, M., Silva, V., Braga, C., Egea, M.: Model-driven security in practice: an industrial experience. In: Proceedings of the 4th European Conference on Model Driven Architecture: Foundations and Applications (ECMDA-FA'06), pp. 326–337. Springer, Berlin (2008)
44. CLUSIF: MEHARI 2010: Fundamental concepts and principles-specifications. Technical Report, Club de la Securite de L'Information Francais (2010)
45. Cockburn, A.: Writing Effective Use Cases. Addison-Wesley, Boston (2001)
46. Dalpiaz, F., Paja, E., Giorgini, P.: Security Requirements Engineering: Designing Secure Socio-Technical Systems. The MIT Press, Cambridge (2016)
47. Damiani, M.L., Bertino, E., Catania, B., Perlasca, P.: Geo-RBAC: A spatially aware RBAC. ACM Trans. Inform. Syst. Secur. (TISSEC) 10, 1 (2007)
48. Danezis, G., Domingo-Ferrer, J., Hansen, M., Hoepman, J.H., Le Métayer, D., Tirtea, R., Schiffner, S.: Privacy and data protection by design – from policy to engineering. Technical Report, ENISA (2014)
49. Davis, A., Overmeyer, S., Jordan, K., Caruso, J., Dandashi, F., Dinh, A., Kincaid, G., Reynolds, P., Sitaram, P., Ta, A., Theofanos, M.: Identifying and measuring quality in a software requirements specification. In: Proceedings of the 1st International Software Metrics Symposium, pp. 141–152 (1993)
50. DCSSI Advisory Office: EBIOS 2010: Expression of Needs and Identification of Security Objectives. Technical Report, Secrétariat général de la défense nationale, Direction centrale de la sécurité des systèmes d'information (2010)
51. De Win, B., Scandariato, R., Buyens, K., Grégoire, J., Joosen, W.: On the secure software development process: CLASP, SDL and Touchpoints compared. Inf. Softw. Technol. 51, 1152–1171 (2009)
52. Dougherty, C., Sayre, K., Seacord, R.C., Svoboda, D., Togashi, K.: Secure Design Patterns. Technical Report, Software Engineering Institute (2009)
53. Dubois, E., Heymans, P., Mayer, N., Matulevičius, R.: A Systematic Approach to Define the Domain of Information System Security Risk Management, pp. 289–306. Springer, New York (2010)
54. Dumas, M., La Rosa, M., Mendling, J., Reijers, H.: Fundamentals of Business Process Management. Springer, New York (2013)
55. Dwork, C.: Differential privacy. In: Automata, Languages and Programming, pp. 1–12. Springer, New York (2006)
56. Dwork, C.: Differential privacy: a survey of results. In: Theory and Application of Models in Computation, pp. 1–19. Springer, New York (2008)
57. Dwork, C.: Differential privacy in new settings. In: Proceedings of the 21st Annual ACM-SIAM Symposium on Discrete Algorithms, pp. 174–183. Society for Industrial and Applied Mathematics, Philadelphia (2010)
58. Easterbrook, S.: Fundamentals of requirements engineering. http://www.cs.toronto.edu/~sme/CSC340F/ (2004). Last Checked 30 May 2016
59. Ekelhart, A., Fenz, S., Neubauer, T.: AURUM: a framework for information security risk management. In: Proceedings of the 42nd Hawaii International Conference on System Sciences (2009)
60. El-Attar, M.: From misuse cases to mal-activity diagrams: Bridging the gap between functional security analysis and design. Softw. Syst. Model. 13, 173–190 (2014)

61. El-Hadary, H., El-Kassas, S.: Capturing security requirements for software systems. Cairo Univ. J. Adv. Res. **5**, 463–472 (2014)

62. Elahi, G., Yu, E.: A goal oriented approach for modeling and analyzing security trade-offs. In: Parent, C., Schewe, K.D., Storey, V.C., Thalheim, B. (eds.) Proceedings of the 26th International Conference on Conceptual Modelling (ER 2007), vol. 4801, pp. 87–101. Springer, Berlin (2007)

63. Fabian, B., Gürses, S., Heisel, M., Santen, T., Schmidt, H.: A comparison of security requirements engineering methods. Requir. Eng. **15**(1), 7–40 (2010)

64. Fernandez-Buglioni, E.: Security Patterns in Practice: Designing Secure Architectures Using Software Patterns. Wiley, New York (2013)

65. Ferraiolo, D., Sandhu, R., Gavrila, S., Kuhn, D.R , Chandramouli, R.: Proposed NIST standard for role-based access control. ACM Trans. Inf. Syst. Secur. **4**(3), 224–274 (2001)

66. Firesmith, D.: Common concepts underlying safety, security and survivability engineering. Technical Report, CMU/SEI-2003-TN-033, Software Engineering Institute (2003)

67. Firesmith, D.: Security use cases. J. Object Technol. **2**(3), 53–64 (2003)

68. Firesmith, D.G.: Engineering security requirements. J. Object Technol. **2**(1), 53–68 (2003)

69. Firesmith, D.: A taxonomy of security-related requirements. In: Proceedings of the Fourth International Workshop on Requirements Engineering for High-Availability Systems (RHAS'05), p. 11 (2005)

70. Firesmith, D.: Engineering safety- and security-related requirements for software- intensive systems. Tutorial, 2007 Carnegie Mellon University (2007)

71. Firesmith, D.: Engineering safety and security related requirements for software intensive systems. In: 29th International Conference on Software Engineering: Companion, p. 169. IEEE Computer Society (2007)

72. Fogie, S., Grossman, J., Hansen, R., Rager, A., Petkov, P.D.: XSS Attacks: Cross Site Scripting Exploits and Defense. Syngress Publishing, Burlington, MA (2007)

73. Fung, B.C.M., Wang, K., Chen, R., Yu, P.S.: Privacy-preserving data publishing: a survey of recent developments. ACM Comput. Surv. **42**(4), 1–53 (2010)

74. Gamma, E., Helm, R., Johnson, R., Vlissides, J.: Design Patterns: Elements of Reusable Object-Oriented Software. Addison-Wesley, Boston (1994)

75. Garcia-Alfaro, J., Navarro-Arribas, G.: A survey on detection techniques to prevent cross-site scripting attacks on current web applications. In: Critical Information Infrastructures Security, pp. 287–298. Springer, Berlin (2008)

76. Gharib, M., Giorgini, P., Mylopoulos, J.: Ontologies for privacy requirements engineering: a systematic literature review. Technical Report, University of Florence and University of Trento (2016)

77. Giorgini, P., Massacci, F., Mylopoulos, J., Zannone, N.: Modeling security requirements through ownership, permission and delegation. In: Proceedings of the 13th IEEE International Conference on Requirements Engineering (RE'05). IEEE Computer Society (2005)

78. Giorgini, P., Massacci, F., Mylopoulos, J., Zannone, N.: Modelling social and individual trust in requirements engineering methodologies. In: Proceedings of the 3rd International Conference on Trust Management. LNCS, pp. 161–176. Springer, Heidelberg (2005)

79. Goldkuhl, G., Lind, M., Seigerroth, U.: Method integration: the need for a learning per-spective. IEEE Proc. Softw. (Special issue on Information System Methodologies) **145**(4), 113–118 (1998). http://ieeexplore.ieee.org/document/729576/

80. Goldstein, A., Frank, U.: Components of a multi-perspective modeling method for designing and managing IT security systems. Inf. Syst. E-Bus Manag. **14**, 101–140 (2016)

81. Gopalakrishnan, S., Krogstie, J., Sindre, G.: Extending use and misuse case diagrams to capture multi-channel information systems. In: Informatics Engineering and Information Science, pp. 355–369 (2011)

82. Graham, D.: Introduction to the CLASP Process. Build Security In (2006)

83. Haibo, S., Fan, H.: A context-aware role-Based access control model for web services. In: IEEE International Conference on E-Business Engineering, pp. 220–223 (2005)

84. Haley, C., Laney, R., Moffet, J.D., Nuseibeh, B.: Security requirements engineering: a framework for representation and analysis. IEEE Trans. Softw. Eng. **34**(1), 133–153 (2008)

85. Hansen, F., Oleshchuk, V.: SRBAC: A spatial role-based access control model for mobile systems. In: Proceedings of the 7th Nordic Workshop on Secure IT Systems (NORDSEC03), pp. 129–141 (2003)

86. Hartong, M., Goel, R., Wijesekera, D.: UsemMisuse case driven analysis of positive train control. In: Advances in Digital Forensics II, pp. 141–155. Springer, Berlin (2006)

87. Herzberg, A., Jarecki, S., Krawczyk, H., Yung, M.: Proactive secret sharing or: how to cope with perpetual leakage. In: Proceedings of the CRYPTO'95, pp. 339–352 (1995)

88. Howard, M., Lipner, S.: The Security Development Lifecycle. Microsoft Press, Remond (2006)

89. Hu, V.C., Ferraiolo, D., Kuhn, R., Schnitzer, A., Sandlin, K., Miller, R., Scarfone, K.: Guide to attribute based access control (ABAC) definition and considerations. Technical Report 800–162, NIST Special Publication (2014)

90. Hu, V.C., Kuhn, D.R., Ferraiolo, D.F.: Attribute-based access control. Computer **2**, 85–88 (2015)

91. Hummer, W., Gaubatz, P., Strembeck, M., Zdun, U., Dustdar, S.: Enforcement of entailment constraints in distributed service-based business processes. Inf. Softw. Technol. **55**(11), 1884–1903 (2013)

92. Hussein, M., Zulkernine, M.: Intrusion detection aware component-based systems: a specification-based framework. J. Syst. Softw. **80**(5), 700–710 (2007)

93. ISO/IEC: ISO/IEC 13335-1:2004. Information technology - Security techniques - Management of information and communications technology security - Part 1: Concepts and models for information and communications technology security management. International Organization for Standardization, Geneva (2004)

94. ISO/IEC: ISO/IEC 27005: 2011: Information Technology: Security Techniques: Information Security Risk Management. International Organization for Standardization, Geneva (2011)

95. ISO/IEC: ISO/IEC 27001:2013: Information Technology – Security Techniques – Information Security Management Systems – Requirements. International Organization for Standardization, Geneva (2013)

96. Jackson, M.: Problem Frames: Analysing and Structuring Software Development Problems. Addison-Wesley, Boston (2001)

97. Jaks, L.: A prototype for transforming role-based access control models. Bachelor thesis, University of Tartu (2012)

98. Janulevičius, J.: Method of information security risk analysis for virtualized systems. Ph.D. thesis, Vilnius Gediminas Technical University (2016)

99. Jensen, J., Tøndel, I.A., Meland, P.M.: Experimental threat model reuse with misuse case diagrams. In: Information and Communication Security, pp. 355–366 (2010)

100. Jürjens, J.: Secure System Development with UML. Springer, Berlin (2005)

101. Karpati, P., Sindre, G., Opdahl, A.L.: Visualizing cyber attacks with misuse case maps. In: Wieringa, R., Persson, A. (eds.) Proceedings of the Requirements Engineering: Foundation for Software Quality (REFSQ 2010). Springer, Heidelberg (2010)

102. Karpati, P., Opdahl, A.L., Sindre, G.: Experimental comparison of misuse case maps with misuse cases and system architecture diagrams for eliciting security vulnerabilities and mitigations. In: Proceedings of the 6th International Conference on Availability, Reliability, and Security (2011)

103. Karpati, P., Sindre, G., Matulevičius, R.: Comparing misuse case and mal-activity diagrams for modelling social engineering attacks. Int. J. Secure Softw. Eng. **3**(2), 54–73 (2012)

104. Karpati, P., Redda, Y., Opdahl, A.L., Sindre, G.: Comparing attack trees and misuse cases in an industrial setting. Inf. Softw. Technol. **56**, 294–308 (2014)

105. Kim, S., Narasimha Reddy, A.L.: Statistical techniques for detecting traffic anomalies through packet header data. IEEE/ACM Trans. Netw. **16**(3), 562–575 (2008)

106. Kissel, R.: Glossary of key information security terms. Technical Report NISTIR 7298 revision 2, NIST (2013)

107. Kolk, K.: An empirical comparison of approaches for security requirements elicitation. Master thesis, University of Tartu (2015)
108. Korman, M., Lagerström, R., Ekstedt, M.: Modeling authorization in enterprise-wide contexts. In: PoEM-SDC 2015: Short and Doctoral Consortium Papers at PoEM 2015, pp. 81–90 (2015)
109. Krogstie, J.: Model-Based Development and Evolution of Information Systems. Springer, London (2012)
110. Kulak, D., Guiney, E.: Use Cases: Requirements in Context, 2nd edn. Addison-Wesley, New York (2004)
111. Lakk, H.: Model-driven role-based access control for databases. Master thesis, University of Tartu (2012)
112. van Lamsweerde, A.: Elaborating security requirements by construction of intentional anti-models. In: Proceedings of 26th International Conference on Software Engineering (ICSE'04), pp. 148–157 (2004)
113. van Lamsweerde, A.: Requirements Engineering: From System Goals to UML Models to Software Specifications. Wiley, New York (2009)
114. Lee, S.W., Gandhi, R., Muthurajan, D., Yavagal, D., Ahn, G.J.: Building problem domain ontology from security requirements in regulatory documents. In: Proceedings of the 2006 International Workshop on Software Engineering for Secure Systems (2006)
115. Leoni, D.: Non-interactive differential privacy: a survey. In: Proceedings of the 1st International Workshop on Open Data (WOD'12), pp. 40–52 (2012)
116. Li, T., Horkoff, J.: Dealing with security requirements for socio-technical systems: a holistic approach. In: Proceedings of International Conference on Advanced Information Systems Engineering (CAiSE 2014), pp. 285–300. Springer, Heidelberg (2014)
117. Lin, L., Nuseibeh, B., Ince, D., Jackson, M.: Using abuse frames to bound the scope of security problem. In: Proceedings of the 12th IEEE International Requirements Engineering Conference (2004)
118. Liu, L., Yu, E., Mylopoulos, J.: Security and privacy requirements analysis within a social setting. In: Proceedings of the 11th IEEE International Requirements Engineering Conference (RE'03), p. 151. IEEE Computer Society (2003)
119. Lodderstedt, T., Basin, D., Doser, J.: SecureUML: a UML-based modeling language for model-driven security. In: Proceedings of the 5th International Conference on the Unified Modeling Language, vol. 2460, pp. 426–441. Springer, Berlin (2002)
120. Lord, N.: Common Malware Types: Cybersecurity 101. https://www.veracode.com/blog/2012/10/common-malware-types-cybersecurity-101/ (2012)
121. Loukas, G., Öke, G.: Protection against denial of service attacks. Comput. J. 53(7), 1020–1037 (2010)
122. Lund, M.S., Solhaug, B., Stølen, K.: Model-Driven Risk Analysis: The CORAS Approach. Springer, Heidelberg (2011)
123. Mahajan, R., Bellovin, S.M., Floyd, S., Ioannidis, J., Paxson, V., S., S.: Controlling high bandwidth aggregates in the network. SIGCOMM Comput. Commun. Rev. 32(3), 62–73 (2002)
124. Marcinkowski, B., Kuciapski, M.: A business process modeling notation extension for risk handling. In: 11th International Conference on Information Systems and Industrial Management. LNCS, pp. 374–381. Springer, Heidelberg (2012)
125. Massaci, F., Mylopoulos, J., Zannone, N.: Security requirements engineering: The SI* modelling language and the tropos methodology. Adv. Intell. Inf. Syst. 265, 147–174 (2010)
126. Matulevičius, R.: Comparing modelling languages for information systems security risk management. In: Seyff, N., Koziolek, A. (eds.) Modellin and Quality in Requirements Engineering: Essays Dedicated to Martin Glinz on the Occasion of His 60th Birthday, pp. 207–220. Monsenstein and Vannerdat (2012)
127. Matulevičius, R., Dumas, M.: A comparison of SecureUML and UMLsec for role-based access control. In: The 9th Conference on Databases and Information Systems (Baltic DB and IS 2010), pp. 171–185 (2010)

128. Matulevičius, R., Dumas, M.: Towards model transformation between SecureUML and UMLsec for role-based access control. In: Databases and Information Systems VI, pp. 339–352. IOS Press, Amsterdam (2011)
129. Matulevičius, R., Lakk, H.: A model-driven role-based access control for SQL databases. Complex Syst. Inform. Model. Q. **3**, 35–62 (2015)
130. Matulevičius, R., Mayer, N., Heymans, P.: Alignment of misuse cases with security risk management. In: Proceedings of the ARES 2008 Symposium on Requirements Engineering for Information Security (SREIS 2008), pp. 1397–1404. IEEE Computer Society (2008)
131. Matulevičius, R., Mayer, N., Mouratidis, H., Dubois, E., Heymans, P., Genon, N.: Adapting secure tropos for security risk management during early phases of the information systems development. In: Proceedings of the 20th International Conference on Advanced Information System Engineering (CAiSE 2008). Springer, Berlin/Heidelberg (2008)
132. Matulevičius, R., Mayer, N., Mouratidis, H., Dubois, E., Heymans, P.: Syntactic and semantic extensions to secure tropos to support security risk management. J. UCS **18**(6), 816–844 (2012)
133. Mayer, N.: Model-based management of information system security risk. Ph.D. thesis, University of Namur (2009)
134. Mayer, N., Heymans, P., Matulevičius, R.: Design of a modelling language for information system security risk management. In: Proceedings of the Research Challenges in Information Science (RCIS 2007), pp. 121–131 (2007)
135. Mayer, N., Dubois, E., Matulevičius, R., Heymans, P.: Towards a measurement framework for security risk management. In: Proceedings of the Workshop on Modeling Security (MODSEC08) held as part of MODELS 2008 (2008)
136. McDermott, J., Fox, C.: Using abuse case models for security requirements analysis. In: Proceedings of the 15th Annual Computer Security Applications Conference (ACSAC '99) (1999)
137. McGraw, G.: Software Security: Building Security In. Addison-Wesley, Upper Saddle River (2006)
138. McGraw, R.W.: Risk-adaptable access control (RAdAC). In: Privilege (Access) Management Workshop. NIST–National Institute of Standards and Technology – Information Technology Laboratory (2009)
139. Mead, N.R., Stehney, T.: Security quality requirements engineering (SQUARE) methodology. In: Software Engineering for Secure Systems (SESS05) (2005)
140. Mead, N.R., Hough, E.D., Stehney II, T.R.: Security quality requirements engineering (SQUARE) methodology. Technical Report CMU/SEI-2005-TR-009, ESC-TR-2005-009, Software Engineering Institute (2005)
141. Mellado, D., Fernández-Medina, E., Piattini, M.: A common criteria based security requirements engineering process for the development of secure information systems. Comput. Stand. Interf. **29**, 244–253 (2007)
142. Mellado, D., Fernández-Medina, E., Piattini, M.: Towards security requirements management for software product lines: a security domain requirements engineering process. Comput. Stand. Interf. **30**, 361–371 (2008)
143. Mellado, D., Blanco, C., Sánchez, L.E., Fernández-Medina, E.: A systematic review of security requirements engineering. Comput. Stand. Interf. **32**, 153–165 (2010)
144. Menzel, M., Thomas, I., Meinel, C.: Security requirements specification in service-oriented business process management. In: International Conference on Availability, Reliability and Security (ARES 2009), pp. 41–49 (2009)
145. MITRE: Common Attack Pattern Enumeration and Classification. https://capec.mitre.org
146. Moffett, J., Nuseibeh, B.: A framework for security requirements engineering. Technical Report 368, Department of Computer Science, University of York (2003)
147. Mouratidis, H.: A security oriented approach in the development of multiagent systems: applied to the management of the health and social care needs of older people in England. Ph.D. thesis, Department of Computer Science, University of Sheffield, UK (2004)

148. Mouratidis, H., Giorgini, P.: Secure tropos: a security-oriented extension of the tropos methodology. Int. J. Softw. Eng. Knowl. Eng. (IJSEKE) **17**(2), 285–309 (2007)

149. Mouratidis, H., Jurjens, J.: From goal-driven security requirements engineering to secure design. Int. J. Intell. Syst. **25**, 813–840 (2010)

150. Mouratidis, H., Giorgini, P., Manson, G.: Integrating security and systems engineering: towards the modelling of Secure information systems. In: Proceedings of the 15th Conference on Advanced Information Systems Engineering (CAiSE'03), pp. 63–78. Springer, Berlin (2003)

151. Mülle, J., Stackelberg, S., Bohm, K.: A security language for BPMN process models. Technical Report 9, Karlsruhe Reports in Informatics (2011)

152. Myagmar, S., Lee, A.J., Yurcik, W.: Threat modeling as a basis for security requirements. In: SREIS (2005)

153. Natan, R.B.: Implementing Database Security and Auditing: Includes Examples for Oracle, SQL Server, DB2 UDB, Sybase. Digital Press, Clifton (2005)

154. NIST: NIST Special Publication 800-39. Managing Information Security Risk: Organization, Mission, and Information System View. National Institute of Standards and Technology, Gaithersburg (2011)

155. NIST: NIST Special Publication 800-30. Guide for Conducting Risk Assessments. National Institute of Standards and Technology, Gaithersburg (2012)

156. Noh, S., Lee, C., Choi, K., Jung, G.: Detecting distributed denial of service (DDoS) attacks through inductive learning. In: Intelligent Data Engineering and Automated Learning, pp. 286–295. Springer, Berlin (2003)

157. Nuseibeh, B., Finkelstein, A., Kramer, J.: Method engineering for multi-perspective software development. Inf. Softw. Technol. J. **38**(4), 267–274 (1996). http://www.sciencedirect.com/science/article/pii/0950584995010548

158. OMG: Unified Modeling Language: Infrastructure and Superstructure, version 2.0. http://www.omg.org/spec/UML/2.0/ (2005)

159. OMG: Business Process Model and Notation (BPMN), version 2.0. http://www.omg.org/spec/BPMN/2.0/ (2011)

160. Onchukova, A.: Security risk management using misuse cases and mal-activities. Master thesis, University of Tartu (2013)

161. Opdahl, A.L., Henderson-Sellers, B.: A unified modelling language without referential redundancy. Data Knowl. Eng. (DKE) (Special Issue on Quality in Conceptual Modelling) **55**, 277–300 (2005)

162. Opdahl, A.L., Sindre, G.: Experimental comparison of attack trees and misuse cases for security threat identification. Inf. Softw. Technol. **51**, 916–932 (2009)

163. ben Othmane, L., Ranchal, R., Fernando, R., Bhargava, B., Bodden, E.: Incorporating attacker capabilities in risk estimation and mitigation. Comput. Secur. **51**, 41–61 (2014)

164. Park, J., Sandhu, R.: The UCON ABC usage control model. ACM Trans. Inf Syst. Secur. (TISSEC) **7**(1), 128–174 (2004)

165. Pauli, J.J., Xu, D.: Misuse case-based design and analysis of secure software architecture. In: Proceedings of the International Conference in Information Technology: Coding and Computing (ITCC'05), pp. 398–403 (2005)

166. Pavlidis, M., Islam, S.: SecTro: a CASE tool for modelling security in requirements engineering using secure tropos. In: Proceedings of the CAiSE Forum (2011)

167. Peeters, J.: Agile security requirements engineering. In: SREIS (2005)

168. Pfitzmann, A., Hansen, M.: A terminology for talking about privacy by data minimization: anonymity, unlinkability, undetectability, unobservability, pseudonymity, and identity management. Technical Report, TU Dresden and ULD Kiel (2010)

169. Radhakrishnan, R.: The Fifth and Final Frontier of Access Control Model (2012). http://www.isaca-washdc.org/presentations/2012/201211-session3_article.pdf

170. Refsdal, A., Solhaug, B., Stølen, K.: Cyber-Risk Management. Springer, Cham (2015)

171. Rodriguez, A., Fernandez-Medina, E., Piattini, M.: A BPMN extension for the modeling of security requirements in business processes. IEICE Trans. Inf. Syst. **90**(4), 745–752 (2007)

172. Rodríguez, A., de Guzmán, I.G.R., Fernández-Medina, E., Piattini, M.: Semi-formal transformation of secure business processes into analysis class and use case models: an MDA approach. Inf. Softw. Technol. **52**, 945–971 (2010)
173. Rodríguez, A., Fernández-Medina, E., Trujillo, J., Piattini, M.: Secure business process model specification through a UML 2.0 activity diagram profile. Decis. Support. Syst. **51**, 446–465 (2011)
174. Rostad, L.: An extended misuse case notation: including vulnerabilities and the insider threat. In: Proceedings of the 12th Working Conference REFSQ'06 (2006)
175. Rrenja, A., Matulevičius, R.: Pattern-based security requirements derivation from secure tropos models. In: Proceedings of PoEM 2015, pp. 59–74 (2015)
176. Sánchez, P., Moreira, A., Fuentes, L., Araújo, J., Magno, J.: Model-driven development for early aspects. Inf. Softw. Technol. **52**, 249–273 (2010)
177. Sandhu, R.S., Coyne, E.J., Feinstein, H.L., Youman, C.E.: Role-based access control models. IEEE Comput. **29**(2), 38–47 (1996)
178. Sandkuhl, K., Matulevičius, R., Ahmed, N., Kirikova, M.: Refining security requirement elicitation from business process using method engineering. In: Joint Proceedings of the BIR 2015 Workshops and Doctoral Consortium (2015)
179. Scandariato, R., Wuyts, K., Joosen, W.: A descriptive study of Microsoft's threat modeling technique. Requir. Eng. J. **20**, 163–180 (2015)
180. Schleicher, D., Leymann, F., Schumm, D., Weidmann, M.: Compliance scopes: Extending the BPMN 2.0 Meta model to specify compliance requirements. In: IEEE International Conference on Service-Oriented Computing and Applications (SOCA), pp. 1–8. IEEE (2010)
181. Schneier, B.: Attack trees. Dr. Dobb's J. (1999). https://www.schneier.com/academic/archives/1999/12/attack_trees.html
182. Schumacher, M., Fernandez-Buglioni, E., Hybertson, D., Buschmann, F., Sommerlad, P.: Security Patterns: Integrating Security and System Engineering. Wiley, New York (2005)
183. Sergeev, A.: Role based access control as secureUML model in web applications development with spring security. Master thesis, University of Tartu (2016)
184. Shafiq, B., Samuel, A., Ghafoor, H.: A GTRRBAC based system for dynamic workflow composition and management. In: Eighth IEEE International Symposium on Object-Oriented Real-Time Distributed Computing (ISORC), pp. 284–290 (2005)
185. Shaikh, R.A., Adi, K., Logrippo, L.: Dynamic risk-based decision methods for access control systems. Comput. Secur. **31**(4), 447–464 (2012)
186. Shen, Y., Pearson, S.: Privacy enhancing technologies: a review. Technical Report HPL-2011-113, HP Laboratories (2011)
187. Shin, M.E., Gomaa, H.: Software requirements and architecture modeling for evolving non-secure applications into secure applications. Sci. Comput. Program **66**(1), 60–70 (2007)
188. Shostack, A.: Threat Modeling: Designing for Security. Wiley, New York (2014)
189. Silver, B.: BPMN Method and Style: A Levels-Based Methodology for BPMN Process Modeling and Improvement Using BPMN 2.0. Cody-Cassidy Press, Aptos (2009)
190. Sindre, G.: A look at misuse cases for safety concerns. In: Situational Method Engineering: Fundamentals and Experiences, pp. 252–266. Springer, Boston (2007)
191. Sindre, G.: Mal-activity diagrams for capturing attacks on business processes. In: Requirements Engineering: Foundation for Software Quality, pp. 355–366. Springer, Heidelberg (2007)
192. Sindre, G., Opdahl, A.L.: Eliciting security requirements with misuse cases. Requir. Eng. J. **10**(1), 34–44 (2005)
193. Sing, E.: A prototype to transform models of secure tropos and misuse case diagrams. Bachelor thesis, University of Tartu (2014)
194. Slavin, R., Lehker, J.M., Niu, J., Breaux, T.: Managing security requirements patterns using feature diagram hierarchies. In: Proceedings of RE 2014, pp. 193–202 (2014)
195. Sommestad, T., Ekstedt, M., Holm, H.: The cyber security modeling language: a tool for assessing the vulnerability of enterprise system architectures. IEEE Syst. J. **7**(3), 363–373 (2013)

196. Soomro, I., Ahmed, N.: Towards security risk-oriented misuse cases. In: Business Process Management Workshops. LNBIP, pp. 689–700. Springer, Heidelberg (2012)
197. Staron, M.: Adopting model driven software development in industry – a case at two companies. In: Model Driven Engineering Languages and Systems, pp. 57–72 (2006)
198. Stålhane, T., Sindre, G.: Safety hazard identification by misuse cases: Experimental comparison of text and diagrams. In: Model Driven Engineering Languages and Systems, pp. 721–735 (2008)
199. Tark, K.: Role based access model in XML based documents. Master thesis, University of Tartu (2013)
200. Tark, K., Matulevičius, R.: Short paper: role-based access control for securing dynamically created documents. In: Business Process Management Workshops. LNBIP, vol. 171, pp. 520–525. Springer, Berlin (2014)
201. Thomas, R., Mark, B., Johnson, T., Croall, J.: NetBouncer: Client-legitimacy-based high-performance DDoS filtering. In: DARPA Information Survivability Conference and Exposition, vol. 12003, pp. 14–25 (2003)
202. Tsipenyuk, K., Chess, B., McGraw, G.: Seven pernicious kingdoms: a taxonomy of software security errors. IEEE Secur. Priv. 3(4), 81–84 (2005). http://ieeexplore.ieee.org/document/1556543/
203. Tsoumas, B., Gritzalis, D.: Towards an ontology-based security management. In: Proceedings of the 20th International Conference on Advanced Information Networking and Applications (AINA'06), vol. 1 (2006)
204. Tsoumas, B., Papagiannakopoulos, P., Dritsas, S., Gritzalis, D.: Security-by-ontology: a knowledge-centric approach. In: Boston, S. (ed.) Security and Privacy in Dynamic Environments, pp. 99–110. Springer, London (2006)
205. Uzunov, A.V., Fernandez, E.B.: An extensible pattern-based library and taxonomy of security threats for distributed systems. Comput. Stand. Interf. 36(4), 734–747 (2014)
206. Viega, J.: Building security requirements with CLASP. In: Proceedings of the 2005 Workshop on Software Engineering for Secure Systems—Building Trustworthy Applications, pp. 1–7 (2005)
207. Wand, Y., Weber, R.: On the ontological expressiveness of information systems analysis and design grammars. J. Inf. Syst. 3, 217–237 (1993)
208. Whittle, J., Wijesekera, D., Hartong, M.: Executable misuse cases for modeling security concerns. In: Proceedings of the 30th International Conference on Software Engineering (ICSE'08), pp. 121–130 (2008)
209. Withall, S.: Software Requirements Patterns. Microsoft Press, Sebastopol (2007)
210. Xin, J.: Applying model driven architecture approach to model role based access control system. Master thesis, University of Ottawa (2006)
211. Xu, D., Pauli, J.: Threat-driven design and analysis of secure software architectures. J. Inf. Assur. Secur. 1(3), 171–180 (2006)
212. Yazar, Z.: A qualitative risk analysis and management tool: CRAMM. Technical Report, SANS Institute (2002)
213. Yu, E.: Towards modeling and reasoning support for early-phase requirements engineering. In: Proceedings of the 3rd IEEE International Symposium on Requirements Engineering (RE'97), p. 226. IEEE Computer Society (1997)
214. Yue, T., Briand, L.C., Labiche, Y.: A systematic review of transformation approaches between user requirements and analysis models. Requir. Eng. J. 16, 75–99 (2011)
215. Zuccato, A.: Holistic security requirement engineering for electronic commerce. Comput. Secur. 23, 63–76 (2004)
216. Zuccato, A.: Holistic security management framework applied in electronic commerce. Comput. Secur. 26(3), 256–265 (2007)
217. Zuccato, A., Endersz, V., Daniels, N.: Security requirements engineering at a telecom provider. In: ARES, pp. 1139–1147 (2008)

Printed in the United States
By Bookmasters